# JUSTICE

# THE DECEPTION OF CHRISTIANITY IN AMERICA

A concise documentation of the suppressed history of church-supported injustice in America

# **Justice**

Copyright © 2023 by Walter B. Pennington. All rights reserved. This book is protected by the copyright laws of the United States of America. No part of this publication may be reproduced, stored in a retrieval system, or transmitted in any form by any means – electronic, mechanical, digital, photocopy, recording, or any other – for commercial gain or profit. The use of short quotations or occasional page copying for personal or group study is permitted and encouraged. Permission will be granted upon request.

Walter B. Pennington
penningtonwalter@bellsouth.net

---

Unless otherwise indicated, all scriptures are taken from The New King James Bible and are printed in italics.

---

## **On the cover**

The cross of Christ is centered in justice. The shackles on top of the Bible symbolize the priority given to injustice over the clearly understood word of God by the European professing church of God in America throughout American history. It represents not just racial injustice throughout America's history but all forms of injustice, including what is identified as social injustice. It also serves as a reminder of how the European population has traditionally used the two together for self-serving advantages. It is representative of the religious hypocrisy throughout the history of America that still exists today. Justice in America has historically been saturated with the innocent blood of humanity.

# Acknowledgments

I am grateful to God Almighty for entrusting me with the responsibility of completing this sensitive, vital work for the end-time season. As with the other two writings before this one ("*The Fanaticism of Christian Discipleship*" and "*Just Like Jesus, Discipleship for Children and Youth*"), He could have selected someone more capable than me. However, I am eternally grateful that He chose me. I credit the Holy Spirit for its completion, realizing that any errors are because of my human nature.

I thank my lovely wife, Jackie, for allowing me the space and time to dedicate to this work. I am grateful for her patience and support during this season of writing and during my difficult season of personal development and building for God's kingdom.

I thank my son Walter III (Tre) for helping with the required formatting. As with all four of my children, I love him dearly and pray that God will continue to develop each of them in His image.

I thank the many prayer warriors who continue to provide the much-needed prayer cover for my family and me.

I pray that God's blessings will remain over the lives of everyone involved.

# JUSTICE

## Contents

Introduction _____ 6

1. Injustice, an American Way of Life _____ 13

2. Personal Stories of Racial Injustice _____ 25

3. The Foundation for God's Throne and Christianity
   _____ 47

4. The Biblical Commandment of Love _____ 63

5. Injustice Perpetrated Against Native Americans
   _____ 73

6. Injustice Perpetrated Against Africans _____ 81

7. The Assassination of President Abraham Lincoln
   _____ 95

8. Injustice Perpetrated Against African Americans
   _____ 101

9. Injustice Perpetrated Against Asian Americans
   _____ 125

10. Injustice Perpetrated Against Hispanics & Latinos
    _____ 139

11. Injustice Perpetrated Through Politics _____ 147

12. Injustice, Deeply Rooted in America's Culture _____ 165

13. Biblical Justice vs. Social Justice _____ 171

14. European (White) Americans for Racial Justice _____ 177

15. The Biblical Response to Injustice by the Oppressed _____ 191

16. The Cost of Restoration _____ 197

17. Conclusion _____ 219

    Epilogue _____ 230

    Appendix (Separate and unequal schools) _____ 231

    Appendix Summary _____ 253

    Personal Reflections and Final Plea _____ 259

    Postscript _____ 265

    Bibliography _____ 271

    Notes _____ 276

# **Introduction**

Most writings that address the ills of Christianity in the United States of America assume the Biblically proven false, yet controversial premise that Biblical Christianity once existed in the United States. Therefore, revival is needed to recapture what has been lost to "Make America Great Again." Contrary to popular belief, Biblical Christianity has never existed in the United States broadly, but primarily a convincing deception disguising the absence of eternal salvation for far too many unsuspecting souls.

This prerequisite for *"The Fanaticism of Christian Discipleship"* is a critical review of the role of the racially segregated institutional White church in America's history in undermining the Biblically required foundation for Christianity.

There are many concerns across racial lines regarding the historical and ongoing rebellion against God and His kingdom design. However, the White race and the White church in the United States remain the focal point where correction must begin because of their dominant role in the United States and their historical role in its human injustice.

In the U.S., we emphasize racial differences, which originated with its first European inhabitants. Racism finds its energy in highlighting racial and cultural differences combined with selfish motives.

Throughout the history of the U.S., many unjust laws have been written, approved, and enforced along racial lines to reinforce and maintain White supremacy, which was born out of racism. These injustices were only possible because of the complicit actions and inactions of the racially segregated White Protestant and Catholic churches, from which everything stemmed that empowered White America and validated their actions and beliefs.

The worldly (satanic) emphasis on racial differences has led to race being a dividing factor in God's professing church and kingdom on earth. As the professing body of Christ, we must remember that in God's kingdom, there is only one race, the human race, descended from one blood, the blood of Adam, bound under one blood, the blood of Christ. As believers in Christ and as Biblically validated, we are a united body of this unique bloodline created by God.

---

[As a clarification, in America, European Americans are identified as "white" and generally, African Americans as "black." The expression "White race," which references the Europeans' light skin color, was first used by Europeans in the seventeenth century. Before that time, no Europeans regarded themselves as white. They identified themselves in terms of their ethnicity, ancestry, or nationality.

The humanity-originated concept of categorizing the human race based on skin color is a misnomer. This categorization is not Biblical nor validated by science. Also, as scientifically proven, no human skin color is purely black or purely white.

To summarize this clarification, as science proves, humanity and the skin color variations identified as races all originated from brown-skinned Africans. The skin color variations resulted throughout centuries from humanity's skin's adjustment to various environmental conditions from long-term inhabitations of different parts of the earth. As Biblically proven, God ordained only one race of humans, and we are made in His image. Also, as Biblically proven and perhaps surprising to many, though we may have different skin color, hair texture, facial and body features, we are all biologically related to each other as blood descendants of Adam.

However, to avoid unnecessary, unproductive confusion and not distract from the critical purpose or diminish the hopeful racial-unifying result of this writing, we will reluctantly continue with the erroneous human-originated, divisive concept of race based on skin color. We will continue to reference those of European descent as "White."]

---

The oneness of the remnant of God's people has always been the foundation that has sustained God's kingdom on earth. The apostle Paul reminded the church of Corinth of the importance of oneness when he wrote in 1$^{st}$ Corinthians 12:12 & 13, *"For as the body is one and has many members, but all the members of that one body, being many, are one body, so also is Christ. For by one Spirit we were all baptized into one body – whether Jews or Greeks, whether slaves or free – and have all been made to drink into one Spirit."*

---

This book takes a Biblical view of how the enemy of God's people, Satan, has effectively used the erroneous concept of racial division as a strategic tool to destroy God's kingdom order for human relations throughout the history of the United States. He accomplished this task by pitting our differences against each other as convenient and effective weapons of spiritual warfare. The bride of Christ is now a divided church, void of God's Spirit, oversight, and leadership, influenced by the deceptive teachings of evilness. Unveiling the hidden strategies of Satan is the first step to racial healing. I pray that this writing will be a spark to ignite the beginning of the much-needed dialog for racial healing and spiritual oneness throughout the church body.

---

Throughout the history of the United States of America, the remnants of the bona fide church of Christ have survived strategic attacks of division by restoring the oneness of God's kingdom design at critical times, though never permanently, only temporarily. After each occurrence of the restoration of oneness, the enemy invariably found means to restore the temporarily interrupted division (A clear-cut example of this successful strategy of Satan was seen after the racial and denominational unifying success of the Azusa Street Revival that began in 1906 and ended in 1909).

Again, the professing Christian church finds itself at the spiritual crossroad where oneness must again be restored, only this time permanently. Spiritual confusion within the professing church of Christ has never been greater than in the present day and time, resulting in national and religious chaos reflected in increasing crime and a growing acceptance of immorality and worldliness within the church body.

Regardless of who you are or your racial or religious affiliation, I hope that as you read this historical accounting of the instrumental role of the professing church of Christ in the deception of Christianity in the United States, you will receive it in the spirit of love in which it was written. Some of the provided information may prove offensive to some. Hopefully, many will be delivered from the spirit of religious confusion permeating the professing body of Christ and genuinely receive the salvation that is freely offered by God to all believers.

Since the initial European occupation of the United States, injustice has been sewn into the complex fabric of its existence and is now an accepted way of life, even within certain segments of the professing body of Christ. As partially revealed in this writing, in many instances, critical spiritual components of history have been omitted or inaccurately reported in historical records. There is now a renewed effort to conceal the uncomfortable aspects of the history of the United States regarding race relations, even within religious institutions of knowledge. God informs His people in Hosea 4:6, *"My people are destroyed for lack of knowledge."*

The role of the White professing church of God in Christ in undermining God's blueprint for Biblical Christianity by disregarding its Biblically-required foundation is now being revealed and must be analyzed, and corrected. All acts of ungodliness by the professing body of Christ will be revealed in this end-time season of revelation, correction, and restoration to allow for repentance before Jesus returns. The painful process of correction can no longer be avoided. The salvation of many lost souls practicing the worldly, self-focused, deceptive, and unbiblical pseudo-Christianity permeating the United States hangs in the balance.

An unbiased review of U.S. history reveals a troubling pattern of human injustice perpetrated against the "least" (those in need) in this prosperous nation of White church-supported inequality. This pattern commenced with the initial European occupation and remains to this day.

Injustice in the United States was only able to exist and continue throughout its history because of the support and, in many instances, initiated actions of the racially segregated White professing church of God in Christ. This rebellion by the professing bride of Christ against the foundation of God's throne has served to open many doors of deception within its understanding and practice of Biblical Christianity.

God's "Great Commandment" of love must be understood as the foundation for Christianity, which was demonstrated in the life and sacrificial death of Jesus Christ (God's "Great Commandment" is discussed in detail in chapter 4). These deceptions were instrumental in the development of a pseudo-Christianity, void of Biblically required guidelines for human justice, sacrificial love, and the Holy Spirit's required presence and guidance. As a result, the professing Christian church remains powerless against the forces of evil that have penetrated its once formidable walls of holiness undergirded with radical obedience. This was the defining character of the first-century church which was led by the Apostles of Christ. God never designed His church to operate without His presence, power, and revealing oversight. His church was designed to reflect His character and life-altering power and provide His entrusted provisions in a sin-sick world full of needs.

As noted, God's creation on earth is now in the end-time season of revelation, correction, and restoration as we prepare for the long-awaited return of Jesus. Indeed, these are serious times that require serious commitment and action. Time is no longer allowed for deceptive religious futility. Correction and restoration must begin within the professing body of Christ.

The required teachings of Biblical scripture, which reveals God's heart, His true character, and kingdom order, have been held hostage by worldly-focused, and in far too many instances, self-focused church leadership. The sacrificial love expressed through the cross of Christ has been rejected as a required way of life by His church, His harlot bride. His harlot bride has lost her spiritual virginity to self-focused desires and motives influenced by greed and worldliness. The ways and values of this world are now revealed within the once formidable and holy walls of God's professing church. We use the term "professing" because accepting any form of worldliness is sinful and must be understood as a rejection of God's requirement for holiness. Accepting any form of worldliness invalidates the Christian association and contradicts God's true kingdom design.

The Indian leader, Mahatma Gandhi, who practiced Hinduism, once stated to professing Christians, "I like your Christ; I do not like your Christianity. Your Christians are so unlike your Christ."

It doesn't require the observation of a Hindu to reveal the hypocrisy of the professing body of Christ in the United States of America. An unbiased review of the history of the racially segregated White institutional church's role in human injustice as revealed within this writing confirms the accuracy of Gandhi's observation.

Hopefully, this writing will be instrumental in developing the true church of Christ and establishing God's true kingdom in the United States and throughout His entire creation. Again, we pray that the church body of Christ will receive the information revealed in this writing as God-initiated acts of love purposed to heal the historical racial divide and finally unite God's splintered body under the sacrificial cross of Christ.

What a joy it will be when God's church body realizes the oneness of His original design, knowing that God is pleased and is truly glorified in the United States of America

As in all things that we do, may God be glorified.

(Also, in this writing, relevant information to a discussed topic is provided as a "**side note**.")

---

*"A church that has lost its voice for justice is a church that has lost its relevance in the world."*

*"Injustice anywhere is a threat to justice everywhere. We are caught in an inescapable network of mutuality, tied in a single garment of destiny. Whatever affects one directly affects all indirectly."*

**- Dr. Martin Luther King, Jr. -**

# **Invocation**

*Eternal and most holy God, creator of all humanity, we praise Your holy name and acknowledge You as King of kings and Lord of lords.*

*Time and time again, You have extended Your mercy to Your unfaithful and unloving creation. We can truly say, Your mercy endures forever.*

*We call upon You in this end-time season of revelation, correction, and restoration within the body of Christ to do what only You can do: instill within us a right relationship with You and Your creation. Historically, we have rebelled against Your holy word and are not worthy to be called children of the Most High God. We have not obeyed Your "Great Commandment" of love for You and all humanity. We have prioritized our selfish desires above the needs of all others.*
*Forgive us, we pray Thee.*

*As I begin this reading that chronicles the sad reality of Your church's rebelliousness, I ask that You give me discernment and clarity of understanding so I may put in proper context the seriousness of our failure to reflect Your love to our dying and sin-sick world.*

*Enable me to become an agent of change that You desire from Your servants so that justice will not just remain a hollow phrase written in a pledge to the nation where I now reside, but will be written in my heart as Your ambassador, and as a citizen of Your heavenly kingdom.*

*I ask this for Your glory in the name of Jesus.*
*Amen.*

# Chapter 1

## Injustice, An American Way of Life

There have been numerous high-profile cases of injustice in the United States of America in recent years, which is not unusual when reviewing its history. The United States has a long history of injustice and resistance to God's designed spiritual order for His kingdom, even within groups of the professing body of Christ. Injustice is a 'hot-button' topic in the United States and practically all other countries worldwide.

World history, including the history of Christianity, reveals that God's creation has consistently rebelled against His designed order for human relations within His kingdom on earth.

After the death of the first-century apostles of Christ, Satan launched an attack against the holy throne of Almighty God, a strategy that, after 2000 years, is still effective in undermining God's design for His kingdom on earth. Satan effectively used the body of Christ, His bride (In the United States, mainly those of European descent), as his vehicle of rebellion against God's heavenly throne grounded on justice and righteousness.

The history of the United States European population has been intertwined with human injustice. Reportedly, the initial European occupation of America was primarily based on a desire for religious freedom. However, their proceeding actions did not reflect the oneness and sacrificial love of God's "Great Commandment" and the Biblical Christianity they professed. Though professing to be Christians, their initial focus on land acquisition resulted in the slaughter and enslavement of millions of Native Americans, the original inhabitants. This early historical sense of Divine entitlement has been reflected in many actions and inactions throughout the history of the United States.

Perhaps difficult to believe, the evil presence and influence permeating the United States throughout its history can be mostly attributed to these initial self-focused sins of greed and murder and other ungodly acts perpetrated against the vulnerable ones of God's creation. Though the slaughter and enslavement of millions of Native Americans by the first European invaders characterized the beginning of the United States experience, these atrocities of ungodly injustice were just the beginning of many more to follow.

This early-history disregard for human justice and sacrificial Biblical love was reflected in a large segment of the body of professing White Christians in the United States throughout the following centuries of its existence.

By and large, conservative White professing Christians did not prioritize or support justice when considering the human rights of racial minorities and the oppressed in the United States of America. Historically, in rebellion against God's word, they primarily supported and/or participated in injustice, condoned it, or remained passive during struggles for justice for the oppressed.

---

Before we continue, we need to clarify the Biblical meaning of "justice." So, what is "**justice**?" In the Biblical perspective, "justice" is defined as lifting the downtrodden [oppressed (Isa. 1:17, Lk. 19:8,9)] to wholeness, honoring and securing the God-given rights of every human being as an equal recipient of God's creation (ref. Mark 12:31).

---

If you want an honest answer to why the United States of America is so divided or why the professing Christian church is ineffective and void of Christ's character, you don't have to look any further than an unbiased analysis of the history and current status of injustice in the United States.

Since time is of the essence as we anticipate the return of Jesus, let's not continue to "beat around the bush" but jump right into it.

---

Practically every Native American, African American, Asian American, Hispanic American, or Latino American has personal stories of racial injustice perpetrated against them or a family member, even those who may be considered financially successful.

Conversely, perhaps because of spiritual unawareness and historical White privilege resulting from being the majority race in a democratic and ungodly society, injustice in America is not seen by most White Americans as a serious problem. Looking through the lens of worldliness and self-focused desires and priorities can easily give a distorted view of spiritual reality as related to required Biblical principles.

When one race is privileged to control the order of a society through a government of majority rule, the government is generally responsive to their needs and desires above all other races within that society. Racial anarchy can easily result when those desires are strictly self-focused with little to no concern for the needs of minority races within the society. This order of priorities usually results in racial inequality. Racial inequality is reinforced by a desire of those in government leadership to please the voting majority in order to receive their support to remain in office. Generally, the desires of an ungodly, unregenerate society are self-focused and not God-focused, resulting in ungodliness and racial division.

For racial justice to manifest in such a society, Godly love must be understood and displayed by the majority race. This love must start with a willingness to reflect the character of Christ grounded on His sacrificial cross as its foundation. In other words, the majority race in every democratic society must convert to true Biblical Christianity and genuinely understand and live according to its sacrificial tenets.

Various polls reflect that the majority of American adults profess to be "Christian." However, as attested by statistical data of institutional, government-endorsed inequality, this nation's character and governmental leadership do not reflect Biblical Christianity as being a majority of the population.

Without interracial dialog, open communication, and a willingness to get to know each other personally, misconceptions are to be expected, which can easily lead to racial stereotyping. Racial stereotyping is having perceptions, ideas, or beliefs about the attributes of a particular race.

"Stereotypes, fiction though they are, sometimes have one foot in reality. That is why many people believe them. Stereotypes arise from headlines that, to an extent, tell some of the story. But they fudge on the details. And in the final analysis, stereotypes fail to justly describe their subjects."[1] The problem of racial stereotyping is prevalent throughout the American society. Racial stereotyping affects every area of life and is often the reason for biases in interracial human relationships and race-focused governmental policies.

---

The results of a Pew Research Center poll released on June 27, 2016, stated, "Black and white adults have widely different perceptions about what life is like for blacks in the U.S. For example, by large margins, blacks are more likely than whites to say black people are treated less fairly in the workplace (a difference of 42 percentage points), when applying for a loan or mortgage (41 points), in dealing with the police (34 points), in the courts (32 points), in stores or restaurants (28 points), and when voting in elections (23 points). By a margin of at least 20 percentage points, blacks are also more likely than whites to say racial discrimination (70% vs. 36%), lower quality schools (75% vs. 53%), and lack of jobs (66% vs. 45%) are major reasons that blacks may have a harder time getting ahead than whites.

Blacks are also about twice as likely as whites to say too little attention is paid to race and racial issues in the U.S. these days (58% vs. 27%)."[2]

It is difficult to understand the plight of minorities in a self-focused and race-focused society unless you "walk in their shoes." Understanding first begins with communication and association.

---

If you are a White American and know any Native Americans, African Americans, Asian Americans, Hispanic Americans, or Latino Americans, and desire to give the impression that you are compassionate and concerned about their concerns, ask them to share their stories of racial injustice with you. If they are open, honest, and comfortable in talking to you, chances are you will get that for which you ask. Meaningful relationships and lasting change begin with open and honest dialog and a willingness to "walk in the shoes" of the oppressed. These bold actions require a desire to break away from the herd to which we belong and its racist and ungodly tendencies. These bold actions can often result in a severed relationship with one's herd, who, though perpetrating the evils of racism, may still feel a sense of betrayal.

---

I am reminded of one such individual who was compassionate and bold enough to do so. His experiences were documented in the book *"Black Like Me."*

In the late 1950s, a White man named John Howard Griffin, a novelist living in Mansfield, Texas had a burning desire to experience and understand what living as an African American in the Deep South would be like. He realized that he had to "walk in their shoes" to gain this understanding. He decided to find out by first transforming his skin color to disguise his whiteness.

Though residing in Texas, he moved to New Orleans, Louisiana, away from his family, where he found a dermatologist to guide him through a temporary skin color transformation from White to Black. After undergoing the required medical treatments to change his skin color, including spending time under ultraviolet lighting, his skin changed to the darkness of an African American. After the skin color transformation, he shaved his head and truly looked like a middle-aged bald-headed African American. He then began a journey throughout four states in the Deep South that lasted six weeks, from November 6 to December 14, 1959. He decided to maintain his name and everything about his true character. The only thing that he changed was his skin color. He wanted to verify if Southern Whites judged and treated African Americans solely by their skin color and not the content of their character. This life-altering journey took him through parts of Louisiana, Mississippi, Alabama, and Georgia.

His motivation for doing this was to determine how the difference gap between the living conditions for Whites and Blacks in the United States could be bridged. He realized that there was no serious communication between the two races and, therefore, no hope of ever coming together as one.

This drastic action truly gave him the experience of living as an African American in the racist Deep South of the late 1950s. This occurred during the time of the Jim Crow laws and open, unwarranted hostility by Whites toward African Americans. Though carefully planned, he was not prepared for what he would experience.

He soon discovered that one's skin color made all the difference in how one was treated in the Deep South. His first experience was realizing the limitations of establishments that he could enter, where he was welcomed before his skin color transformation. He experienced a complete attitude change towards him from Whites, whom he had encountered before his transformation. Whereas before, they treated him with dignity and respect as one of their own, now they treated him just the opposite. He was now hated and disrespected by his own race simply because of the color of his skin.

It became a serious struggle to find public places where he could eat or locations where he could stay or simply use a restroom. While traveling on public transportation, he experienced, for the first time in his life, what it was like to have to sit in the back area of buses and the inability to exit the bus during rest stops to use "White-only" restrooms. He witnessed firsthand the hatred of his White race towards African Americans simply because of the color of their skin.

He experienced the darker side of humanity that he was oblivious to beforehand. For the first time in his life, he experienced and saw how institutional racism was a reality in the Jim Crow Deep South. Most Whites of today truly believe that institutional racism does not exist in the United States and that equal opportunity is afforded to all who are willing to take advantage of it. Many feel that African Americans are exaggerating when they acknowledge the reality of institutional racism. Many Whites view the African American acknowledgment as an attempt to gain local and worldwide sympathy and advantage by creating, in their minds, a problem that does not exist.

Concerned Whites of today need to take a page from his life-altering journey. You can only see and understand the reality of life for others when you place yourself in their position and truly "walk in their shoes."

After surviving this dangerous ordeal that included many perils and transforming his skin back to white, he was not prepared for what would happen next.

He revealed his experience in writing and many public interviews on national and international radio and television talk shows. He brought awareness to the seriousness of the racial divide in the Deep South states of the United States of America and the unlikeness of the White race ever receiving African Americans as their peers and equals.

It is common in race relations in the United States that when one breaks away from their "herd" and does something contrary to the herd's interests, the herd will turn against them and no longer view them as one of their own. Though many people praised him for his bold action, not everyone was pleased. The White citizens of Mansfield united in expressing their hatred of him. This attitude is commonly seen throughout the history of the United States toward Whites who seek justice and righteousness for minority race groups and the oppressed.

He and his family started receiving hate calls and death threats from members of the White race who felt that he had betrayed them. They viewed him as one who exaggerated the extent of their "dirty laundry" and exposed it to the world. They felt they had been blindsided without an advanced warning of his intentions. As he realized, an advanced warning would have allowed them the necessary time to determine an effective explanation and course of action as a countermeasure. So, understandably, he did not reveal what he was planning to do. As to be expected, when the dark side of their character was revealed to the world, they lashed out in anger. He was hanged in effigy from a red light wire in downtown Mansfield, Texas. A dummy, half white, half black, with his name on it with a yellow streak painted on its back, was hung from a wire. After many threats from angry Whites who felt betrayed, he and his entire family had to eventually move from Mansfield, Texas, out of fear for their safety.

This experience truly changed his life and his understanding of the plight of African Americans in the Deep South from the injustices of his own race. He discovered that in the Deep South, the content of one's character did not matter for the treatment of African Americans. The only thing that mattered was the color of their skin.

Though some feel that times have changed, many will agree that the injustices that he experienced back then while briefly living as an African American, to varying extents, are still being experienced by minorities in America today.

---

**Hopefully, this writing will be helpful to all White and minority Americans who genuinely believe that human injustice is a reality and desire a spiritual reality change. We hope to show that injustice was sewn into the very fabric of the United States from its inception and maintained throughout its history primarily by the support, and in many instances, orchestrated activities of the historical racially segregated White institutional church. We hope to show that its support of injustice reflected a direct spiritual attack orchestrated by Satan against God's heavenly throne. We also hope that Christianity can establish its footing on the Biblical foundation of justice and righteousness grounded on God's "Great Commandment" of love for the first time in the United States and before the long-awaited return of Jesus.**

---

As stated, practically every minority in the United States of America has personal stories of racial injustice.

My personal stories of racial injustice in my family are numerous. I don't have to look any further than my household while growing up to see the effects of White-initiated institutional injustice against minorities in the United States. I will share them in the next chapter.

---

However, as a brief history, I was born and raised in a part of Mississippi called the Delta, a part of the area that was informally known as the "Bible Belt." The term "Bible Belt" is believed to have been introduced in 1924. Merriam-Webster defines the "Bible Belt" as an area chiefly in the southern U.S. whose inhabitants are believed to hold uncritical allegiance to the literal accuracy of the Bible broadly: an area characterized by ardent religious fundamentalism. The term was derived from an ardent determination for the way of life based on the literal interpretations of the Bible in Evangelical denominations. To make this understanding as simple as possible, the religious majority, comprised mostly of Whites, believed in living according to the requirements of the Holy Word of God.

As I matured in life and gained more awareness of spiritual reality, I began to question the legitimacy of the characterization of the Mississippi Delta as part of the "Bible Belt." As I read and better understood the Bible, I never saw or experienced any positive influence of the Bible in race relations and everyday life and the then racially segregated White institutional church. The perpetrators of racism and inequality seemingly were not influenced by the teachings of Holy Scripture, though most of them were actively involved in institutional religion and professed to believe in the Bible as the inerrant word of God.

I never understood the spiritual blindness of someone who professed Christianity but could not love anyone of the opposite race since the foundation for Christianity was passionate, sacrificial, and unconditional love for all humanity, in other words, loving as Jesus loved.

I never understood the boldness of sin, how an individual could rebel against God by disobeying His commandments and then desire and expect His acceptance of their unbiblical life-focus of hate-inspired evilness.

I never understood how an individual could disguise his identity to humanity by putting on a white robe and hood of hate and burning crosses as a means of terror on Saturday night and serve as a church deacon on Sunday morning for the One Who died on a cross, demonstrating unconditional love for all humanity and obedience to the Father.

I could never understand the self-considered superiority that many Whites felt towards other races and the fear and hatred Whites had for African Americans rather than remorse for their forced labor and genocide through the injustice of African slavery. This forced and unjust labor was instrumental in building the wealth of the United States and its economy. The U.S. continues to reap benefits from its ungodly history of slavery and racial injustice against its minority race groups.

I could go on listing the things I could not understand regarding the White race in the "Bible Belt." In summary, I could never understand the immorality and religious hypocrisy throughout the "Bible Belt" by those of the White race who professed Christianity but hated all minorities in the U.S. and lived in open rebellion against God's heavenly throne.

As I began to see the vastness of this spiritual confusion and the fact that to differing degrees it existed throughout the United States, I began to discern it as an institutional strategy of evilness orchestrated by Satan against the then racially segregated institutional White church system in the U.S., a strategy that still exists today. As Paul wrote in the book of Ephesians chapter 6, verse 12, *"For we wrestle not against flesh and blood, but against principalities, against powers, against the rulers of the darkness of this world, against spiritual wickedness in high places."* **Our spiritual battles are not with humanity but with Satan and his evil forces operating through humanity.**

I realize that my experiences and understandings will be refuted by many and perhaps, to some, will seemingly border on racism, but don't draw any conclusions at this point. We are just beginning, so stay with me until the end as we review many suppressed facts of America's history for spiritual clarity.

---

[(As a clarification, in this writing, we will often use the expression **"White church."** In doing so, we are referencing those churches with European (White) leadership and primarily

European (White) membership. It is important to note that as a means to maintain racial segregation, before the 1970s, most White churches in the Deep South Bible Belt were racially segregated (They did not allow African American attendance or membership), in opposition to the foundational tenets of Christianity. In 1959, nearly a century after slavery was abolished, less than two dozen of the South's 100,000 White churches were known to have any Black members. Today, 86% of American churches lack any meaningful racial diversity.[3]]

(Also, to clarify, we will frequently use the description **"conservative White professing Christians."** In doing so, we are referencing White professing Christians who believe in the entirety of the Bible but disregard the total inclusiveness of God's 'Great Commandment' in their daily life, especially when referencing race relations and what is identified as social justice issues, which we will address later in this writing. As earlier noted, the term **"White"** references those of European descent with light skin color. Also, we use the term **"professing"** simply because honoring these exclusions invalidates the Christian association. In fairness, those who honor these exclusions represent a large segment of the White professing Christians in the U.S.; however, they do not comprise the entirety of this group. God always establishes a remnant for His glory and the survival and advancement of His true kingdom on earth. Also, in the context of this writing, the term **"conservative"** references those who desire to maintain the traditional moral values of their forefathers, and in many instances, instead of clearly understood foundational Biblical principles.**)**

(Finally, throughout this writing, we will alternate between the names "America," "United States," and "U.S." Each instance denotes the country of the United States of America.)

---

Throughout the history of the United States of America, in rebellion against the "Great Commandment" of God and His heavenly throne, the historical racially segregated institutional White Church mirrored the general ungodly, unjust, and self-focused ways and values of the White atheistic society in the U.S. rather than being a model and source of hope for their eternal salvation. In reality, though professing Christ as Lord and Savior, as undiscerning and mostly disguised agents of evilness, the racially segregated institutional White church modeled a false, but convincing, version of Christianity, thus, enhancing the deception of Christianity in America and creating a false sense of salvation.

---

*"Evil men do not understand justice, But those who seek the LORD understand all."*
**Proverbs 28:5**

---

*"Keep justice, and do righteousness, for My salvation is about to come, and My righteousness to be revealed."*
**Isaiah 56:1**

---

*"For the LORD loves justice, and does not forsake His saints. They are preserved forever, but the descendants of the wicked shall be cut off."*
**Psalm 37:28**

---

# Chapter 2

## Personal Stories of Racial Injustice

As stated in the previous chapter, practically every African American, Asian American, Hispanic American, Latino American, or Native American has personal stories of racial injustice perpetrated against them or a family member.

I can recall many injustices in my lifetime, from growing up in the 1950s and 1960s in the Jim Crow segregated South to becoming the first generation of African Americans hired in management in the telecommunications industry in New Orleans, Louisiana, and the state of Louisiana.

My hiring resulted from a federal mandate, which resulted from a successful NAACP lawsuit against a major telecommunications company because of a lack of African Americans in management. After accepting this position in management and moving to New Orleans from Atlanta, Georgia, I was not prepared for what was to follow.

My first supervisor was an elderly White male with a high school degree who felt threatened by my presence because I had a college degree in mathematics, of which he had little understanding. Obviously, he was unqualified to be a manager in engineering, and his newly-hired African American subordinates often questioned how that could have happened. However, as so often seen in America, the required qualifications for upper management were raised to a higher standard after African Americans were hired into management. Much of my employment experience was spent fighting for justice in a racially hostile work environment due to institutional racism. Racism was prevalent against all of the newly hired African American management employees throughout that company. The overt racism resulted in several lawsuits filed by African American management employees seeking justice, including my own.

I can utilize this chapter to detail my experiences of injustice even while serving as a pastor in a major White-controlled denomination. However, I will forgo detailing my personal experiences and use the remainder of this chapter to highlight my parents' experiences and tireless work. To honor them and the many unsung heroes for justice whose stories will never be told, I will share abbreviated accounts of their experiences. In doing so, I hope others who have stories to tell will be encouraged to do likewise.

---

I was blessed to have two parents who dedicated their lives to making the lives of others better during the evil time of Jim Crow-ordered segregation. Though now deceased, my father was a pastor in a major denomination, and my mother was a public school principal/teacher in Holmes County, Mississippi. They both were dedicated to their professions and served the Lord, first and foremost, with all diligence. By God's grace, they were able to persevere under the unbearable weight of the White church-supported Jim Crow laws reflecting racial hatred and institutional racism throughout the Southern Bible Belt.

---

*"May the LORD our God be with us, as He was with our fathers."*
### 1st Kings 8:57

---

*"Our fathers trusted in You; They trusted, and You delivered them."*
### Psalm 22:4

# Rev. Walter B. Pennington, Sr. (1923-2004)

My dad pastored for 44 years in a multi-racial denominational religious institution in the state of Mississippi. Many of those years were also spent working for civil rights for African Americans in Noxubee County, where he pastored in Macon, Mississippi, for a while. He received much credit for improving the conditions of injustice against African Americans in Noxubee County in the 1960s. He viewed racism in Macon as atrocious and realized that something had to be done.

Rev. Pennington was instrumental in organizing protests against White merchants because of their mistreatment of African Americans. Though welcoming African Americans as customers to receive their finances, many White merchants refused to employ or accept them in their segregated residential communities, schools, and churches. He formed the first NAACP branch in Noxubee County and was actively involved in organizing resistance to segregation and other areas of injustice.

Eventually, his leadership for civil rights in Noxubee County became a source of friction between him and the White-controlled denomination in which he pastored. Rather than supporting his Bible-based activism for human rights and equality, his denomination reassigned him to a church in another county. This "underhanded" move severed his leadership and activism in the Noxubee County African American community and was a setback for the progress made under his community leadership. This open rebuke of his activism by his White-controlled denomination deeply troubled him regarding the legitimacy of their profession of faith. As can be witnessed in many religious institutions today, their allegiance to the concerns and fears of their race was prioritized above their commitment to God Almighty, thus reinforcing the deception of Christianity.

Indeed, as throughout the history of America, the 1950s and 1960s were turbulent times for African Americans seeking racial justice. As is today, racial hatred and institutional racism were prevalent throughout America. However, in the 50s and 60s, they were more openly revealed and obvious.

---

In response to the civil rights movements of the 1950s, the state of Mississippi secretly formed "The Sovereignty Commission." This commission was a state-funded agency founded in the 1950s to fight integration in Mississippi. This immoral, White church-supported commission was secretly funded with public funds and approved by a racist all-white state legislature. During its existence, the commission profiled more than 87,000 persons associated with or suspected to be associated with the civil rights movement (which they opposed). It investigated the work, credit histories, and even personal relations of the persons it investigated. The secret files for this organization were closed under a secrecy order by the Mississippi Legislature in 1977. However, a federal judge ordered them to be released and opened to the public in March 1998 following years of legal battles. The files included nearly 132,000 pages detailing this commission's secret and immoral workings in fighting integration in Mississippi.

When reviewing these files, Rev. Walter B. Pennington's name appears more often than any other name, reflecting his leadership's seriousness and effectiveness in activism for racial equality.

An abbreviated accounting of his activism was published in a local newspaper in 1998 under the front page title "Preacher sought positive change." This article stated:

"There's a good reason Rev. W. B. Pennington's name appears so many times in the recently opened records of the Mississippi Sovereignty Commission.

Long before Reecy Dickson and Ike Brown started championing the rights of Noxubee County blacks, there was Pennington.

His name appears more often than any other when searching through nearly 132,000 pages of documents opened by a federal court order on March 17.

And even today, Pennington receives much of the credit for improving conditions for blacks in Noxubee County.

"When I first came to Noxubee County in 1962, I was appalled at how blacks were treated," said Pennington, now semi-retired and living in Starkville.

"A black man couldn't walk down Jefferson Street wearing a white shirt without being chased off the street," said Pennington.

Pennington came to Macon as pastor of St. Paul United Methodist Church. The King Street church was then, and still is, one of the largest black churches in Noxubee County.

"It didn't take me long to figure out that Noxubee County needed change," he said. "There were no civil rights activities going on, and whites were awfully cruel to blacks."

Pennington credits longtime sheriff Emmett Farrar with keeping Noxubee County behind the rest of the state in racial tolerance. "He ruled Noxubee County with an iron fist," Pennington said.

Pennington, who said he had never been involved in civil rights activities before coming to Macon, said he began his mission slowly. "Every time I'd preach at a different church around the county, I'd drop a few little hints," he said. "Finally, in 1966, after a service at Shuqualak, a man named Titus Tippett came up to me and said he and a group of men wanted to meet with me at Miller's Chapel Church in Macon," Pennington said. "When I got to the meeting, there were six or seven black men there, and they said they wanted to start a movement for change in Noxubee County, and they wanted me to be their leader," he said. "That's when it all started."

"Pennington remembers in detail the massive task that began that night and climaxed with the prize, the federally supervised, first-ever voter registration for blacks in the basement of the Macon Post Office in 1967.

"Nobody had a clue we were going to do it," said Pennington. "We had made a vow among all of us to move about our business quietly during the process." He said, "But when we were ready to do it, the last thing I did was to make a call to Washington, D.C. That's all it took to get the federal protection we needed."

"The best thing that ever happened to Noxubee blacks came the next year when Doc Taylor was elected sheriff," Pennington said. "When Doc Taylor was elected, the selective arrests, jail beatings, and mistreatment of blacks all came to an end."

Pennington said Taylor had approached him just prior to the election, asking for support and pledging to end the mistreatment of blacks by the sheriff's department if he would help him get elected. "I believed him, and he kept his word," Pennington said.

With help from the newly registered black voters, Taylor won a landslide victory in the 1967 election, earning more than twice that of his next closest opponent, Mrs. Emmett Farrar.

"Doc Taylor sent the Farrars back to the farm," Pennington said.

Taylor, who served from 1968 until 1972, hired the first black to ever wear a police uniform in Noxubee County when he named Garrett Doss as a deputy. Doss died in 1969 when he was shot by another black man while trying to make an arrest near Macon's Baptist Hill Community.

Taylor, who returned to his successful farming career after the one term in office, remembers those years as tough. "I have a lot of fond memories of those years, but I also remember how tough it was on my family," he said in an interview this week. "I'm glad someone remembers me favorably."

Taylor said his only goal when he took over as sheriff in 1968 was to bring about fair and honest law enforcement for all of Noxubee citizens. "But, change in Noxubee County has never been easy," he said.

One of the most prominently mentioned aspects of Pennington's tenure as leader of Noxubee's black population is his relationship with one of his followers, the late Rev. John Wesley Hunter of Shuqualak.

"If I have one regret about my years in Noxubee County, that would be it," Pennington says.

Sovereignty Commission records from the late 60s refer often to the rift that developed between Pennington and Hunter.

"I recruited him, and I formed the first Noxubee branch of the NAACP, and I put him in charge," said Pennington. "And, then, I found him a church and got him installed as pastor – the biggest mistake I've ever made."

But, Pennington said Hunter quickly became jealous and began a scheme to take away the power he had developed in the black community. "He saw what I had done, and he wanted it for himself."

Pennington agrees with Sovereignty Commission reports that say he and Hunter had contrasting styles. "I was a behind-the-scenes kind of leader, and Hunter was very confrontational," he said.

Pennington also agrees with reports that say the county's black population soon became divided over the split.

When the United Methodist Conference transferred Pennington to a church in Louisville, it opened the door for Hunter to take over.

"He never developed the following he hoped for," Pennington said

Pennington, who is a longtime subscriber to "The Beacon," says he still keeps a close watch on Noxubee County even though he hasn't visited here in years.

"I'm disturbed by a lot of the things I see happening, especially the fact that blacks are now totally controlling politics there," Pennington said. "I never dreamed of the day it would come to that. I always preached that we needed to involve our people in the political process – not take it over."

Pennington said he hopes the Noxubee County government can one day be more diverse. "You won't see positive change until that happens," he said.

Pennington said he still remembers well his last few days in Macon when word got out that he would be leaving. "I had developed a lot of friendships with white people in Noxubee County," he said. "Not many of them agreed with me, but they appreciated the fact that I wasn't a radical."

Pennington said many whites came to see him as he began making moving plans. He said they said they feared what would happen if Hunter took charge.

"I can still see Supervisor Mullins (District Two's Bill Mullins) stopping by my television repair shop and telling me he hated to see me go," he said. "I remember his words like it was yesterday. He said, 'Rev. Pennington, you've freed a lot of white folks in Noxubee County, too.'"[1]

(The Mississippi Sovereignty Commission files can be accessed at https://da.mdah.ms.gov>sovcom)

---

As throughout the Bible Belt, integration never worked in Noxubee County. Whites, while primarily professing Christianity, fled the residential communities and public schools for private schools following integration, and today, the public schools remain almost totally black.

Rev. Pennington truly hoped that through his efforts of compassion in seeking justice for African Americans, many Whites would also be delivered from their spiritual confusion, turn from their evil ways, and receive the salvation that God was offering. He was genuinely concerned and often prayed for the spiritual direction of his multi-racial yet segregated denomination. He hoped they would one day be able to recognize the 'errors of their way' and turn from their wicked ways and genuinely represent God's kingdom in all its glory as drum majors and spiritual leaders for justice and righteousness.

Though the denomination he was affiliated with was multi-racial, the White-dominated leadership supported segregation efforts to the delight of their professing White constituents and White financial supporters.

His denomination was multi-racial but White-controlled. African Americans had very little input into the decision-making process. Rather than be a beacon of light and hope for God's will during the darkness of that time, the leadership primarily honored the Jim Crow laws of that era. (The Jim Crow laws will be discussed in more detail in Chapter 8.)

All pastoral church appointments and leadership positions remained strictly along racial lines. African American pastors were paid less than White pastors mainly because of inadequate resources within their assigned churches. By and large, the White churches were more affluent and financially stable. As in some churches today, African American pastors were never allowed to pastor White churches throughout the "Bible Belt," and White churches would never accept an African American pastor.

Though this denomination professed Christianity, like most others with substantial White involvement during that era, they rebelled against its foundation of passionate, sacrificial, and unconditional love for all humanity. In other words, they were instrumental in preserving the pseudo-Christianity of this nation's European founding fathers. Their refusal to accept God's word and commit to Christianity's Biblical tenets must be seen as a primary cause for the continuation of the deception of the existence of true Biblical Christianity throughout the "Bible Belt" and the entirety of America.

---

***"Throughout history, it has been the inaction of those who could have acted; the indifference of those who should have known better; the silence of the voice of justice when it mattered most; that has made it possible for evil to triumph."***

**- Haile Selassie**

# **Mrs. Susie B. Pennington (1921-1991)**

My mother served as a principal in the racially segregated and unequal school system in Holmes County, Mississippi, for many years of her teaching career. The inequality in the school system in Holmes County during the 1950s and 1960s was without parallel.

She taught in the small towns of Cruger and Tchula, Mississippi, where racial injustice was the accepted way of life. There were no similarities between the public schools for African Americans and the public schools for Whites.

The public school for African Americans in Cruger was deplorable even by the unacceptable standards of that era.

The school did not have running water, a hot lunch program, or indoor bathroom facilities. Eventually, she convinced the school board to provide a snack and milk machine so that the students would at least have some nourishment, even though it would be subpar.

Behind the school building were two outhouse-type structures used as bathroom facilities, one for boys and the other for girls. The teachers were also required to use them. Obviously, this inconvenience presented health concerns and challenges during periods of rain and adverse weather conditions. If you are unfamiliar with outhouses, they had no disposable waste mechanism or sanitary treatment for waste material. They were simple wood structures comprised of a simple hand-made toilet situated over a dug-out pit to collect untreated waste material. To those of us who have never experienced using odious outhouses as bathroom facilities, it is difficult to imagine the horribleness of having to do so.

The all-white Holmes County school board would have the poorly constructed wood floors of the school periodically coated with motor oil to protect the wood. Obviously, there was no regard for children and teachers breathing the hazardous fumes. I recall how slippery the floors were after a fresh coating of oil, which required caution while moving around. There was no Board of Health oversight for the concerns of African Americans in Holmes County.

The building had no insulation and no consistent outer covering. The light of day would often shine through the many cracks in the poorly-constructed walls. In the winter, the building was insufficiently heated by coal-burning heaters that were located in the center of the classrooms. There were no safety rail guards or protection to keep the teachers and children from accidentally touching these hot heaters during their times of use. Students would often receive burns from accidentally touching them. There were only three coal-burning heaters for the entire building. One classroom was unheated. Most children had to keep their coats on during the cold winter months. I remember my mother and the other two teachers arriving early during the winter seasons to start the fire in the heaters to warm the building, which was never comfortable or evenly heated. The first children to arrive for school were responsible for going outside to bring in the necessary coal for the heaters. The coal was usually dumped in a pile on the side of the building. Breathing the air from the indoor burning of coal that escaped from the heaters' exhausts presented another health hazard.

I remember her often having to go into her purse to provide for a child's needs. The town of Cruger was considered to be poor by normal standards of prosperity during that time frame. There were few jobs available, and many African Americans lived on White-owned plantations. Many others were not employed or underpaid. The African American teachers and employees in Holmes County were paid less than their White counterparts. Often, she would have to provide a child with some item of clothing. She often remained late to ensure the fire in the heaters was completely out, and the children were safely home.

The two main rooms of the school building were separated by sheets strung together and were lighted by a single light bulb connected to an unprotected electrical wire hanging from the ceiling. Needless to say, this dangerous and irresponsible lighting was inadequate for reading and learning, and noise from the adjacent classroom was often distracting.

There was no air conditioning. Therefore, windows had to remain open during the hot Delta months. The windows did not have screens, so wasps and other insects were a constant nuisance and obstacle to learning.

The school was isolated on the opposite side of the busy main highway that ran adjacent to the town. So, students had to cross the highway to get to and from school each day. They were instructed to always look both ways and run when the traffic was clear when crossing alone. The school board did not provide crossing and safety measures for the school, nor did the county or town. Accidents were always a major concern as there were no "caution" or "reduce speed" signs to warn motorists of children crossing the highway.

Once the White school received new textbooks, their old ones were sent to the African American school for their use. Many of those textbooks were often missing pages and covers or were littered with markings. She never expressed anger to her students and teachers regarding these injustices but prayed for and trusted God's oversight. Complaining to the racist all-white school board could result in dismissal.

She required excellence and did not accept excuses from her students or teachers (Philippians 4:13). Many of her students were successful in life, as proof that with determination and God's favor, all obstacles in life can be overcome. I can go on with the inequities of this school and system, but I think that you get the picture.

In contrast, the White school was on the other side of the highway in the affluent, racially segregated White community. Everything we mentioned that the African American school did not have was found at the White school, which was a much better learning and childhood development environment. The White school was constructed out of brick and mortar and was a much better-constructed and designed building. They had a cafeteria with a hot lunch program, indoor bathroom facilities with public running water, cold water fountains, etc.

I know it sounds like I am exaggerating the conditions at the African American school because this sounds like the conditions in a third-world country where extreme poverty limits resources and the things that can be done. I knew you would think so. Therefore, I have included some available pictures for your review in the appendix.

These inequities resulted from a racist, White church-supported, all-white school board whose only interest was the education of White children. These types of injustices were prevalent throughout the "Bible Belt" and the entire nation, perhaps not to the degree of atrociousness and ungodliness as existed in Holmes County, Mississippi. However, they were experienced to some degree by all minorities throughout America. This ungodly reality of White church-condoned race relations in America's history must not be ignored or suppressed, but highlighted so as to never be repeated.

---

According to Gallup, 95% of adults in America professed Christianity in 1955 (Gallup, Inc. is an American analytic and advisory company known for its public opinion polls conducted worldwide). As recently as 1990, 90% of Americans identified as Christians compared to about two-thirds today, as the Pew Research Center reported. Considering that Holmes County was a part of the "Bible Belt," we can rightfully assume that many members of the all-white Holmes County School Board were professing Christians or had influential friends or family members who professed Christianity. This likely reality highlights the widespread spiritual confusion that existed in America's history and the racially segregated White professing Christian church. Regretfully, it continues to this day among White professing Christians throughout America and beyond.

---

The inequities described in Holmes County, Mississippi, were not unique. They were prevalent in practically all public school systems throughout the South. They were the primary impetus for increasing public protests throughout the South for integration and racial equality. Many of these public protests resulted in violence perpetrated against African American protesters by all-white police forces and unrestrained, angry White citizens. Many of these hateful White citizens erroneously professed Christianity, thus enhancing its deception in America through their rebellious misrepresentations.

These inequities and the resulting protests were the impetus for the Federal court order mandating nationwide public school integration. The U.S. Supreme Court mandated the legal ending of public school segregation in 1954 in its Brown vs. Board of Education ruling. On May 17, 1954, U.S. Supreme Court Justice Earl Warren delivered the unanimous ruling.

In this milestone decision, the Supreme Court ruled that separating children in public schools based on race was unconstitutional. It signaled the end of legalized racial segregation in public schools throughout America. This decision overruled the "separate but equal" principle set forth in the 1869 Plessy v. Ferguson case.

As expected, this Supreme Court order was not well-received by Whites throughout the racially segregated Southern "Bible Belt." Whites throughout the South were determined not to allow their children to integrate with African American children. They immediately took action to counter this Supreme Court decision. Meetings were held in White churches throughout the South to devise strategies and long-term solutions. This forced, court-ordered desegregation led to the formation of many private academies throughout the South (most of them are still active today, and the student bodies and administrations are overwhelmingly White). These academies were organized solely to prevent White children from integrating into the public school systems with African American children.

In an article written in "The Atlantic Daily Newspaper," the author wrote, "More than four decades after they were established, "segregation academies" in Mississippi towns like Indianola continue to define nearly every aspect of community life. Hundreds of these schools opened across the country in the 20 years after the Brown v. Board decision, particularly in southern states like Mississippi, Arkansas, Alabama, and Virginia. While an unknown number endure outside of Mississippi, the Delta remains their strongest bastion.

A Hechinger Report analysis of private school demographics (using data compiled on the National Center for Education Statistics website) found that more than 35 such academies survive in Mississippi, many of them in rural Delta communities like Indianola. Each of the schools was founded between 1964 and 1972 in response to anticipated or actual desegregation orders, and all of them enroll fewer than two percent black students. (The number of Mississippi "segregation academies" swells well above 35 if schools where the black enrollment is between three and 10 percent are counted.) At some of them, including Benton Academy near Yazoo City and Carroll Academy near Greenwood, not a single black student attended in 2010, according to the most recent data. Others, like Indianola Academy, have a small amount of diversity."

It would be easy to see Indianola and Mississippi, more generally, as an anomaly when it comes to education: hyper-segregated, fraught with racial mistrust, and stuck in the past. But in some respects, the story of education in Indianola is becoming the story of education in America.

Indianola, like other segregated communities across the country, is defined not only by two school systems and two sides of town but by two competing narratives that attempt to explain segregation's stubborn persistence."[2]

---

The White institutional church played a vital role in forming and supporting the academy school system throughout the South.

In an article entitled "The Academy Stories," the author stated, "White churches rarely preached loyalty to public schools. In fact, Protestant churches gave essential support to segregation academies in community after community.

Typically, churches helped new academies by volunteering use of their Sunday School rooms until an actual academy's construction.

Briarcrest Baptist School in Memphis, which proclaimed itself the biggest non-Catholic Christian school system in the nation, initially spread out its classes between about a dozen Southern Baptist churches in the area. The school, organized for students to flee 1973 court-ordered busing in Memphis, was the setting for the book and film "The Blind Side." The motto of its building campaign as busing began was: "With God, nothing is impossible."

White churches were involved with segregation academies at every step. Many academies sprung up almost overnight in small towns where Sunday School classrooms were the only place that could house students and teachers."[3]

Indeed, White churches throughout the "Bible Belt" opened their doors to desperate parents fleeing forced school desegregation as temporary school facilities until the private academies could be built. Their willful involvement accounted for the success of the segregated academy system.

---

I included my parents' career inequities and involvement in the struggle for racial justice because, like so many unsung heroes and drum majors for racial justice, their stories of involvement will never be documented or known.

So, I salute all of the unknown heroes for racial justice whose shoulders we now stand on. We must thank God for their courage, commitment, and favor over their lives, as it was He Who protected and guided them through their struggles.

I want to express my gratitude for the lives of Mrs. Amy Thurmond, Ms. Doris Smith, Mrs. Susie B. Pennington, and Rev. Walter B. Pennington, Senior. Their faithful commitment and service to the African American race made a difference in the lives of the White and African American communities they served. God strategically placed them in areas of desperate need as representatives of His holy throne. They truly made a difference in the lives of many innocent victims, both African American and White.

These four individuals represented the entire faculty and staff of the Cruger African American school in the 1950s and early 60s. They perfected a system of teaching three different grade levels in a single classroom while covering all required study courses. They did so while enduring the injustices of the White church-supported, all-white racist Holmes County School Board. The accomplishments of these individuals, like so many unsung heroes who persevered while enduring the evilness of racial injustice, may never be recorded in history books of American heroes. However, the impact of their tireless and courageous service will be felt for generations to come.

---

My mother's involvement with racial hatred and injustice did not end with her school tenure in Cruger, Mississippi.

After the Federal court order mandating the integration of all public schools in America, White students abandoned public schools en masse throughout the Bible Belt. The White students in the adjacent small towns of Cruger and Tchula, Mississippi, did likewise.

In an instance, the student body and staff of the abandoned all-white public school facility in Tchula became totally African American.

Mrs. Susie B. Pennington, the principal of the African American school in Cruger, was appointed the new principal of the public school in Tchula.

As expected, all did not go well with this new arrangement. This public school facility was located in an all-white community. Also, as expected, White resistance and backlash to African Americans utilizing this facility and coming into their community were intense. As Mrs. Pennington's son, I recall how our family feared for her safety as she would often be required to remain at school after hours for various reasons and often alone. We thank God she was not physically harmed during this overt racial hatred and chaos.

Unsurprisingly, the main building of the Tchula facility was destroyed by an arson-set fire on August 15, 1969. The all-white fire department did not save the burning building. It is amazing that with the widespread design of the building, none of it was saved. It was totally destroyed, mostly due to the lack of a serious effort by the all-white Tchula Fire Department.

After the hate-inspired burning of the main building, the then all African American student body started using the gymnasium for classrooms.

Also, and unsurprisingly, when the surrounding White community realized this adjustment, action was again taken. On December 12, 1969, the gymnasium was completely destroyed by a second arson-set fire. After this second burning, the African American student body was relocated from this facility and out of the White community to another facility for their safety.

In response to these two burnings, Representative Robert Clark, the only African American member of the State Legislature, organized a march and protest rally in the town of Tchula since the school board or local police had taken no action. Other African American civil rights leaders participated in the march and rally. Joining Clark in the march were Fannie Lou Hamer of the Mississippi Freedom Democratic Party, and Aaron Henry, State NAACP president. This march and protest rally drew widespread attention to these atrocities of racial hatred. Perhaps because there was no loss of life and the suppression of these events by the local press, these unjust school burnings did not receive the national and world attention as some of the other race-related burnings of that era.

In response to the attention that the march and rally brought to these school burnings, the all-white Board of Supervisors met in January 1970 to decide their official response. In this meeting, they determined the fires to be deliberately set, which was obvious. They offered a paltry $500.00 reward for information leading to the apprehension of the perpetrator(s). To this day, no one has been charged for these hate crimes. It is important to note that the Board of Supervisors took no action after the first burning of the main building. It was only after the second burning of the gymnasium and the demonstration march and protest rally by African American leaders that they decided to take a course of action. Even then, their action was inconsequential and reflected a lack of serious interest.

This example of White hatred and injustice was prevalent not just throughout the Bible Belt, but the entirety of America. Each state in America has stories of racial hatred and injustice that were not documented or were omitted from American history recordings. None of these injustices would have happened if the segregated White churches in Cruger and Tchula had taken a stand for righteousness and boldly stood against them as ambassadors of Christ. Regretfully, their rebelliousness against Christ was reflected in their unyielding support for them and unrighteousness.

Unbelievably, the White citizens of these two towns were able to utilize what was the public White school facility in Cruger as the first private academy in the state of Mississippi. It was used by the White students of Cruger and the White students of Tchula who had abandoned the previously all-white public school facility in Tchula. Still today, it is uncertain how the public White school building facility in Cruger legally became a private White school academy because records were not made public. But what is certain is that a newly constructed gymnasium for this academy was built on land that a local racially segregated White denominational church previously owned. In opposition to and rebellion against the word of God, White church support was instrumental in maintaining the segregated educational system of these two towns. This pattern of White church support for racial segregation and rebellion against the word of God existed throughout the Bible Belt.

The Cruger-Tchula Academy was the beginning of what would develop into a trend throughout the state. Many more private academies were formed for the purpose of avoiding integration with African Americans and, to varying degrees, were supported by the racially segregated White institutional churches. Many of the private academies formed in Mississippi during that era are still in existence (estimated to be 42). The Cruger-Tchula Academy was closed in 1971.

The evilness and injustice of that era were reflected not only in the residential White communities and churches but also in the local and state government, as is still experienced today in Mississippi and throughout the Bible Belt.

For example, through an act of the Mississippi legislature, the state of Mississippi supported the segregated academy schools by providing state-funded tuition payments until this immoral system of support was blocked in the federal court. The current immoral acts perpetrated by the Mississippi state government against the vulnerable ones in God's kingdom are simply a continuation of a White church-supported historical trend of open rebellion against God. Not only the perpetrators, but also those who condone and vote for this sinfulness will be held accountable. Even today, most professing White Christians throughout the Southern Bible Belt remain rebellious against God's requirements for human justice and defiantly unrepentant thus, reinforcing the deception of Christianity in America.

---

Reflecting on those dark days of overt racial hatred and injustice throughout Mississippi and the Bible Belt, I remain thankful that God protected my parents and our family from physical harm. I applaud them and the many unsung heroes who, through providential appointment by God, bravely honored His calling on their lives. There were many obedient servants of God, both African American and White, who made a tremendous difference during the racial chaos of the 1950s and 60s. Most of their stories will not be documented or recorded by historians. However, and more importantly, their faithfulness is recorded in the annals of Heaven. God was glorified through their obedience.

---

As I made comparisons reflecting the inequities within the public school systems of the 1950s and 60s, we can make these same comparisons of inequities and injustice in every other area of life throughout the Southern "Bible Belt" during that era.

Whether comparing employment opportunities, incarceration rates, quality of health care, or any other area of life, injustice was and still is the way of life in the Southern "Bible Belt" and, to varying degrees, the entirety of the United States. Sadly, as noted, the injustices experienced by minorities throughout American history were only possible because of the support of the racially segregated White institutional church from which everything else in the White communities stemmed. The White church was not just a worship facility but also the preferred location for community meetings, especially in times of interracial crises. In far too many instances, the racially segregated White institutional church was the perpetrator of many acts of injustice.

---

Throughout America's history, the racially segregated White institutional church has distorted Biblical Christianity, which will be further revealed and reviewed in the remainder of this writing. As stated, without its support, injustice against the minority races of this society, as it existed throughout America's history, would not have been realized.

---

*"A democracy cannot thrive where power remains unchecked and justice is reserved for a select few. Ignoring these cries and failing to respond to this movement is simply not an option.*
*Peace cannot exist where justice is not served."*

*- John Lewis -*

*"Therefore we also, since we are surrounded by so great a cloud of witnesses, let us lay aside every weight, and the sin which so easily ensnares us, and let us run with endurance the race that is set before us, looking unto Jesus, the author and finisher of our faith, who for the joy that was set before Him endured the cross, despising the shame, and has sat down at the right hand of the throne of God."*
**Hebrews 12:1, 2**

---

*"The LORD executes righteousness and justice for all who are oppressed."*
**Psalm 103:6**

---

*"Who can utter the mighty acts of the LORD? Or can declare all His praise?*

*"Blessed are those who keep justice, and he who does righteousness at all times!"*
**Psalm 106:2, 3**

# Chapter 3

## The Foundation for God's Throne and Christianity

As revealed throughout the history of the United States of America and documented in this writing, there is confusion within the body of professing White Christians in the U.S. regarding the importance of human justice, especially racial justice. Many don't realize its importance in validating their profession of Christian faith, or understand it to be a salvation requirement. Therefore, clarity is vitally important.

An excellent place to center all discussions regarding justice and injustice is the Bible because the professing body of Christ must be solely guided by His holy word.

So, what does the Bible say about justice and its relation to Christianity and God's designed order for His kingdom?

Psalm 89:14 states, *"Righteousness* (judgment) *and justice are the foundation of Your throne; Mercy and truth go before your face"* (also, Genesis 18:19, Psalm 97:2). The foundation of God's throne is righteousness and justice ['tsedeq' (Hebrew); the right; equity; even].[1] The NIV version states, *"Righteousness and justice are the foundation of your throne; love and faithfulness go before you."*

**God's 'Great Commandment' of love is rooted in justice and righteousness (judgment) and originated from His heavenly throne.**

# God's Throne

## ** Righteousness and Justice **

Love and Faithfulness

## ** Christianity **

Regarding Psalm 89:14, Barnes Bible Commentary states, "Justice and judgment are the habitation of the throne – Margin, 'establishment.' The Hebrew word 'mâkôn' means properly a place where one stands, then, a foundation or basis.

The idea here is, that the throne of God is founded on justice and right judgment, it is this which supports it. His administration is maintained because it is right. This supposes that there is such a thing as right or justice in itself considered, or in the nature of things, and independently of the will of God, that the divine administration will be conformed to that, and will be firm because it is thus conformed to it.

**Even omnipotent power could not maintain permanently a throne founded on injustice and wrong. Such an administration would sooner or later make its own destruction sure.**

Mercy and truth shall go before thy face literally, anticipate thy face, that is, thy goings. **Wherever thou dost go, wherever thou dost manifest thyself, there will be mercy *(love)* and faithfulness *(truth)*.** Thy march through the world will be attended with kindness and fidelity. So certain is this, that His coming will, as it were, be anticipated by truth and goodness."

---

It is important to note that the writer states an important Biblical truth in this commentary. "Even omnipotent power could not maintain permanently a throne founded on injustice and wrong. Such an administration would sooner or later make its own destruction sure." In other words, any movement or organization founded on or characterized by injustice and wrongdoing is destined for destruction.

This warning is especially relevant for religious institutions. **As applied to this writing, we may say that any religious organization founded on injustice and wrongdoing is destined for destruction, as is reported and witnessed in the deception and further demise of institutional religion in the United States today.**

With the clarity of the foundation of God's throne, we can see the importance of Jesus' statement to the scribes and Pharisees in Matthew 23, verse 23. Jesus recognized their hypocrisy in performing their sacred obligations to God. They were more focused on religious duties of the Law than the more important matters of the faith, which reflected the heart-concerns of God for His kingdom. Jesus stated to them in verses 23-28,

*"Woe to you, scribes and Pharisees, hypocrites! For you pay tithe of mint and anise and cumin, and have neglected the weightier matters of the law: justice and mercy and faith. These you ought to have done, without leaving the others undone. Blind guides, who strain out a gnat and swallow a camel!*

*Woe to you, scribes and Pharisees, hypocrites! For you cleanse the outside of the cup and dish, but inside they are full of extortion and self-indulgence. Blind Pharisee, first cleanse the inside of the cup and dish, that the outside of them may be clean also.*

*Woe to you, scribes and Pharisees, hypocrites! For you are like whitewashed tombs which indeed appear beautiful outwardly, but inside are full of dead men's bones and all uncleanness. Even so you also outwardly appear righteous to men, but inside you are full of hypocrisy and lawlessness."*

---

It is amazing how relevant the holy scriptures are throughout eternity. Though these statements of Jesus were made over 2,000 years ago, it seems as if He is addressing much of the leadership in the twenty-first- century professing church of God in Christ in the United States of America.

The words of Solomon in Ecclesiastes 1:9-10 are proven time and again to be true. Solomon stated, *"The thing that hath been, it is that which shall be; and that which is done is that which shall be done: and there is no new thing under the sun. Is there anything whereof it may be said, See, this is new? It hath been already of old time, which was before us."* In other words, Solomon is simply saying that history repeats itself. Therefore, the statements of Jesus will be relevant until His return, as the professing church of Christ remains in rebellion as throughout the history of Christianity.

---

When we look closer at Jesus' statements to the scribes and Pharisees, two things immediately stand out more than all others.

First, Jesus's disdain for religious hypocrisy was revealed by His response to the religious priorities of the scribes and Pharisees. As is also reflected throughout the twenty-first-century professing church of Christ in the United States, they were more concerned with outer purity than the heart's purity.

Second, as was with the scribes and Pharisees, we can become so preoccupied with the requirements of scriptures that we can easily overlook the guiding spiritual principles of scriptures. We can become so preoccupied with the requirements that we overlook the required relationship with the source of the scriptures. The scribes and Pharisees tithed on herbs which was required by the Mosaic Law, but overlooked the more important matters of Justice and love for God and humanity. Like many religious leaders today, they learned what God said but never knew Who God was or how what He said applied to them personally. They never understood the eternal importance of their representation of God's holy throne.

Like many twenty-first-century religious leaders, the scribes and Pharisees knew the word of God because they had dedicated themselves to studying, but they never developed a personal relationship with God. When you develop a personal relationship with God, you share your intimate thoughts and concerns with Him, and He shares His intimate thoughts and concerns with you. As God shares His intimate thoughts and concerns with you, you begin to know and understand His heart, His ways, and His priorities. You begin to take on His character. This is what the scribes and Pharisees had failed to do. Their confusion was the result of them not realizing and honoring the foundation of God's heavenly throne.

---

As a **side-note** of clarification, Jesus' statement in verse 23 acknowledging the fact that the scribes and Pharisees paid tithes on mint, anise, and cumin must not be misunderstood as Jesus condoning the paying of financial tithes to a post-resurrection religious organization. Jesus' statement acknowledged the fact that the Mosaic law required the paying of tithes. However, the Mosaic law required paying tithes on agricultural products, including livestock (ref. Deuteronomy 14:22-29, Leviticus 27:30-32). Financial giving to God for the needs of ministry has always been voluntary [("free-will") (e.g., Exodus 25:1-3, 35:4-5, $2^{nd}$ Corinthians 9:6,7)]. There is no Biblical basis for the twenty-first-century teaching of paying financial tithes to a religious organization. Financial tithing to the church was ordered by the Council of Macon and instituted by the Roman Catholic Church in 585 A.D. Their decision was not based on the word of God but on a desire to secure significant and consistent financial support (refer to *"The Fanaticism of Christian Discipleship"* by this same writer for more detail on Christian financial stewardship).

---

As revealed throughout this writing, there is much confusion and deception in the United States of America regarding Christianity. Most professing Christians in the U.S. define "Christian" as a follower of Jesus. Though this is true, it does not reveal the required character trait. A partial truth is deceptive and misleading. From the Biblical perspective, anything misleading is considered erroneous.

It is generally believed among most professing believers in America that we become a "Christian" when we ***"confess with our mouth the Lord Jesus and believe in our heart that God has raised Him from the dead"*** (Rom. 10:9). This erroneous belief only enhances the deception of Christianity in America. We become believers when we repent our sins and sincerely receive Jesus as the Lord of our lives. However, we are not yet "Christian." Christianity results from a commitment to Christian discipleship (ref. *"The Fanaticism of Christian Discipleship for more information"*).

So, what is the Biblical understanding of the term "Christian?" **The character-revealing definition of "Christian" is manifesting the qualities and spirit of Jesus, or "Christlike."** The character of Christ is the aggregate of His beliefs, attributes, and traits that form His nature based on the sacrificial love of God. **In the Biblical perspective, a "Christian" is not just a person who follows or believes in Christ, but a person whose life is an image of the character of Christ."** <u>This is foundational.</u>

---

*"For no other foundation can anyone lay than that which is laid, which is Jesus Christ." (1ˢᵗ Cor. 3:11)*

*"Nevertheless the solid foundation of God stands, having this seal: "The Lord knows those who are His," and, "Let everyone who names the name of Christ depart from iniquity." (2ⁿᵈ Tim.2:19)*

---

I would like to briefly share my God-initiated experience in realizing and understanding the importance of foundations in life and religion.

After pastoring in the denominational setting for many years, the Lord brought me away to develop the Louisiana Prayer Institute in Covington, Louisiana. He could have chosen someone more capable with construction experience and Bible knowledge. But He chose me.

After questioning God's choice of me as the best person to do this, He informed me that He chose me not because of my qualifications but because of my heart (1ˢᵗ Sam. 16:7). He looked beyond my many faults, lack of knowledge, and building experience and saw me as one whose heart was for Him, and one who would obey His instructions in faith.

I proceeded in faith with enthusiasm for the hopeful outcome. However, my enthusiasm was soon dashed by the reality of the difficulty of this assignment. I did not realize I would spend a year working on the foundation. The fact that this development would be in what is defined as "wetlands" created many challenges for which I was not prepared. The instability of soil in "wet Lands" presents challenges for construction. I was required to get soil samples from different depths below the ground surface. Soil sampling was required because there are many issues below the ground surface that can affect the stability of the building, just as there are many issues below the surface of our lives that affect our spiritual stability.

I think God purposefully chose this location to teach me the importance of foundations. After the first year, all of my labor had resulted in only a concrete slab on which to build a building. Since this represented most of my building budget, I began to see that this project was truly going to be a faith challenge, especially since I was no longer employed. As I had taught others how God has a way of putting you in challenging situations to increase your faith, I realized that I was now experiencing what I had taught others during my pastoral ministry season.

At this point in the construction, the only thing visible was a concrete slab. What could not be seen was the underneath requirements for that slab. As the engineers I contracted realized, the building would be unstable if the foundation was not secure. Initially, the building would look presentable, but eventually, foundational issues would surface, which could jeopardize the stability of the building.

Applying this understanding to religion, particularly Christianity, if our spiritual foundation is unstable, our life's journey will lack spiritual stability and be unfruitful. Salvation for many lost souls to whom we share and model the gospel of Christ may be jeopardized, including our own.

---

Jesus stated in the "Parable of the Two Builders," *"Therefore whoever hears these sayings of Mine, and does them, I will liken him to a wise man who built his house on the rock: and the rain descended, the floods came, and the winds blew and* beat on that house; and it did not fall, for it was founded on the rock.

*But everyone who hears these sayings of Mine, and does not do them, will be like a foolish man who built his house on the sand: and the rain descended, the floods came, and the winds blew and beat on that house; and it fell. And great was its fall"* (Matthew 7:24-27.

In its commentary on this parable, the NKJV Study Bible states, "The key difference in the two houses is not their external appearance. Pharisees and scribes may seem to be as righteous as the heirs of the kingdom. The key in the story is the foundations The house on the rock pictures a life founded on a proper relationship to Christ (16-18), 1 Cor. 10:4, 1 Pet. 2:4-8). It will stand the test of Christ's judgment, but the house on the sand will fail the test (see 1 Cor. 3:12-15)."[2]

---

It is important to note that a house built on an improper foundation or an improper relationship with Christ will fail His judgment test. A foundation built on injustice is in opposition to God's will and the foundation for His throne. Its builder will fail his end-time judgment test. An improper relationship is one that condones and is built on injustice.

---

The Barna Group released the results of a survey on September 15, 2020, addressing the motivation level of White Christians to address Racial injustice. The survey was titled "White Christians Have Become Even Less Motivated to Address Racial Injustice."

The report stated, "This year, the killings of George Floyd, Ahmaud Arbery, and Breonna Taylor and the shooting of Jacob Blake have sparked a nationwide conversation about racial justice. Some of the more prominent responses include a series of marches with historic attendance, a players' strike in the NBA and WNBA, and new policies concerning issues such as Confederate symbols on flags and reparations for Black residents. Social media has swirled with resources and hashtags, books on anti-racism have risen to the top of the best-seller lists, and leaders in government, business, and religious institutions have invited deep and, at times, public examination of their actions and influence.

One might assume that the events of 2020 have increased awareness of racial injustice in the United States and motivation to address it. But the story isn't so straightforward, new Barna research (conducted in partnership with Dynata) suggests. Yes, there are signs the past year has clarified how Americans think about racial injustice – but that doesn't mean they see the issue, or their role within it, with greater urgency. **In the Church especially, there is a sense that people are doubling down on divides.** Motivation to address racial injustice has declined in the past year.

When Barna asks, "How motivated are you to address racial injustice in our society?" we see numbers moving out from the middle – toward being less motivated. In 2019, one in five U.S. adults was "unmotivated" (11%) or "not at all motivated" (9%); just a year later, in the summer of 2020, that percentage has increased to 28% percent (12% unmotivated, 16% not at all motivated). Meanwhile, the number of those who are "somewhat motivated" has shrunk, and the number of those who are motivated has held fairly steady over the past year, indicating **some of those who might have previously been on the fence about addressing racial injustice have become more firmly opposed to engaging.**

The unmotivated segment has seen growth among both practicing and self-identified Christians. Among self-identified Christians, the unmotivated group has shifted from 19 percent in 2019 (10% unmotivated, 9% not at all motivated) to 30 percent (12% unmotivated, 18% not at all motivated) in 2020. For practicing Christians, those who were unmotivated in 2019 (9% unmotivated, 8% not at all motivated) have also increased to 30 percent (12% unmotivated, 18% not at all motivated) in 2020. **In one year, that's more than an 11 percent point increase overall in Christians who are uninspired to address racial injustice, including a doubling of those who say they are "not** at all motivated" in both practicing and self-identified groups.

Some Christians are willing to admit uncertainty on the topic; one in five is "unsure" about whether they are motivated to address racial injustice (10% in 2019, 9% in 2020).

Some minority groups are, naturally, highly motivated to address the racial injustices that may affect them. Among self-identified Christians, **Black adults in particular (46% "very motivated"), followed by Hispanic adults (23% "very motivated"), are eager to be involved – something few white self-identified Christians express (10% "very motivated")."**

---

The results of this survey should serve as a wake-up call to the twenty-first-century institutional church and its leaders. It reveals either an unawareness of the foundation of God's throne and their primary purpose as God's representatives or/and a willingness of far too many professing Christians not to truly represent the just God they profess as Lord. Any professing Christian who condones injustice and is not actively involved in fighting for racial justice for God's entire creation does not represent God's kingdom and knows not, or cares not about the heart and will of God. **Therefore, they have not truly received Jesus as the Lord of their lives.** Their lives are in opposition to the foundation of the holy throne of God. Their profession is without merit, and their hopes for salvation are dashed. Acceptance of injustice and a lack of involvement in securing justice for everyone clearly show that they do not truly understand and believe in Jesus.

The results of this survey reflect a spiritually confused church that is moving farther away from God and His heart's concern and requirement for human justice.

---

**Every professing Christian must prioritize securing human justice for God's entire creation, regardless of racial or cultural differences or required sacrifice(s).** As

**Christians, the needs of others must always be considered before our own** (John 13:34,35).

---

God's 'Great Commandment' is understood as the Biblical foundation for all believers in Christ (It is important to note that Jesus elevated God's requirements of love and sacrifice for all humanity for Christian discipleship and Christianity as clarified in the following chapter). This foundation proceeds from His heavenly throne and is rooted in justice and righteousness.

As a reminder, the 'Great Commandment, as stated in Mark 12:30-31 reads, *"And thou shalt love the Lord thy God with all thy heart, and with all thy soul, and with all thy mind, and with all thy strength: this is the first commandment. And the second is like, namely this,* **Thou shalt love thy neighbor as thyself.** *There is none other commandment greater than these."* In summarizing an often disregarded Biblical reality, Paul stated in Galatians 5:14, *"For all the law is fulfilled in one word, even in this: 'You shall love your neighbor as yourself.'"*

God's 'Great Commandment' requires passionate, sacrificial, and unconditional love for God and the entirety of humanity, regardless of their differences. In race relations, passionate, sacrificial, and unconditional love for all humanity is rarely reflected among White professing Christians in the United States of America in their relationships with minorities. This required level of love is foundational for all believers of Christ. However, as evidenced throughout the European history in the United States, it is not evident in the lives of most White professing believers. We must question the primary spiritual focus of the White institutional church in the U.S. Without this required foundation, all other spiritual focuses and efforts are in vain and will not be honored by God.

The apostle Paul clarified this eternal requirement of God in 1$^{st}$ Corinthians 13:1-3, *"Though I speak with the tongues of men and of angels, but have not love, I have become sounding brass or a clanging cymbal. And though I have the gift of prophecy, and understand all mysteries and all knowledge, and though I have all faith, so that I could remove mountains, but have not love, I am nothing. And though I bestow all my goods to feed the poor, and though I give my body to be burned, but have not love, it profits me nothing."*

**The disheartening reality of this dilemma is that the eternal salvation that many assume they have may not be realized because this proof of one's belief in Jesus is not realized in their life. In fact, many professing Christians throughout the history of the U. S. have opposed it.**

---

The twentieth-century world-renowned evangelist Smith Wigglesworth stated, "Accepting Christ as Savior builds the character of a person in purity until his inward heart is filled with divine love and has nothing but thoughts of God alone."[1]

---

If we say that we believe in Jesus and have not experienced this transformation in our hearts, this is an indication that we do not truly believe in Jesus. As earlier noted, this masterful strategy of Satan has accounted for the loss of eternal salvation for many unsuspecting souls. Throughout America's history, they practiced his deceptive, enticing, and self-focused version of his false Christianity.

The good news for all who are alive today is that deliverance and the opportunity for repentance are available to all who choose to turn from their Satan-inspired wicked ways of rebellion against the holy throne of God. Our wicked, self-focused ways result from not loving all others as much as we love ourselves which manifests through our actions and inactions.

---

**Again, Biblical love is rooted in justice and righteousness and proceeds from God's throne. Christianity does not exist without justice and righteousness.**

---

In concluding this chapter, we ask the vital question, "Where does the twenty-first-century church stand in its understanding of the importance of Justice in establishing the kingdom of God?" Obviously, there are many concerns that must first be highlighted, understood, and then addressed with Biblical solutions. Hopefully, this writing will provide an acceptable response to this question and give Bible-based answers to some of these major concerns. From the beginning of creation, God has stated His commandment for His servants to keep His ways. Genesis 18:19 reminds us, *"The way of the LORD is to do righteousness and justice."* **This verse also notes that this was a requirement for Abraham to realize God's promise. Children of God, beware!**

---

**If you have received Jesus as Lord, committed your life to God, and are actively pursuing His calling upon your life, be mindful of this key requirement for success.**

---

The next chapter is primarily a slightly altered and condensed reprint of a section from *"The Fanaticism of Christian Discipleship"* transcribed by this same writer. It is included in this writing because of its importance to understanding the foundation for Christianity, which a long history of accepted injustice, unrighteousness, and spiritual deception resulting from erroneous teachings has distorted.

Professing Christians must not forget that the foundation for Biblical Christianity has always been, and will forever be, passionate, sacrificial, and unconditional love for God and the entirety of humanity. Without clarity of this understanding, the remainder of this writing may not be fully understood and elevated to its required level of importance. Because of the current spiritual confusion in religion, lives may remain unchanged.

If you have read *"The Fanaticism of Christian Discipleship"* and received the next chapter as Biblical truth, you may view the next chapter as a reminder. We must keep its importance afresh within us to live the true meaning of the sacrificial cross of Christ in our daily lives and reveal its reality to this sinful, hurting world. If you have not read *"The

*Fanaticism of Christian Discipleship,"* we encourage you to do so, as this writing on *"Justice"* may be viewed as a prerequisite. This writing gives clarity to why Christianity has never existed in the U.S. broadly. Its companion, *"The Fanaticism of Christian Discipleship,"* clarifies Christianity for the edification of the professing body of Christ.

**Without the required foundation of God's heavenly throne firmly established within His kingdom on earth, Biblical Christian discipleship and Christianity will not be realized. This reality has been evident throughout the ungodly history of the United States. It was fueled by the spiritual deception within the institutional church, as revealed and discussed throughout this writing.**

---

*"There is only one secure foundation: a genuine, deep relationship with Jesus Christ, which will carry you through any and all turmoil. No matter what storms are raging all around, you'll stand firm if you stand on His love."*

- Charles Stanley -

---

*"The foundation upon which one builds their life will determine the effectiveness and sustainability of their influence throughout and after their life."*

- Walter B. Pennington -

*"According to the grace of God which was given to me, as a wise master builder I have laid the foundation, and another builds on it. But let each one take heed how he builds on it. For no other foundation can anyone lay than that which is laid, which is Jesus Christ. Now if anyone builds on this foundation with gold, silver, precious stones, wood, hay, straw, each one's work will become manifest; for the Day will declare it, because it will be revealed by fire; and the fire will test each one's work, of what sort it is."*

1$^{st}$ Corinthians 3:10-13

---

*"The just shall live by faith."*
Romans 1:17

*"You cannot live by faith until you are just and righteous."*
- Smith Wigglesworth -

---

*"If the foundations are destroyed, what can the righteous do?"*
Psalm 11:3

---

# Chapter 4

## The Biblical Commandment of Love

As believers in Christ, all of our actions and beliefs must be solely guided by the Word of God. An important question must be addressed for us to know and understand Jesus' requirements for love, His heart, and His 'true' character. The question is, **"What is the Biblical command that addresses the focus and level of love that Jesus requires of believers?"**

As previously stated, Jesus provided the answer to this question in God's "Great Commandment."

However, it is important to note that Jesus altered God's "Great Commandment" as a requirement for Christian Discipleship and Christianity. Jesus stated to His disciples in John 13: 34 & 35, *"A new commandment I give unto you, that ye love one another; as I have loved you, that ye also love one another. By this shall all men know that ye are my disciples, if ye have love one to another."*

Before we address the implications of this new commandment of Jesus to all professing Christians, it is important to review the Biblical origin of God's commandment of love for His creation.

God first stated His commandment of love, which applied to all of His creation, to His servant Moses in Deuteronomy 6:5 and Leviticus 19:18. Deuteronomy 6:5 states, *"And thou shalt love the LORD thy God with all thine heart, and with all thy soul, and with all thy might."* Leviticus 19:18 states, *"But thou shalt love thy neighbor as thyself."* Jesus later identified these commandments as the summary of God's entire law. These commandments as given by God, were later combined and referred to as the "Great Commandment," which was the foundational requirement of love for all believers in Christ.

Jesus' restatement of these commandments of God is recorded in the books of Matthew, Mark, and Luke. As noted in the previous chapter, in the 12$^{th}$ chapter of Mark's gospel, Jesus responded to a question from a scribe. Verses 28-31 read, *"And one of the scribes came, and having heard them reasoning together, and perceiving that he* (Jesus) *had answered them well, asked him, Which is the first commandment of all? And Jesus answered him, The first of all the commandments is, Hear, O Israel; The Lord our God is one Lord: And thou shalt love the Lord thy God with all thy heart, and with all thy soul, and with all thy mind, and with all thy strength: this is the first commandment. And the second is like, namely this, Thou shalt love thy neighbor as thyself. There is none other commandment greater than these."*

Again, we have a popular passage of scripture to all 'true' believers. Most believers have heard sermons preached from these scriptures. There has been much preaching and teaching on these foundational scriptures of love, from the Sunday morning pulpit to the Wednesday night Bible study. Still, with all of the focus given to them, the professing body of Christ has struggled to embrace the magnitude and the associated demands of their meaning since the end of the first-century Apostolic church.

A major problem that partly led to this dilemma was the subconscious and perhaps unintentional deletion of the word **'all'** and the phrase **'as thyself.'** So, the message that was understood within the professing Christian church could best be seen by the following rewrite of these scriptures. The accepted theology read, "Thou shalt love the Lord thy God with thy heart, and with thy soul and with thy mind, and with thy strength. And the second is like, unto it, thou shalt love thy neighbor." This spiritual deletion from God's Holy Word reflected, at best, an oversight or, at worse, an act of selfish defiance by institutional religion.

Though this action may not have been intentional, the results did undermine the integrity of God's foundation for relationships in His creation. What the religious institutions perhaps subconsciously deleted from God's requirements of love made **'all'** the difference in God's creation by altering His design for our relationships with Him and each other.

Technically, this spiritual deletion was an act of disobedience. God clearly stated in Deuteronomy 12:32, *"What thing soever I command you, observe to do it: thou shalt not add thereto,* ***nor diminish from it***" (Also: Deut. 4:2, Prov. 30:6, Eccles. 3:14, and Rev. 22:18, 19). As previously stated, what was perhaps subconsciously, and unintentionally deleted, made **'all'** the difference in God's creation.

The deleted requirements of **'all'** in our relationship with God and **'as thyself'** in our relationship with our neighbor began the downward spiral and eventual dismantling of the foundation that God developed for human relations within His kingdom. Regretfully, the professing church of Christ was oblivious to these spiritual deletions that perhaps were orchestrated by Satan. These deletions had to be reinstated as the 'driving force' behind all of the actions and teachings of God's people to re-establish the foundation of His design for relationships within His kingdom. Regretfully, this required reinstatement was never accomplished, so the Biblically required intensity of our love for God and humanity was not realized or maintained within the body of Christ. Therefore, without His firm foundation of total and unconditional love as was modeled by Jesus, professing Christians did not continue to project the true character of Christ as did the first-century Apostolic church.

To this day, God's professing church has struggled to comprehend, teach, and model what God meant when He included the word **'all'** in our relationship of love for Him and the phrase **'as thyself'** in our relationship of love for humanity. As a clarification, the relevant definition of the word **'all'** (Greek "holos") is "the whole, entire, throughout, completely."[1] Simply stated, it means 'everything one has.' Nothing is omitted in expressing our total love for God.

The required love for God as expressed through His commandment is much more than an affirmation or a strong feeling; it is total obedience, loyalty, and sacrificial service above all else.

This commanded relationship requires **all** of our time, **all** of our energy, **all** of our efforts in life, and **all** of our entrusted resources to be utilized in expressing our total love for God.

The phrase, '**as thyself,**' as applied to our love for humanity, means 'even as, like' (ref. Strong's Concordance). It is implied that we do love ourselves. At a minimum, God requires that we love all others as much as we love ourselves, not just in words but in our hearts and deeds.

Before we proceed, we must address a concern of the early believers that remains a concern of many believers today. An important three-part question of clarification had to be addressed regarding these foundational commandments of love from God. The relevant question for professing believers was, **"What is implied in loving God with all my heart, soul, mind, and strength and loving my neighbor as myself, and how are these requirements of love lived out in everyday life?**

The best answer to this question is found in 'Clarke's Commentary.'

It states, "**He loves God with all his heart**, who loves nothing in comparison to him, and nothing but in reference to him: -who is ready to give up, do, or suffer anything in order to please and glorify him: -who has in his heart neither love nor hatred, hope nor fear, inclination, nor aversion, desire, nor delight, but as they relate to God, and are regulated by him.

**He loves God with all his soul**, or rather, with all his life, who is ready to give up life for his sake, to endure all sorts of torments, and to be deprived of all kinds of comforts, rather than dishonor God: - who employs life with all its comforts, and conveniences, to glorify God in, by, and through all: -to whom life and death are nothing, but as they come from and lead to God. From this Divine principle sprang the blood of the martyrs, which became the seed of the Church. They overcame through the blood of the Lamb, and loved not their lives unto the death (see Rev. 12:11).

**He loves God with all his strength** who exerts all the powers of his body and soul in the service of God: -who, for the glory of his Maker, spares neither labor nor cost – who sacrifices his time, body, health, ease, for the honor of God his Divine Master: -who employs in his service all his goods, his talents, his power, credit, authority, and influence.

**He loves God with all his mind** (intellect) who applies himself only to know God and his holy will: -who receives with submission, gratitude, and pleasure, the sacred truths which God has revealed to man: -who studies no art nor science but as far as it is necessary for the service of God, and uses it at all times to promote his glory – who forms no projects nor designs but in reference to God and the interests of mankind: -who banishes from his understanding and memory every useless, foolish, and dangerous thought, together with every idea which has any tendency to defile his soul, or turn it for a moment from the center of eternal repose.

In a word, he who sees God in all things – thinks of him at all times – having his mind continually fixed upon God, acknowledging him in all his ways – who begins, continues, and ends all his thoughts, words, and works, to the glory of his name: -this is the person who loves God with all his heart, life, strength, and intellect.

He is crucified to the world, and the world to him: he lives, yet not he, but Christ lives in him. He beholds as in a glass the glory of the Lord, and is changed into the same image from glory to glory. Simply and constantly looking up to Jesus, the author and perfecter of his faith, he receives continual supplies of enlightening and sanctifying grace, and is thus fitted for every good word and work.

**The love of our neighbor** springs from the love of God as its source; is found in the love of God as its principle, pattern, and end; and the love of God is found in the love of our neighbor as its effect, representation, and infallible mark. In a word, we must do everything in our power, through all the possible varieties of circumstances, for our neighbors, which we would wish them to do for us, were our situations reversed."[2]

In his commentary on these two commands of God, Matthew Henry gives additional clarification when he states, "Our love of God must be a sincere love, and not in word and tongue only, as theirs is who say they love him, but their hearts are not with him. It must be a strong love; **we must love him in the most intense degree;** as we must praise him, so we must love him, **with *all that is within us,*** Ps. 103:1.

We must love our neighbor as ourselves, as truly and sincerely as we love ourselves, and in the same instances, nay, in many cases, we must deny ourselves for the good of our neighbor and must make ourselves servants to the true welfare of others, and be willing to spend and be spent for them to lay down our lives for the brethren."[3]

**Our love for all humanity must be at least equivalent to our love for ourselves.**

*************************************

As previously mentioned, the "Great Commandment" of God is rooted in justice, which, along with righteousness, is the foundation for His heavenly throne (ref. Ps. 89:14, 97:2). **If human justice is not a passion and central focus in our lives, we do not represent, or perhaps, know, understand, or truly accept the essence of God**.

The desire for justice for everyone validates our Christian association. There are many available resources for clarity of justice; however, we recommend:

"We Cry Justice," edited by Liz Theoharis
"Little Book of Biblical Justice," by Chris Marshall
"Good News to the Poor," by Theodore W. Jennings, Jr.

*************************************

With this background summary of God's original commandments for love as our Biblical foundation, we can now put in perspective the change to one of God's commands (Lev. 19:18) that Jesus stated to His disciples in the 13th chapter of John, verse 34. Again, Jesus said to His disciples, *"A new commandment I give unto you, That ye love one another; as I have loved you, that ye also love one another."*

At first observation, Jesus seems to be repeating God's original commandment of love that all believers must have for each other (Mark 12:31, the 2nd commandment of the 'Great Commandment"). However, there is a notable difference. A closer observation reveals that Jesus changed the original requirement of **'as thyself'** to **'as I have loved you.'** This change to God's 2nd commandment of love elevated the intensity of love that we must have for each other to become Christians or "Christlike." It is important to note that Jesus did not change the 1st commandment of God (Mark 12:30), only God's second commandment (Mark 12:31).

Regarding this new commandment given by Jesus, Clarke's Commentary states, "In what sense are we to understand that this was a *new commandment? Thou shalt love thy neighbor as thyself,* was a positive precept of the law, Lev. 19:18, and it is the very same that Christ repeats here; how then was it new? Our Lord answers this question, *Even as I have loved you.*

Now Christ more than fulfilled the Mosaic precept; he not only loved his neighbor *as himself,* but he loved him more than *himself,* for he laid down his life for men. In this, he calls upon the disciples to imitate him; to be ready on all occasions to lay down their lives for each other. This was, strictly a *new* commandment: no system of morality ever prescribed anything so pure and disinterested as this. Our blessed Lord has outdone all the moral systems in the universe in two words: 1. Love your enemies; 2. Lay down your lives for each other."[4]

**Jesus made this new commandment, in addition to the original 1st commandment of total love for God, His foundation for Christian discipleship and Christianity.** Jesus stated to His disciples in verse 35, *"By this shall all men know that ye are my disciples."*

Regarding this verse, Clarke's Commentary states, "From this time forward, this mutual and disinterested love shall become the essential and distinctive mark of all my disciples. When they love one another with pure hearts, fervently, even unto death, then shall it fully appear that they are disciples of that person who laid down his life for his sheep, and who became, by dying, a ransom for all."[4]

Indeed, Jesus elevated God's requirement of love that Christians must have for each other and all humanity to a level of intensity that had never before been Biblically required. Throughout the history of the United States of America, professing Christians have not 'truly' modeled God's original requirements of love. Therefore, the new requirement given by Jesus for Christianity will prove to be an even greater challenge to accept, teach, and model. Contrary to historical trends by religious institutions in the United States, this new requirement of Jesus must not be diminished or altered and is foundational to 'true' Christianity.

**In summary, as first-century Christians realized, and perhaps to the dismay of many twenty-first-century professing Christians, the Biblical requirement of love for God and humanity is fanatical and all-consuming (Webster's Ninth New Collegiate Dictionary defines "fanatical" as marked by excessive enthusiasm and often intense, uncritical devotion). This was the defining character as modeled by Paul and the Apostles of Christ (ref. Lk. 22:33, Jn. 11:16, Acts 5:40-41, 15:26, 21:13, $2^{nd}$ Cor. 11:23-33). The controversial and mostly misunderstood term "fanatical" has been mainly associated with ungodly religious extremism as opposed to total love for God and humanity as reflected in God's "Great Commandment" and Jesus' new commandment (ref.** *"The Fanaticism of Christian Discipleship"* **for clarification).**

To many unsuspecting ministries, this revelation requires a major change to the focus of their teaching and modeling of Biblical Christian love. This revelation also requires a reevaluation of the legitimacy of their claim to the title of "Christian."

At any cost, we must eliminate all hypocrisy in our relationships with God and humanity to restore His designed foundation of love. **To be considered a Christian ("Christlike"), we must love each other as Christ loved us. Another way that this may be stated is, we must love all others more than we love ourselves, even to the point of death. This, indeed, is the love that proceeds from God's throne that Jesus demonstrated on the cross.**

*******************************

As a <u>side note</u>, though not generally taught and modeled in institutional churches in the United States and most industrialized countries worldwide, this identifying attribute reflects the true meaning of the cross of Christ. It reveals the Biblical requirement for authentic Christianity: total giving of self in love, obedience, and faith. Institutional religion, by and large, has embraced a demonically orchestrated pseudo-Christianity that does not adhere to the required Biblical standards revealed in the "Great Commandment" and the new commandment of Christ as referenced in this chapter. This pseudo-Christianity's development commenced in Europe after the first-century Apostolic church and should be understood as a demonically orchestrated strategic attack against the holy throne of Almighty God. To the detriment of God's kingdom, the spiritual-damaging results are still evident today in churches worldwide and are maintained by deceptive, self-focused erroneous, teachings.

***************************

Whatever we do, wherever we go, and unto all humanity, we must reflect the sacrificial love of God. All that we do must reflect His character and be done for His glory (1$^{st}$ Cor. 10:31). His love is rooted in justice and righteousness, which is the foundation for His heavenly throne. The Bible gives many cautions about injustice (e.g., Prov. 16:8, 29:27, Isa. 10:1,2, Jer. 22:13, Lk. 16:19-31), but still, the racially segregated White institutional church throughout its history in America rebelled against this eternal requirement of God for human relations as will be further revealed and analyzed in this writing.

*******************************

**A professing Christian does not believe in Jesus nor possess eternal salvation without a life commitment to human justice. It must be expressed through sacrificial love addressing the needs of all humanity.**

*******************************

Throughout its existence, the racially segregated White institutional church in the United States failed to inform its membership of this eternal truth. Thus, its leadership will be held accountable for the eternal consequences of its membership's unjust actions or inactions that resulted from the lack of withheld Biblical instruction (ref. Ezekiel 3:18,19).

We will review some of the inadequately documented and suppressed injustices of the racially segregated White institutional church in America's history that mainly and arguably contributed to the deception of Christianity throughout the history of the United States of America.

---

*"Love suffers long and is kind; love does not envy; love does not parade itself, is not puffed up; does not behave rudely, does not seek its own, is not provoked, thinks no evil; does not rejoice in iniquity, but rejoices in the truth; bears all things, believes all things, hopes all things, endures all things. And now abide faith, hope, love, these three; but the greatest of these is love."*

**1st Corinthians 13:4-7, 13**

---

*"Beloved, let us love one another, for love is of God; and everyone who loves is born of God and knows God. He who does not love does not know God, for God is love."*

**1st John 4:7-8**

---

*"The only thing that counts is faith expressing itself through love."*

**Galatians 5:6**

# Chapter 5

## Injustice Perpetrated Against Native Americans

As previously stated, the European occupation of this country was characterized by injustice perpetrated against Native Americans, the original inhabitants. The total number of Native Americans before the European invasion is uncertain. However, because of centuries of injustice perpetrated by White Americans, historians agree that the present number of Native Americans in the U.S. is a small fraction of the number before the European invasion. Historians agree that the Native Americans were sovereign owners of 100% of what is now the United States. As a result of White church-supported U.S. government genocide throughout the following centuries, today, the remaining 2 million Indians hold sovereignty over only 2% of the land.[1]

It is important to note that many of the Native Americans captured in battle conflicts with the European invaders were held or sold into slavery.

"A study by Linford D. Fisher, associate professor of history at Brown University, found that Native Americans, including noncombatants, who surrendered during King Philip's War to avoid enslavement were enslaved at nearly the same rate as captured combatants.

Native American slavery "is a piece of the history of slavery that has been glossed over," Fisher said. "Between 1492 and 1880, between 2 and 5.5 million Native Americans were enslaved in the Americas in addition to 12.5 million African slaves."

While Africans who were enslaved did not know where they would be taken, Native Americans understood that they could be sent to Caribbean plantations and face extremely harsh treatment far from their homes and communities, according to the study. Fear of this fate spurred some Native Americans to pledge to fight to the death, while others surrendered, hoping to avoid being sent overseas, the study found.

"Even contemporary official histories of the war all point to the same thing: Indians were enslaved en masse and either distributed locally or sent overseas to a variety of destinations," Fisher wrote in the study."[2]

"It seems that as soon as Europeans showed up on the coasts of the United States, they started reading from a formal document called the "Requierimento" that declared themselves to be Christians and by nature superior to the uncivilized heathens that they encountered. The indigenous people were then informed by the "Requierimento" that if they accepted Christianity, they would become the Christian's slaves in exchange for the gift of salvation; if they did not accept the gospel of Christianity, they would still become slaves but that their plight would be much worse. Everywhere that explorers such as Ponce De Leon, Vazquez De Ayllon, and Hernando De Soto went on their explorations throughout the American Southeast, they carried with them bloodhounds, chains, and iron collars for the acquisition and exportation of Indian slaves. A Cherokee from Oklahoma remembered his father's tale of the Spanish slave trade, "At an early stage, the Spanish engaged in the slave trade on this continent and in so doing kidnapped hundreds of thousands of the Indians from the Atlantic and Gulf Coasts to work their mines in the West Indies.

No sooner had they set foot on the shore near Charleston, S.C., that the English set about upon establishing the peculiar institution of Native American slavery. Seeking the gold that had changed the face of the Spanish Empire but finding none, the English invaders of the Carolinas quickly seized upon the most abundant and available resource they could attain. The indigenous peoples of the Southeastern United States became a commodity of the open market. Applying the same rhetoric that they had used in their genocidal campaign against the "heathens" and "Barbarian" of Scotland and Ireland, the Carolinians cited Indian "savagery" and "depredations" as justification for "Indian wars" to dispossess and enslave the Yamasee, the Tuscarora, the Westo and eventually the Cherokee and the Creek.

Charleston and Savannah quickly became the centers of this North American commercial slavery enterprise. In the latter half of the seventeenth century, Native American nations throughout the South were played against each other in an orgy of slave dealing that decimated entire peoples. The Indian slave trade in the Carolinas, with these southern ports as their centers, rapidly took on all of the characteristics of the African slave trade.

Many of the Indian slaves were kept at home and worked on the plantations of South Carolina; by 1708, the number of Indian slaves in the Carolinas was nearly half that of African slaves."[3]

---

After centuries of forced land acquisition, mostly by violence, the Indian reservation system was established.

"The Indian reservation system established tracts of land called reservations for Native Americans to live on as White Europeans took over their land. The main goals of Indian reservations were to bring Native Americans under White-established U.S. government control, minimize conflict between Indians and White Europeans, and encourage Native Americans to take on the ways of the White man. But many Native Americans were forced onto reservations with catastrophic results and devastating, long-lasting effects. (More information on the reservation system is given later.)

In 1785, the Treaty of Hopewell was signed in Georgia, the largest state at the time, placing the native Cherokees under the protection of a young United States and setting boundaries for their remaining land."[4]

---

[As a side note, hypocritically, as with Hispanics and Latinos who are coming to America today seeking a better life, at their initial occupation of America, Europeans came in overwhelming numbers for the same reason. Native Americans were overwhelmed by their large numbers and superior weaponry. The Native Americans were forced, more often by violence, to unjustly give up their lands to accommodate the self-focused and aggressive desires of the increasing European population. As history confirms, and regretful for the early Native Americans, there were no border walls or border security to prevent European invaders from entering their country as is being proposed primarily by conservative politicians and supported primarily by conservative White professing Christians and White supremacists today. The ungodly intent of this proposal is to bar entry into the U.S. for needy Hispanics and Latinos, disregarding the fact that many are professing Christians, and Biblically, are brothers and sisters to the conservative White professing Christians who desire to keep them out. This rebellion against God's kingdom order of sacrificial love for all humanity reinforces the deception of Christianity.]

---

It wasn't long before European invaders intruded on Cherokee land. The Cherokees cried foul and revolted against the Europeans. To reestablish peace between the Cherokees and the Europeans, the Treaty of Holston was signed in 1791 in which the Cherokees agreed to give up all land outside of their U.S. government-established borders.

Not only did the federal government want Native Americans to give up their land, but they also encouraged them to become farmers and Christians. In the early 19$^{th}$ century, Europeans moved into southern Cherokee territory en masse and wanted their government representatives to claim the land.

The United States acted to remove all Indian nations from the southeast forcefully. Georgia agreed to cede her western land to the government in return for Indian land title.

After the Louisiana Purchase, Thomas Jefferson hoped to move eastern Indian tribes past the Mississippi River, but most Indians rejected his idea. When Georgia held lotteries to allocate seized Indian land, the battle-weary Creeks who'd sought sanctuary in east Alabama fought for their independence against the militia of Andrew Jackson, which included so-called "friendly Indians."

[As a **side note**, it is important to note that all of the U.S. Presidents that we mention in this chapter professed Christianity. Also, all of them, except Grover Cleveland, owned slaves and profited financially from the unjust forced misery and deaths of human slavery that unmercifully decimated entire families. Unfortunately, the false Christianity that they modeled was self-focused and void of human justice and the required foundational love of God's 'Great Commandment' for all humanity. This orchestrated evilness enhanced the ongoing deception of Christianity in America. through their deceptive, hypocritical, immoral leadership (ref. Chapter 11 for more detail)].

***********************

After suffering a devastating defeat at what became known as the Battle of Horseshoe Bend, the Creeks yielded more than 20 million acres of land to the U.S. federal government.

Over the next several years, the government passed several acts to diminish Indian autonomy, despite the Cherokee forming a new constitution-based government of their own. In December 1828, Georgians ordered the seizure of the remaining Cherokee land in their state.

On May 28, 1830, the Indian Removal Act was signed by President Andrew Jackson **(Presbyterian).** Unbelievably, the Act allowed the U.S. government to divide what was originally Indian land west of the Mississippi to give back to Indian tribes in exchange for their other land that was taken by the U.S. government. The U.S. government even picked up the cost of relocating the Indians and helped them resettle. The Indian Removal Act was controversial, but Jackson argued, without remorse, that it was the best option since Europeans had rendered Indian lands incompatible with sustaining their way of life.

Over the next few years, the Choctaw, Chickasaw, and Creeks were forced to move westward on foot, often in chains and with little or no food and supplies. Even some Indians in the North were forced to relocate by the U.S. government.

In 1838, President Martin Van Buren **(Dutch Reformed)** sent federal troops to march the remaining southern Cherokee holdouts 1,200 miles to Indian territory in the Plains. Disease and starvation were rampant, and thousands died along the way, giving the tortuous journey the nickname "Trail of Tears."

A group of Seminoles, however, refused to leave and hunkered down in Florida. They fought federal troops for almost a decade before their leader was killed, and they finally surrendered.

As White Europeans continued westward and desired more land, Indian territory continued to shrink, but there was no more land for the U.S. government to move them to.

In 1851, the U.S. Congress passed the Indian Appropriations Act, which created the Indian reservation system and provided funds to move Indian tribes onto farming reservations and hopefully keep them under control.

Daily living on the reservations was hard at best. Not only had tribes lost their native lands, but it was almost impossible to maintain their culture and traditions inside a confined area. Feuding tribes were often placed together, and Indians, who were once hunters, struggled to become farmers. Starvation was common, and living in close quarters hastened the spread of diseases brought by White European invaders.

Indians were encouraged or forced to wear non-Indian clothes and learn to read and write English, sew, and raise livestock. White missionaries attempted to convert them to their deceptive pseudo-Christianity and give up their spiritual beliefs.

In 1887, the Dawes Act was signed by President Grover Cleveland **(Presbyterian)**, allowing the U.S. government to divide reservations into small plots of land for individual Indians. The government hoped the legislation would help Indians assimilate into White culture easier and faster and improve their quality of life. But the Dawes Act had a devastating impact on Native American tribes. It decreased the land owned by Indians by more than half and opened even more land to White Europeans and railroads. Much of the reservation land wasn't good farmland, and many Indians couldn't afford the supplies needed to reap a harvest.

Prior to the Indian reservation system, female Indians farmed and took care of the land while men hunted and helped protect the tribe. Now, men were forced to farm, and women took on more domestic roles.

After a review of life on Indian reservations known as the Meriam Survey, it was clear the Dawes Act was severely detrimental to Native Americans. The law was ended in 1934 and replaced with the Indian Reorganization Act with the goals of restoring Indian culture and returning surplus land to tribes. It also encouraged tribes to self-govern and write their own constitutions and provided financial aid for reservation infrastructure.

Today, living conditions on reservations aren't ideal and are often compared to those of a third-world country. Housing is overcrowded and often below standards, and many people on the reservations are stuck in a cycle of poverty.

Health care on reservations is provided through Indian Health Services, but it's underfunded and, in some cases, practically non-existent. Many Native Americans die from lifestyle-related diseases such as heart disease and diabetes.

Infant mortality rates are significantly higher for Indians than for Whites, and alcohol and drug abuse is on the rise. Many people leave the reservations for urban areas in search of employment and improved living conditions. Others are forced to remain and endure poverty because their reservation is the only land that they have and can afford.

The Indian reservation system was originally established as a result of the greed and prejudice of the early European invaders and their newly formed U.S. federal government.[4]

The institutional White church-supported injustice against the Native Americans was purposed for taking the American land from Indians for use by European invaders and to utilize Native American labor through forced slavery to build White wealth, this nation, and its economy. The self-focused evilness reflected through these White church-supported acts was without measure. White historians and religious leaders must not continue to suppress or alter the facts of this vital part of America's history, but with remorse and repentance before Almighty God, learn from and correct the resulting damaging spiritual results.

It is important to note that through all of America's government and racially-segregated White church-supported injustices perpetrated against the Native Americans, the invading Europeans sought to convert Native Americans to their unbiblical and rebellious form of Christianity. They disregarded the evilness of their self-focused sins of racial injustice, greed, and genocide which were not seen as contradictory to the Christianity they professed, reflecting the persuading blindness of satanic influence.

The White church-supported injustices, characterized by genocide perpetrated against Native Americans, were the beginning of a pattern of institutional hatred and injustice against minority races that would continue throughout the history of the United States of America.

[As a side note of revelation and framework for this writing, it is important to note that while professing Christianity, this historical pattern of European invasions of occupied foreign territories, unjustly taking the land, often by violence, and forcing the indigenous people to provide labor for their self-serving desires is witnessed throughout world history.

Throughout world history, Europeans violently invaded the lands of North, South, and Central America, Australia, New Zealand, China, the Philippines, the Caribbean, most of South East Asia, India, the Middle and Near East, and the entire continent of Africa in pursuit of slave labor, spiritual dominance, and the theft of natural resources to supply European economies. Their evil-inspired hunger to dominate and seize complete control was the primary desire revealed in these invasions. This disguised satanic effort and strategy for worldwide control of God's creation was without moral restraint as Satan utilized, and continues to utilize, every unjust tool in his limited arsenal against humanity and the professing church of God in Christ and God's kingdom. His many injustices throughout world history were undergirded with his most effective tool and weapon, religious deception.

Europe's invasion of America was reflective of a much larger and more comprehensive evil strategy by Satan to subvert God's kingdom order worldwide and seize control of His creation. This strategy was launched in Rome after the death of the first-century Apostles of Christ. It gained traction in the fourth century through the Roman Catholic Church during the reign of Emperor Constantine who was the first Roman emperor to convert to Christianity. He provided many positive changes, however, Satan was able to capitalize from his political and financial influence and unbiblical oversight to subvert Biblical tenets and secure a stronghold over the Roman Catholic Church and the continent of Europe.

This deceptive historical worldwide strategy of Satan laid the spiritual groundwork for the chaos and spiritual turmoil that America and the world are encountering today.]

---

As a closing **side note** of concern, it is a well-known and proven fact that African Americans are killed in police encounters in America at higher rates than White Americans. What may be surprising to most Americans is the troubling fact that Native Americans are killed in police encounters at higher rates than any other racial group in America, according to data from the Centers for Disease Control and Prevention. These deaths often don't get much media attention or, as with African American deaths, consideration for intervention by conservative White professing Christians and conservative lawmakers.

---

*"The hope of a secure and livable world lies with disciplined nonconformists who are dedicated to justice, peace, and brotherhood."*
- Dr. Martin Luther King, Jr. -

# Chapter 6

## Injustice Perpetrated Against Africans

Though rarely discussed and often suppressed, the involvement of the professing White Christian Church in America in the African slave trade is well documented in American history. Their involvement resulted in much wealth gained through the use and sale of slaves, resulting in the holocaust of millions of innocent Africans, including children. "In fact, the White Catholic Church in America was the backbone of the slave trade."[1]

Forced slavery, characterized by cruel, inhumane treatment, is perhaps the most dehumanizing experience that any human being can endure. The atrocities perpetrated against African slaves in America cannot be understood by the rational, God-fearing mind. The depravity of humanity reflected by White professing Christian slave owners cannot be understood outside of the understanding of the mesmerizing power of demonic influences. Native American, African, and under-reported Asian slavery in America was simply evil by design and would not have happened or survived but for the support and oversight of the racially segregated White professing church of God. This successful strategy of Satan, though perpetrated through the White professing Christian Church, reflected a direct spiritual attack against the foundation of the Holy throne of God. This demonic strategy resulted in the loss of eternal salvation for many unsuspecting souls deceived by a deceptive, demonic-influenced form of a false religion that was erroneously identified as "Christian."

Indeed, African slavery was a degrading, dehumanizing, and devastating experience as children were often separated from their parents, and families were torn apart, never to see each other again. The unjust treatment of slaves in America often included sexual abuse and rape by White slave masters and, though rarely discussed and mostly suppressed in America's history, often secretly by their fantasizing wives and in rare instances, by their daughters. Many of these spiritually dysfunctional slave-owning families were professing Christians.

[As a side note, forced sexual encounters with male slaves by wives and White female companions of slave masters were an unanticipated "thorn in the flesh" for both Africans and White Americans during and in the aftermath of African slavery. The loss of the fidelity of the White female that originated with African slavery remains an incendiary spark that ignites White male rage and racial animosity. It is primarily an undiscussed stimulus for many of his perpetrated racial injustices against African American males. This fidelity loss remains as an arrow penetrating the heart of his manhood which compounds his inner struggle in determining how to respond. His historically displayed response of hatred, rage, and violence against African American males has compounded the deception within his relationship with God. In not repenting before Almighty God and seeking His spiritual direction and inclusion within His kingdom, his evil-induced response has proved detrimental to his relationship with God. His self-inflicted spiritual bondage resulted from the sin of human slavery that was masterfully orchestrated by Satan to ensure his eternal damnation. This spiritual bondage, which has primarily been unrecognized and undiscussed within the White institutional churches in America has remained throughout the many years since slavery commenced. It was enhanced by a satanic-influenced deceptive but convincing humanity-altered false religion that disregarded the human relations requirements of Holy Scripture. Rather than being the source of Godly spiritual guidance, the racially-segregated White church throughout America's history primarily condoned his ungodly behavior. By condoning his ungodliness, the White church further separated itself from God by making itself complicit in his sins of rage. The spiritually damaging results are still evident throughout America's White professing Christian body and society as his rage remains. However, in this end-time period of revelation, correction, and restoration, God is presenting perhaps a final opportunity for the development of the elusive racial oneness that has rarely existed between African American and White males in America.]

---

Slaves were often unmercifully beaten with whips as a means of punishment and maintaining control. However, punishments often took other forms, including mutilation, imprisonment, and being sold away from the plantation and their families. Most slaves were forced to work from sunrise to sunset. To maximize their wealth, some cruel owners and slave masters made their slaves work every day. As noted, this cruel and inhuman treatment of humanity could only have been orchestrated by Satan, the prince of death, theft, and destruction (John 10:10). No other explanation regarding the participation by professing Christians for selfish and evil monetary gains can survive Biblical scrutiny.

In describing his visit to the Cape Coast and Elmina castles in Ghana, the author of *"Church Involvement In The Trans-Atlantic Slave Trade"* wrote:

"The discussion of the extent to which slavery has been unjust and inhuman to the society cannot be exhausted. Slavery denied people of their freedom and rights to live as human beings. Some of the plaques in the castles are evidence of the denial of the human rights of the slaves. One of them points out how these slaves were kept in such a dirty and unfavorable environment. The slaves were given little food, just enough to sustain them. We discovered small conduits on the floor of the dungeons, which, according to the tour guides, were meant to carry their feces and urine into the sea. The statement, "May humanity never again perpetrate such injustice against humanity," on the plaque in the Cape Coast castle declares the consequence of the slave trade.

Many slaves died in the dungeons. Some slaves were put in condemned cells in the castles to die for acts that were seen by the slave masters to be punishable. Some female slaves were sexually abused in the castles. The slaves were treated and transported like wares of trade. They were "shackled in chains like beasts, underfed" before and during transportation through the hazards of the seas. Men, women, and children were crammed in the decks to such an extent that the slave ships became "floating coffins," and half of the slaves died of disease and mistreatment. Some slaves committed suicide in the crossing of the Atlantic. On arrival at the ports of destination, the slaves were rendered commercial commodities. They had to be displayed in the slave markets to attract buyers. The slaves were conscripted to inhuman and oppressive labor on their arrival at the home of the slave masters.

The slave trade deprived people of their original religious practices, alienated them from their cultural roots, and "deprived them of their sense of place in the world. The slaves were uprooted from their cultures and introduced to the alien cultures of their masters. They eventually recognized their non-belongingness to the culture of their slave masters. They suffered social and racial discrimination that haunted them for so long. The slave masters' interest was only in the acquisition of wealth at the expense of the human rights of the slaves.

The church's involvement in such an atrocious economic venture seems paradoxical and contrary to its mission of love for humanity. Hence, the church's contribution to the trans-Atlantic slave trade needs a thorough discussion to unravel the motives of such a paradox."[2]

---

"Christianity was proslavery," said Yolanda Pierce, the dean of the divinity school at Howard University. "So much of early American Christian identity is predicated on a proslavery theology. From the naming of the slave ships, to who sponsored some of these journeys, including some churches, to the fact that so much of early American religious rhetoric is deeply intertwined with slaveholding: It is proslavery." Some Christian institutions, notably Georgetown University *(A Roman Catholic institution)* in the District, are engaged in a reckoning about what it means that their past was rooted in slaveholding. But others have not confronted the topic. "In a certain sense, we've never completely come to terms with that in this nation,"[3]

---

The Roman Catholic church played a vital role in the trans-Atlantic slave trade, according to historians and several published theses on the topic.

"The tans-Atlantic slave trade was introduced by the coming of the Europeans, who came with the Bible in the same manner that Arab raiders and traders from the Middle East and North Africa introduced Islam through the Trans-Saharan slave trade, according to AfricaW.com, a premier informational website available throughout the continent.

'In fact, the Church was the backbone of the slave trade,' the authors wrote. 'In other words, most of the slave traders and slave ship captains were very 'good' Christians.'

For example, Sir John Hawkins, the first slave ship captain to bring African slaves to the Americas, was a religious man who insisted that his crew serve God daily and love one another. His ship, ironically called 'The Good Ship Jesus,' left the shores of his native England for Africa in October 1562. Some historians argue that if churches had used their power, the Atlantic slave trade might have never occurred.

By the same logic, others argue that the Catholic church and Catholic missionaries could have also helped to prevent the colonization and brutality of colonialism in Africa. However, according to a 2015 Global Black History report, the Catholic Church did not oppose the institution of slavery until the practice had already become infamous in most parts of the world."[4]

---

The slave trade in America, a primary source of wealth for the Roman Catholic Church, many racially segregated Southern White Protestant churches and institutions, and many White Southern families, was interrupted by the presidency of Abraham Lincoln, which will be briefly discussed in the following chapter.

---

"In most cases, the churches and church leaders did not condemn slavery until the 17th century.

The five major countries that dominated slavery and the slave trade in the New World were either Catholic, or still retained strong Catholic influences, including Spain, Portugal, France, England, and the Netherlands.

'Persons who considered themselves to be Christian played a major role in upholding and justifying the enslavement of Africans,' said Dr. Jonathan Chism, an assistant professor of history at the University of Houston-Downtown.

Many European Christian slavers perceived the Africans they encountered as irreligious and uncivilized persons. They justified slavery by rationalizing that they were Christianizing and civilizing their African captives. They were driven by missionary motives and impulses,' Chism said.

Further, many Anglo-Christians defended slavery using the Bible. For example, white Christian apologists for slavery argued that the curse of Ham in Genesis Chapter 9 and verses 20 to 25 provided a biblical rationale for the enslavement of Blacks, Chism said.

In this passage, Noah cursed Canaan and his descendants, arguing that Ham would be 'the lowest of slaves among his brothers' because he saw the nakedness of his father. A further understanding of the passage also revealed that while some have attempted to justify their prejudice by claiming that God cursed the black race, no such curse is recorded in the Bible.

That oft-cited verse says nothing whatsoever about skin color.

Also, it should be noted that the Black race evidently ascended from a brother of Canaan named Cush. Canaan's descendants were evidently light-skinned, not black. Truly nothing in the biblical account identifies Ham, the descendant of Canaan, with Africans. Yet, Christian apologists determined that Africans were the descendants of Ham,' Chism said.

Nevertheless, at the beginning of the sixteenth century, the racial interpretation of Noah's curse became commonplace, he said."[4]

*****************************************

The involvement of the Catholic Church in African slavery is well-documented. Though less documented, the racially segregated White Protestant Church in America was also involved and benefited financially and socially from slave labor and the African slave trade. The role of the racially-segregated White Protestant professing Christian church in America in African slavery must not be overlooked in American history.

As an example to be highlighted, all four of the founders of the Southern Baptist Theological Seminary, the first and oldest institution of the nation's largest Protestant denomination, enslaved Africans and profited financially and socially from African slavery. Among them, they legally owned more than 50 African slaves without any opposition from the Southern Baptist Convention.

The Southern Baptist denomination was formed because the Northern Baptists refused to appoint slaveholders as missionaries. The Northerners understood the sinfulness of human slavery and would not yield regarding God's Biblical commandment of sacrificial love for all humanity. However, the Southerners rebelled against God by disregarding the sinfulness and degradation of human slavery because of the financial implications and their desire to maintain White supremacy. Therefore, they would not yield to the Northerner's demand for Biblical justice and righteousness.

The seminary was founded in 1859 by slaveholding members of the Southern Baptist Convention. In addition to providing moral and spiritual justification for slavery, they also defended it in practice, denying that abuses, violence, assaults, and rapes were in any way commonplace or systematic. Many of their successors on the faculty, throughout the period of Reconstruction and well into the 20th century, advocated the inferiority of African Americans and openly embraced the ideology of the 'Lost Cause of Southern Slavery.' Seminary leaders argued that slavery was essential to a civil society, "an institution of heaven," that benefitted enslaved people, whose inferiority "indicated God's providential will for their enslavement." In 1882, founder John Broadus wrote, "Black moral inferiority was connected to biological inferiority." The seminary's early faculty and trustees created and perpetuated the elaborate mythology of racial difference that was created by God to sustain slavery in America.[5]

Today, Southern Baptists recognize and admit to many of the errors of their past but, regretfully, have chosen to take modest, inconsequential steps to resolve them before Almighty God. Their longstanding opposition to God's Holy throne and the "Great Commandment" of Christ is still reflected in their refusal to utilize their tremendous influence and leadership in opposing all forms of injustice. By taking a stand and exerting their tremendous influence throughout the South as ambassadors of God's Holy throne of justice and righteousness and modeling the love of Christ....

- All forms of voter suppression would cease in the Southern Bible Belt, and voter protection laws could be restored.
- As with all professing Christians in America, they could and should mandate that all unjustly drawn voting districts be redrawn to accurately reflect their racial percentages to allow just representation.
- They could and should be a passionate voice for fair and just immigration policies and encourage their members and supporters to open their private homes and lives to needy immigrants and the poor within our society as sanctuaries of Godly love and hope (Isa. 58, Matt. 25:31-46) and thus receive His promised blessings.
- They could and should oppose the current efforts to roll back social programs and laws that aid and protect the welfare and rights of minorities and the financially poor who are victims of institutional injustice and racism.
- As did Zacchaeus in Luke 19:8, they could and should renounce all generational wealth and privileges gained

- through the injustice of human slavery and the genocide of minority races by White Americans for personal gain and social status and pursue and recommend meaningful avenues of restitution as required by God.
- In summary, they ~~could and should~~ **"must"** sacrificially model themselves after the One they profess as Lord and turn from all historical hypocrisy to validate their verbally stated repentance and legitimacy to the world and God Almighty.

These are just some of the things that not just Southern Baptists should do, but all who have been influenced by this evil virus of deception to condone, perpetuate, or continue to accept the benefits of injustice. There are many things that they could do to align themselves with the heart and will of God in obedience to His Holy Word. This new sacrificial commitment to God and righteousness would finally end their historical and ongoing religious futility and end their role in disguising the longstanding deception of Christianity in the Bible Belt of America. These and other visible actions of justice and righteousness would reveal to Almighty God, their spiritually confused leadership, membership, supporters, and the world that they have truly repented of their past and finally received Jesus as their Lord and the salvation He offers.

In doing so, they should expect to lose many longstanding members and financial supporters. However, once purged of their present hindrances to Godliness and obstacles to justice and righteousness, the Spirit of God can then manifest within their institution, validating His approval. This would facilitate the end of the deception of Christianity within the body of White professing Christians within the Southern Bible Belt of America who would also be willing to honor this new cross-centered, sacrificial commitment to God (Judges 7:1-22).

****************************************

[As a **side note**, this required action must not be understood as the final solution to the longstanding divide between God and themselves but as the necessary beginning to realizing true Biblical Christianity. Though not the focus of this writing, their next concern to be addressed must be "How do they address the divisiveness of denominationalism that humanity instituted, but God never ordained?" [ref. John 17:20-23, Deut. 4:2, 12:32, Prov. 30:6, Eccles.

3:14, Rev. 22:18, 19] This global problem must become a concern and priority of all denominations before Jesus returns to receive His spiritually united and unspotted bride. Heaven is not segregated by race or earthly religious denominations, however, it remains uncertain about separations in Hell.]

*****************************************
Merciful Father, *"He who has ears to hear, let him hear!"*
*****************************************

**It would be correctly stated to say that nearly all racially segregated White professing Christian institutions that existed during the time frame of African slavery in America, rebelled against God by distorting Holy Scripture and Biblical Christianity. This was purposefully done to reap the financial and social benefits from the enslavement of Africans.** Even the Quakers (Society of Friends), who were leaders in the abolitionist movement, took a century to disown enslavers from their congregations.

African slavery was a continuation of the ungodly strategy of White supremacy launched against minority race groups in America that commenced with the initial European occupation of this nation. Many ungodly strategies to maintain White supremacy continue by various means today among White professing Christians and within many religious institutions.

---

An example of the distortion of Holy Scripture by White professing Christian institutions to reinforce White supremacy, and gain financial and social benefits and the resulting religious hypocrisy can easily be seen in the documented history of the Mormon Church in America. From its inception, like nearly every other racially segregated White religious institution that existed in America during the time frame of slavery, the Mormon Church also profited financially and socially from African slavery and human injustice.

Though the Book of Mormon taught that slavery was against God's law (Mosiah 2:13, Alma 27:9), in 1836, in agreement with the erroneous teaching of the Southern Baptist and many other racially segregated religious institutions, Joseph Smith, the founder of Mormonism, wrote in the *"Messenger and Advocate"* an article supporting slavery and affirming that it was God's will. He said that the Northerners had no right to tell the Southerners whether they could have slaves. Joseph Smith defended slavery, arguing that the Old Testament taught that blacks were cursed with servitude, and the New Testament defended slavery. Like many White American religious leaders of that era, and as earlier noted, in 1836, Smith taught that the Curse of Ham came from God and that it demanded the legalization of slavery. Both Joseph Smith and Brigham Young (who succeeded Joseph Smith after he was murdered) taught that Mormons were not abolitionists *(those who want to end human slavery)*. After the church base moved to Missouri and gained Southern converts, church leaders began to own slaves. In response to the Emancipation Proclamation issued by President Abraham Lincoln freeing African slaves, Brigham Young taught that efforts to abolish slavery were contrary to the decrees of God and would eventually fail. He also encouraged members to participate in the Indian slave trade.[6]

As with many historical White religious institutions in America, much of the historical wealth of the Mormon church is stained by the sin of human slavery and the associated unjust miseries and deaths. Regardless of all outward appearances of success and prosperity as seen today, as with many primarily White religious institutions in America, the wealth of the Mormon church (estimated to exceed $100 billion) is not blessed, honored, or received by our holy, omniscient God. Hypocritically, while hoarding massive wealth in opposition to God's 'Great Commandment' of sacrificial love which has enhanced much unnecessary, unjust suffering of humanity, the Mormon church teaches: *"Part of repentance is to make restitution. This means that as much as possible, we must make right any wrong that we have done. For example, a thief should give back what he has stolen. A liar should make the truth known."*[7]

Included with other documented Mormon church immoralities, they all contribute to the historical deception of spiritual blessings and true Christianity existing in America. (Reference *"The Fanaticism of Christian Discipleship"* for Biblical clarity of God's designed purpose for amassing wealth in Christianity).

---

**This mostly suppressed history and spiritual status of the Mormon church, by and large, is the shared history and spiritual status of the White institutional church in America as it remains under God's wrath** (Rom. 1:18, Eph. 5:6).

Many benefits gained from African slavery by America and its various institutions are still reaping benefits today.

The two most famous buildings in Washington, D.C., the United States Capitol and the White House were built by enslaved Africans. Also, the Smithsonian Institution, Wall Street in New York, Fort Sumter in South Carolina, and, perhaps hard to believe, many historic racially segregated White churches in America were built by enslaved Africans.

Profits from African slavery were used to build some of the most prestigious colleges and universities in America: Princeton, Harvard, Brown, University of Virginia, University of Georgia, University of North Carolina, Rutgers University, Yale, Columbia, and Georgetown, just to name a few. In addition to using the profits from slavery to build these institutions, African slaves were used to serve the needs of the then all-white faculty and administration of many of them.

Twelve U.S. presidents owned African slaves at some point in their lives. Only two of the first twelve presidents never owned slaves, John Adams and John Quincy Adams.

Indeed, the legacy from the ungodly wealth gained from African slavery is sewn deeply into the fabric of the United States of America, generating more financial wealth today for descendant White families, churches, government, and private and public institutions.

Though seldom realized or accepted by most professing Christians today, the blood of enslaved Africans, Native Americans, and Asians has been crying out to the Lord from the soil of this nation for long, overdue justice (Genesis 4:10, Isaiah 26:21). In this end-time period of revelation, correction, and restoration, long-overdue accountability is required and is already being effected by God throughout America and its institutions.

---

"While Baptists in the South played the most vocal role in defending the institution of slavery before the Civil War, other denominations, including the Presbyterian Church, the Episcopal Church, the Lutheran Church and the Catholic Church, and other religious educational institutions all benefited from enslaved labor in some way. Whether it was members of the clergy or the churches themselves owning enslaved people, or the churches receiving taxes from congregants in the form of tobacco farmed by enslaved people, the wealth of the churches was deeply intertwined with the slave trade.

Well into the 20th century, churches and their clergy also played an active role in advocating policies of segregation and redlining *(discriminatory practices)*."[8]

---

There has been much writing documenting African slavery in America. But to this day, there has not been a comprehensive study and spiritual evaluation of the dominant role of the racially-segregated White institutional church in America's history and its effect on hindering the establishment of true Biblical Christianity. True Christianity is validated by God's presence, power, and sacrificial love, which requires interracial oneness in America's professing body of Christ.

Hopefully, this concise writing will not just bring awareness of the primary cause of the long-standing divide between God and religion in America. Our fervent prayer is that it will become a much-needed spark to ignite open and honest dialog by professing Christians of all races across all lines of division. Prayerfully, it will generate a focused and more comprehensive approach to establishing true Biblical Christianity in America and throughout the world as was revealed and modeled in the first-century church of the Apostles of Christ. Though ignored throughout America's history, God's eternal kingdom design for human relations has not changed.

Again, we pray that with the guidance of the Holy Spirit, an open and honest dialog will lead to the establishment of true Biblical Christianity in America, reflecting the required sacrificial love for all humanity, justice, and interracial oneness of God's eternal kingdom design. These Biblical requirements for race relations have not existed throughout America's history of White church-condoned hatred, racism, violence, and White supremacy.

Establishing God's requirements of sacrificial love for all humanity, justice, and interracial oneness must become the primary focus of the professing body of Christ before Jesus returns to claim His united, unspotted bride, the Biblically bona fide church of God in Christ. The salvation of many unsuspecting souls who unknowingly are victims of this historically successful, evil, deceptive strategy 'hangs in the balance.'

The required resolutions are beyond the scope of humanity's limited understanding. They require individual and corporate efforts of repentance and seeking God through fervent prayer for a revelation of His required resolution(s), which obviously must include restitution wherever possible.

---

*"Father God, open the eyes of the spiritually blind so they may recognize the errors of their way, change and turn from their historical evil-inspired ways, and receive Your salvation that is freely offered.*

*This we ask for Your glory in the name of Jesus. Amen."*

---

*"We have deluded ourselves into believing the myth that capitalism grew and prospered out of the Protestant ethic of hard work and sacrifices. Capitalism was built on the exploitation of black slaves and continues to thrive on the exploitation of the poor, both black and white both here and abroad."*

**- Dr. Martin Luther King, Jr. -**

*"Where justice is denied, where poverty is enforced, where ignorance prevails, and where any one class is made to feel that society is an organized conspiracy to oppress, rob and degrade them, neither persons nor property will be safe."*

- **Frederick Douglass** -

---

*"Slavery is founded in the selfishness of man's nature. Opposition to it is in his love of justice. These principles are an eternal antagonism, and when brought into collision so fiercely, as slavery extension brings them, shocks, and throes, and convulsions must ceaselessly follow."*

- **President Abraham Lincoln** -

---

*"Every man knows that slavery is a curse. Whoever denies this, his lips libel his heart."*

- **Theodore Dwight Weld** -

---

# Chapter 7

## The Assassination of President Abraham Lincoln

In the book entitled *"The Suppressed Truth About the Assassination of Abraham Lincoln,"* the author revealed many suppressed facts that implicated the Roman Catholic Church in the assassination of President Abraham Lincoln in 1865. Though never proven in a court of law, an acceptable motive for his assassination and the Roman Catholic Church's involvement and support of the perpetrators was well documented.

It is a well-known and proven fact that the Roman Catholic and Protestant churches in America participated in and profited from the injustice of African slavery in America. Many resources have documented this deplorable fact that is perhaps hard to believe by the twenty-first-century rational God-fearing mind. More recently, Georgetown University (A Roman Catholic University in Washington, D.C., with a reported 2.6 billion dollar endowment) has admitted to its involvement in owning and selling African slaves for profit. Also, the College of the Holy Cross (A Roman Catholic college in Worcester, Massachusetts, with a reported 1 billion dollar endowment) has confessed to its involvement with African slavery in America. For spiritual oneness with God, many other institutions must take their lead and step forward with confession, resulting in repentance and restitution.

In *"The Suppressed Truth About the Assassination of Abraham Lincoln,"* the author focuses on the involvement of the Roman Catholic Church in African slavery and their response to the effects of the changing political landscape of that era regarding institutional slavery in America.

The author revealed that the Roman Catholic Church's historical involvement in human slavery did not start with the African slave trade. The Roman Catholic Church has a long history of profiting from human injustice and slavery. He stated, "From the earliest times, the Roman Church advocated human slavery. In the Middle

Ages, when feudal slavery flourished, the church fattened on the exploitation of the serfs who were bought and sold with the land. These serfs were supposed to have no souls and were in precisely the same category as cattle. The great monasteries and nunneries were among the largest owners of serfs. For instance, had Joan D' Arc lived four hundred years before her time, she and her family would have been among the serfs attached to the Monastery of San Ramey. In short, serfdom was the basis of the wealth of the papacy.

It is true that in rare cases, the church lifted out of serfdom a boy in whom it recognized some peculiar native talent or personal trait which might be cultivated and turned to its own advantage, but the act was simply the removal from the thralldom of serfdom to that of ecclesiastical slavery for further and more useful exploitation by more exacting taskmasters, for the Roman church has always enslaved the minds of its followers and victims.

---

The Society of Jesus, also known as the Jesuits, is a religious order of the Catholic Church headquartered in Rome. It was founded in 1540 by Ignatius of Loyola and six companions, with the approval of Pope Paul III.

The Jesuit Oath exacts the obedience of "cadavers."

[A portion of the Jesuit Oath reads, "I do further promise and declare, that I will have no opinion or will of my own, or any mental reservation whatever, even as a corpse or cadaver, but will unhesitatingly obey each and every command that I may receive from my superiors in the Militia of the Pope and of Jesus Christ.

That I may go to any part of the world whithersoever I may be sent, to the frozen regions of the North, the burning sands of the desert of Africa, or the jungles of India, to the centers of civilization of Europe, or to the wild haunts of the barbarous savages of America, without murmuring or repining, and will be submissive in all things whatsoever communicated to me."]

---

The Jesuits believed that "Slavery did not constitute a crime before any law, divine or human. What reasons can we have for undermining the foundations of slavery with the same zeal that ought always to animate us in overcoming evil? When one thinks of the state of degradation in which the hordes of Africa live, the slave trade may be considered as a providential act, and we almost repudiate the philanthropy which sees in a man but one thing – material liberty."

"This Jesuit virus that "Slavery does not constitute a crime before any law, divine or human," was the deadly drug that set the blood of the slave owners on fire, justified their "cause," distorted their vision, controlled their ethics, and appealed so strongly to their economic interest, and it was the one big urge underlying the whole progress of the treason of secession."[1]

---

Regarding the African slave trade and the assassination of President Abraham Lincoln, the author noted that the immorality of slavery drew Abraham Lincoln into the field of candidates for President of the United States. The author stated, "He was drawn into the field by the infamous Dred Scott Decision rendered by the fanatical Romanist, Judge Taney, Chief Justice of the United States Supreme bench. The Taney decision, in a nutshell, was that the "Negro had no rights which the white man had to respect." This virtually placed the government's endorsement of black slavery and aroused Mr. Lincoln to action.

Also, during this time frame, Mr. Lincoln, an attorney, accepted a court case to represent a Catholic priest who was falsely accused by a 'perjuring gang of priests' for crimes he did not commit. This trial became well-known and celebrated. It was thought to be closely monitored by the Roman Catholic hierarchy. After winning this case and exposing the perjuring priests, Mr. Lincoln spoke to the court. He said, "As long as God gives me a heart to feel, a brain to think, or a hand to execute my will, I shall devote it against that power which has attempted to use the machinery of the courts to destroy the rights and character of an American citizen." This promise made by Abraham Lincoln in his maturer years he also kept. That same year, when he entered the political field, tearing to tatters, as no other man could, Taney's Dred Scott Decision, in favor of black slavery, he fully understood the motive power behind it was Rome.

From that time on, the black clouds of Jesuitism were fast gathering about the life of Abraham Lincoln. These enemies followed his path as a shadow follows sunshine. From that moment, his doom was written in letters of blood."

After winning this case for the innocent priest, Mr. Lincoln noticed that the priest was crying and asked him why was he crying (perhaps thinking that these were tears of joy)? The priest replied, "I am not weeping for myself, but for you, sir. They will kill you, and let me tell you this, if I were in their place and they in mine, it would be my sole, my sworn duty, to take your life myself, or to find a man to do it."[2]

Abraham Lincoln ran a successful campaign and became the 16th President of the United States in 1861.

Years later, on the evening of April 14, 1865, shortly after his reelection and the end of the Civil War, Abraham Lincoln was assassinated by John Wilkes Booth, a **Roman Catholic** convert. Lincoln was shot at the Ford's Theater in Washington, D.C. and died the next morning. His assassination happened just days after General Robert E. Lee surrendered his Confederate forces to General Ulysses S. Grant on April 9, 1865 at Appomattox Court House, thus ending the Civil War, and after delivering a speech that detailed his Reconstruction Plans for the United States. In planned acts of long overdue justice, President Lincoln was going to give citizenship and voting rights to newly freed African Americans. These decisions were unpopular throughout the racist South and its religious institutions, which were reeling from the economic impact of the loss of slave labor and the fear of receiving newly freed African slaves into their society. It has been more than one and a half centuries since President Lincoln was assassinated. Still, voting rights for African Americans remain under attack by conservative Republican law makers (Lincoln's political party) and their primary supporters and spiritual accomplices, most conservative White professing Christians. These evil-induced, rebellious acts against God's "Great Commandment" of love for all humanity opposes President Lincoln's design for his political party.

Also, as a little-known footnote in America's history, Abraham Lincoln was credited for building the Republican Party into a strong national organization with a focus on justice for the "least." This focus can be contrasted to today's Republican Party whose political platform is riddled with injustice, spiritual deception, and rebellion against the heavenly throne of Almighty God. Their ungodliness is disguised by the party's anti-abortion and anti-gay rights stances which are purposed to influence a public perception of righteousness.

Abraham Lincoln's fault was that he was a morally upright and just man fighting for justice in an immoral and unjust society which was, and still is, controlled by an enemy whose only desire is to kill, steal, and destroy (John 10:10). Satan will not hesitate to use his most effective and preferred weapon of spiritual warfare to do so, which is false and deceptive religion. His hatred for God and those who serve Him is without measure, which was blatantly revealed at the crucifixion of Christ.

In this highlighted publication, the author noted many other acts of ungodliness perpetrated by the Roman Catholic Church throughout American and world history that accounted for Christianity's deception. Many other available writings are in agreement with the author's assessments, and some present other troubling unbiblical concerns.

The author also noted, "The church of Rome has for centuries been a large manufacturer of wine, liquors, and beers. The most expensive European wines are made by the monks and nuns of that church. The finest champagne, for instance, is manufactured by the Carthusian Monks. "Benedictine," that beverage of hell, the sole purpose of which is intended to increase prostitution, was concocted by a monk of the Benedictine order eleven centuries ago. He was later created a cardinal by the Pope for the valuable service which he thereby rendered to his "Holy" church.

The cross is blown in the glass of every bottle of Benedictine; the coat of arms of the order is impressed upon the wax which seals it, and the Latin motto dedicates it "To God, the purest and the best."

Fifty percent of the wines manufactured in the United States were made in California, and about fifty percent of this was manufactured by the Roman Catholic Church in its monasteries in that state."[3]

---

(For additional information regarding the suppressed history of President Abraham Lincoln's assassination, we recommend the book entitled *"Rome's Responsibility for the Assassination of Abraham Lincoln."* By Thomas M. Harris)

---

## *"For the wrath of God is revealed from heaven against all ungodliness and unrighteousness of men, who suppress the truth in unrighteousness."*
## Romans 1:18

---

## *"You are those who justify yourselves before men, but God knows your hearts. For what is highly esteemed among men is an abomination in the sight of God."*
## Luke 16:15

*"If God now wills the removal of a great wrong, and wills also that we of the North as well as you of the South, shall pay fairly for our complicity in that wrong, impartial history will find therein new cause to attest and revere the justice and goodness of God."*

- President Abraham Lincoln -

---

*"America's regretful history should not be suppressed, but revealed and acknowledged and result in unregretful repentances before Almighty God."*

- Walter B. Pennington –

---

*"Familiarize yourselves with the chains of bondage and you prepare your own limbs to wear them. Accustomed to trampling on the rights of others, you have lost the genius of your own independence and become the fit subjects of the first cunning tyrant who rises among you."*

- President Abraham Lincoln -

(This latter statement and perhaps prophecy by President Abraham Lincoln can be witnessed in the United States of America today.)

# Chapter 8

## Injustice Perpetrated Against African Americans

Two years before his assassination by John Wilkes Booth, a Roman Catholic convert, President Abraham Lincoln signed the Emancipation Proclamation on January 1, 1863, during the timeframe of the American Civil War. He signed this document against the advice of his closest advisors. He realized the economic impact that this document would have on the Roman Catholic Church, White institutions, White slave owners, and their families throughout the Confederacy, whose financial viability depended on slave labor. He also realized the negative political impact of this proclamation but realized it was the morally right thing to do and was long overdue.

Throughout the history of African slavery in the United States, it was noted in different writings that the Roman Catholic Church profited from the enslavement of Africans, as did practically all other White religious groups and institutions throughout the South. As noted in *"The Suppressed Truth about the Assassination of President Abraham Lincoln,"* the economic impact of African slavery in America was felt all the way to the Vatican in Rome, which had become a primary source of revenue for its global operation.

African slavery had become a contentious issue between the northern states and the Confederacy, which led to the American Civil War. Though enslaved Africans were held in some northern states, the Confederacy was recognized as the epicenter for African slavery in the United States of America.

The Civil War was fought from April 1861 to the spring of 1865 between the Union ("the North") and the Confederacy ("the South") over the moral and economic issue of African slavery. Slave labor had provided much wealth to White families and religious and non-religious institutions throughout the South. The Confederate states were unwilling to yield to the North's political pressure and moral concerns because African slavery had become the backbone of their economy. It was the economics of slavery and political control of that system that was central to the conflict.

During the timeframe of this conflict, slavery was legal in the states of Alabama, Arkansas, Delaware, Florida, Georgia, Kentucky, Louisiana, Maryland, Mississippi, Missouri, North Carolina, South Carolina, Tennessee, Texas, and Virginia. Primarily, these states were later hypocritically labeled the "Bible Belt," a deception of God's character and Biblical Christianity, void of Christ's sacrificial love for all humanity.

---

The Emancipation Proclamation freed nearly four million Africans who were held as slaves within the rebellious Confederate Southern states. The proclamation stated, "All persons held as slaves are, and henceforward shall be free."

Though this proclamation freed African slaves held in Confederate states, it was through the Thirteenth Amendment to the U.S. Constitution that the U.S. Senate passed on April 8, 1864, and the House passed on January 31, 1865, that emancipation became national policy. The Thirteenth Amendment to the U.S. Constitution is recognized as the formal abolition (end) of slavery in the United States.

Understandably, enslaved Africans throughout the South received this declaration of freedom with excitement and hope for a new, better, and more inclusive future of America's prosperity that they had been forced to build. However, this excitement was soon dashed by a new reality of White church-supported terror.

---

The American Civil War was the bloodiest war ever fought on American soil. It accounted for a reported loss of more than 620,000 human lives. Most of the fighting during the war took place in the Confederate states. After the bloody and destructive Civil War ended in 1865 in defeat for the Confederacy, the economy of the Confederacy was literally in shambles. Combined with the end of legalized White church-supported slavery, the backbone of the southern economy, the Confederacy found itself in a seemingly hopeless situation regarding economic recovery. In addition, there was a major concern and fear by Southern Whites of integrating the millions of newly freed slaves into a new relationship of equality and shared prosperity (Christian tenets that Southern White professing Christians could never accept or honor). Other than economic instability, this had become the greatest fear of Whites throughout the Confederacy. **This fear took precedence over faith in God, justice, and righteousness, like many documented fears today.**

White supremacy and racial inequality were in jeopardy and, in their fearful and hate-filled minds, had to be maintained at any cost. Indeed, this was a trying and stressful time for Whites throughout the Confederacy. It was recognized throughout the South and the spiritually confused racially-segregated Southern White institutional church that a new strategy and major change were desperately needed in order to maintain economic stability, governmental control, and White supremacy.

Until this point in America's history, there had not been a major organized White church-supported institution of terror, even though the racially segregated White institutional church had shared responsibility for much of the terror and injustice of America's past. However, as stated, this desperate time required major and radical change.

This sense of desperation led to the formation and rise of the most feared and successful Southern White church-supported hate group in the history of the United States of America.

On December 24, 1865, six ex-Confederate soldiers, who were professing Christians, put aside their religious and denominational differences and met in Pulaski, Tennessee, to formulate a new strategy. The result of this meeting was the formation of the organization known as the Ku Klux Klan. The Klan was a vigilante group mobilizing a campaign of violence and terror against the progress of Reconstruction. The Klan's name became synonymous with terrorism and violence, primarily toward newly freed African Americans.

The six Ku Klux Klan charter members (founders) were:

1. Captain John C. Lester, **Methodist** (He was an official in the Methodist Church and a member of the Tennessee State Legislature. He and Rev. D. L. Wilson, a noted **Presbyterian** pastor in Broadway, Virginia, put aside their denominational differences and co-authored a book detailing the history and the evil orchestrated constitution of the Ku Klux Klan).
2. Major James R. Crowe, **Presbyterian** (He was an official in the Presbyterian Church and held a high rank in **Freemasonry.** He was elected a Grand Turk in the KKK.)
3. Adjutant Calvin E. Jones, **Episcopalian**
4. Captain John B. Kennedy, **Presbyterian**
5. Frank O. McCord, **Methodist;** Grand Cyclops in the KKK.
6. Richard Reed, **Presbyterian**

---

**It is important to note that the only time recorded in the history of these religious denominations that they united, including Freemasonry, was not as an obedient response to Jesus' prayer to the Father for oneness (Jn. 17:21), but for a rebellious unifying cause of evilness orchestrated by Satan, thus exposing his hidden agenda and strategy and their disguised hidden evil association** (Also note Hiram Wesley Evans' religious association and high rank and association with Freemasonry on the next page). **It would be naïve and could prove fatal and eternally damning if discerning believers continue to disregard the facts when Satan mistakenly "overplays his hand" and reveals himself, his strategies, and his kingdom composition. Again unbiblical man-devised denominationalism and secret societies are proven to be a convincing deception for evilness and are revealed time and again to not be aligned with God's kingdom design. Believers beware!**

If you have been deceived and victimized by the divisiveness of denominationalism or Catholicism or an ungodly association with a secret society organization, or any other ungodly association, now is the ideal time for separation and seeking God for spiritual deliverance and oneness. (ref. Page 210 for more information). **This was an eye-opening God-given revelation that required a personal and life-altering decision by this writer as an active member of Freemasonry and as serving as a pastor in a major denomination. Indeed, God truly blessed my voluntary separations (Rom. 12:1-2, $2^{nd}$ Cor. 6:11-18).** (ref. *"The Fanaticism of Christian Discipleship"* for more information and clarity on Christian consecration.)

As the group gained members from all strata of the Southern White society, they used violent intimidation to prevent African Americans - and any White people who supported Reconstruction - from voting and holding political office. **("Reconstruction"** was the period after the Civil War when several U.S. administrators sought to reconstruct the Confederate states by establishing and protecting the legal rights of the newly freed African slaves.)

In an effort to maintain control of the government and reinforce White supremacy, the members of the Ku Klux Klan, joined by other White Southern professing Christians and non-believers, engaged in a violent campaign of deadly voter intimidation during the 1868 presidential election. From Arkansas to Georgia, thousands of African Americans were killed. Similar campaigns of lynchings, tar-and-featherings, rapes, and other violent attacks on those challenging White supremacy became a hallmark of the Klan.

[As an alarming and suppressed **side-note** of history, it can arguably be stated that the United States, supported by its racially segregated White religious institutions, taught and modeled terrorism to many of its twenty-first-century foreign adversaries of terror. The Biblical principles that *"God is not mocked"* and *"You reap what you sow"* (Gal. 6:7-9), are again proven. The wrath of God against the U.S. should not be surprising but expected (Rom. 1:18, Eph. 5:6)]

After a short but violent period, the "first-era" Klan disbanded when it became evident that the Southern White church-supported Jim Crow laws would secure White supremacy across the country.[1]

After disbanding in 1869, the Klan was revised at the start of its $2^{nd}$ era by the Reverend Colonel William Joseph Simmons, a White **Methodist** preacher in Atlanta, Georgia. He served as the imperial wizard of the KKK and was later elected emperor for life.

Hiram Wesley Evans, a member of the **Christian Church (Disciples of Christ) and a $32^{nd}$-degree Freemason**, succeeded him. Evans sought to promote a form of nativist, protestant nationalism.[2]

(**"Nativism"** is the policy of protecting the interests of native-born or established inhabitants against those of immigrants.
**"Protestant nationalism"** is an ideology that seeks to create and maintain a legal fusion of Protestant Christian religion with a nation's character. Advocates of protestant nationalism desire their view of

Christianity to be an integral part of their country's identity and want the government to promote or enforce their position.)

\*\*\*\*\*\*\*\*\*\*\*\*\*\*\*\*\*\*\*\*\*\*\*\*\*\*\*\*\*\*\*\*\*\*

**The twenty-first-century conservative White professing Christians' focus on nativism, White Protestant nationalism, voter suppression and intimidation, and racial injustice is not a recent phenomenon of religious rebellion against God's designed kingdom order. It originated with the Ku Klux Klan, with whom they have a historical, kindred spiritual relationship.**

\*\*\*\*\*\*\*\*\*\*\*\*\*\*\*\*\*\*\*\*\*\*\*\*\*\*\*\*\*\*\*\*\*\*

It is spiritually alarming to observe how Satan will utilize those under his influence to publicly reflect his disdain for Christ and God's kingdom through mockery and other insulting and degrading means. The Ku Klux Klan eventually chose a burning cross as its symbol of fear and hatred in opposition to the cross of Christ, which represented unconditional, sacrificial love for all humanity. The Ku Klux Klan often burned crosses on African American and African American sympathizers' property to display hatred and terror to invoke fear, which is mockingly contrary to the cross of Christ. The burning cross became one of the most potent hate symbols in America and was a vivid sign and symbol of America's spiritual hypocrisy and religious deception.

\*\*\*\*\*\*\*\*\*\*\*\*\*\*\*\*\*\*\*\*\*\*\*\*\*\*\*\*\*\*\*\*\*\*

From its inception, under Satan's influence, the Ku Klux Klan deceptively disguised itself as a "Christian" organization. This evil, hate-filled organization was embraced by the racially segregated White institutional church, which resulted in a kindred relationship of mutual support. As all professing Christian groups have a statement of belief, so did the Ku Klux Klan. Portions of The Klan Creed read:

"I believe in God, Ineffable; Infinite; Eternal; Creator and Sole Ruler of the universe; and in Jesus Christ, His Son our Savior, who is the Divine Word made manifest in flesh and demonstrated in life.

I believe that God created races and nations, committing to each a special destiny and service; that the United States, through its White Protestant citizens, holds a Divine commission for the furtherance of free government, **the maintenance of white supremacy,** and the protection of religious freedom; that its constitution and laws are expressive of this Divine purpose."[3]

Obviously, the Klan views White supremacy as a Divine entitlement to be maintained at all costs, even to the point of murder, which the racially segregated White Protestant churches in America did not openly oppose.

It has always been a membership requirement that each member is a professing White Protestant Christian. The application form reads:

"The requirements for membership are that you be White, Native-born, Protestant Gentile American who believes in the United States of America above any other Government, civil, political or ecclesiastical; who will support the principles of Free Public Schools, Free Speech, Free Press, Separation of Church and State, Liberty, **White Supremacy**, Just Laws, the Pursuit of Happiness and the Sanctity of the Home."

It concludes with the question, "**To what church do you belong?**"[4]

The Klan was involved in every aspect of the White Protestant church in the United States of America, with members occupying many top leadership positions (e.g., **Southern Baptist, Presbyterian, etc.**). **Indeed, institutional hatred was sewn deeply into the spiritual fabric of White religion throughout America's history.**

It was relatively normal for Klansmen to attend church service in full uniform (hoods and robes). The practice both asserted their predominance and implied their connection to local church leaders. As an act of their kindred spiritual connection, the Ku Klux Klan often hosted church revivals. As an appreciation, Klansmen would offer cash contributions to the host church congregations. In their evil-inspired revivals, White professing Christians recommitted themselves to White supremacy and racial division in rebellion against God's "Great Commandment" of love and interracially unifying Word. Their blatant rebelliousness against God reinforced the deception of Christianity throughout the influential body of undiscerning White professing Christians throughout America.

**************************

Pictured at the top of the following page is a typical church revival held by the Ku Klux Klan. This revival was held at a racially segregated White **Presbyterian** church in Evergreen, Alabama, in April 1927. On the first night, 100 people registered to join as official members of the Klan. This ten-day revival resulted in an additional 600 new members to the local chapter of the Klan.

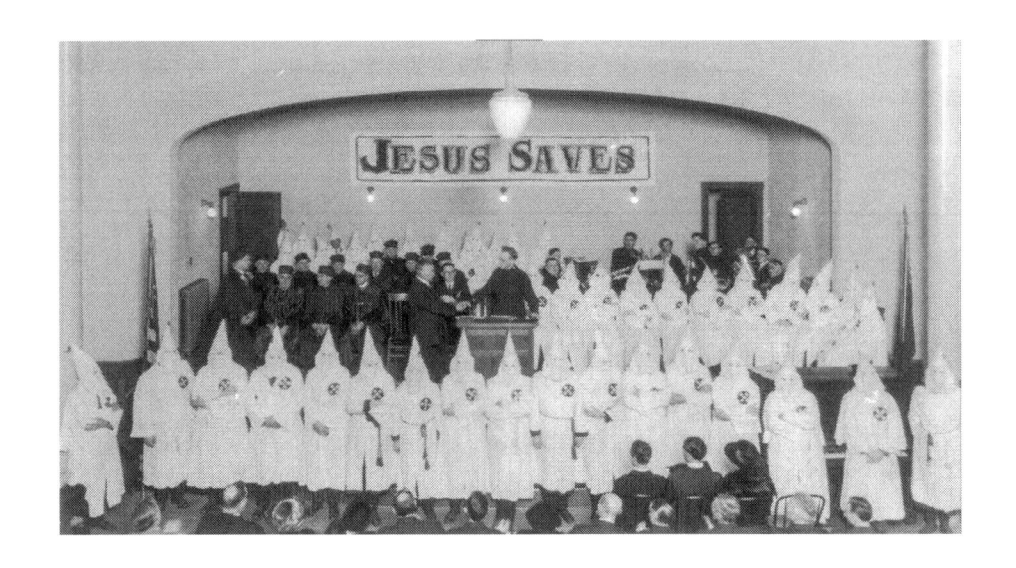

Pictured below is a typical Ku Klux Klan gathering before the start of a Sunday morning worship service. This particular gathering was held at a White federated denominational church in New Jersey in June 1926. The church became federated when the White racially segregated **Methodist** and **Presbyterian** churches suffered economic difficulties and decided to unite. Most White Protestant denominational churches in the Deep South Bible Belt embraced the Ku Klux Klan. The fact that this church was not in the Southern Bible Belt reflects the widespread acceptance and influence of the Klan throughout the United States of America.

**[Their processions into worship always included the U.S. flag (as pictured) reflecting and revealing the original version of the evil-inspired White Protestant professing Christian nationalism that is prevalent in the U.S. today.]**

As noted, Satan utilizes those under his evil influence to make a mockery of Christ and God's holy kingdom. The initiation ceremony for new converts into the KKK included a demonically orchestrated deception of the "laying on of hands" to supposedly invoke godly blessings and the bestowing of his authority as the other converts remained prayerful (as pictured) to their evil god. Their evil god is still orchestrating the deception of Christianity in America and the world today. This evil orchestrated ceremony was always performed at a supposedly blessed altar draped with a U.S. flag and often a burning cross in the background (as seen below), again, revealing the original version of today's White Protestant professing Christian nationalism and the continuation of the historical deception of Christianity in America.

It was through the involvement of the Ku Klux Klan and their acceptance by the racially segregated White Protestant churches in the United States of America that White supremacy, nativism, Protestant nationalism, racial division, and racial injustice were normalized in the White professing church of God. This masterful strategy that supplanted God's holy Word and His kingdom order for human relations is still reaping benefits for Satan's deceptive kingdom in the United States today through segments of Christ's deceived White professing body as they remain under Satan's blinding evil influence.

By embracing the Klan and supporting them, the racially segregated White Protestant churches in the U.S. willingly made themselves spiritual accomplices to their evilness, and by association, the KKK's god was proven to also be their god. As pictured above and on the following page, their evilness ranged from mocking Christ by burning his sacrificial cross as a means of terror and a symbol of hate while displaying the U.S. flag (as seen), again, demonstrating the original version of today's White Protestant nationalism in America.

Under Satan's evil influence and supported by the racially segregated White Protestant churches of America, thousands of innocent victims were murdered by the KKK to maintain White supremacy, economic, and deceptive religious control of the U.S. **Many of their victims were professing Christians who were martyred as servants of Almighty God. Their blood has been crying out to God for long overdue justice from the soil of the entirety of the U.S.** (ref. Gen. 4:9-11, Isa. 26:21). Assuredly, Satan orchestrated this evilness through the historical undiscerning, racially segregated White Protestant church, reinforcing his deceptive pseudo-Christianity in America. **In this end-time period, Jesus' harlot bride (His rebellious professing church) in America must undergo a painful, God-ordained purging and fidelity correction which has already begun and regretfully, will intensify in the coming days.**

The passiveness and oftentimes involvement of White Catholic and White Protestant churches in America's injustice was sadly exemplified during the documented lynchings of over forty-four hundred African Americans after slavery ended. The actual total is believed to be much higher, with lynchings still being recorded in some rural areas of America today. [This sad reality of America's history and the current state of race relations in America is well documented at the Legacy Museum, Memorial, and Monument Park located in Montgomery, Alabama (eji.org). Professing Christians of all races should prioritize visiting these sites to view the results of the complicit actions and inactions of the historical racially segregated White church in America and regretfully, many undiscerning and spiritually confused professing White Christians in America today. Viewing and understanding history can be a first step to interracial reconciliation and realizing the Biblical design of one body in Christ.]

Church leaders were active participants in many of these documented lynchings. Many participated physically, while many supportive pastors participated by encouraging the perpetrators from the pulpit of their church.

Vocal encouragement by misusing the Bible to justify these atrocious, ungodly acts was prevalent, such as in the case of the lynching of George White in Wilmington, Delaware, on June 23, 1903. The Rev. Robert A. Elwood, the pastor of the White racially segregated Olivet **Presbyterian** church, preached a fiery sermon that was blamed for the lynching. The text of the sermon was widely distributed and was believed to have had much influence on the lynching of George White that followed. Rev. Elwood took his text from 1st Corinthians 5:13, ***"Therefore put away from among ourselves that wicked person."*** He purposefully and erroneously used this scripture to encourage the lynching even though George White had not been found guilty of any crime or had even had a court trial. After this sermon, a mob of approximately 300 demon-influenced White men and boys stormed the jail where George White was being held, forcefully took him away, and lynched him.[5]

This was not an isolated event. The purposeful misuse of the Holy Bible was common in the historical racially segregated White churches throughout America to justify acts of injustice and ungodliness to maintain White supremacy. The misuse of sacred scripture to justify their actions of injustice was a blatant, demonically orchestrated rebellion against God's holy and righteous throne.

---

Many graphic photographs of actual mob lynchings and public burnings of African Americans are documented at the Legacy Museum and published in the book, *"Without Sanctuary."* Though painful and difficult to view, this museum and publication documents a sad reality of America's history that must not be suppressed or forgotten. **America's history must be accurately acknowledged to enable spiritual change to be orchestrated by the Holy Spirit.**

George Santayana, in *"The Life of Reason"* (1905), stated, "Those who cannot remember the past are condemned to repeat it," as proven by the current resurgence of hate in America, exacerbated by conservative political rhetoric without objections from the national body of conservative White professing Christians. Winston Churchill stated, "Those that fail to learn from history are doomed to repeat it."

**The point to be made is that we must not forget, alter, or continue to suppress or whitewash America's history, and we must learn from our mistakes.** We must learn from our mistakes so that we do not run the risk of repeating them, especially as professing Christians, servants of Almighty God, who are entrusted ambassadors of His holy throne. As chosen and dedicated servants of God, we must not be influenced or continue to fall prey to the deceptive strategies of Satan and the ways of this evil world, as revealed throughout America's history and documented in this writing. Instead, we are required to be a light of righteousness unto this dark and evil world, reflecting the sacrificial love of God to all humanity and obedience as modeled by Christ and the first-century apostolic church. Regretfully, the professing church of God in Christ in the United States of America, across denominational and racial lines, has faltered in this regard.

---

In reference to the lynching of African Americans by White Americans in the United States, the late Congressman John Lewis asked the question, "What is it in the human psyche that would drive a person to commit such acts of violence against their fellow citizens?" Indeed, this is an important question.

**Perhaps a more important question we should ask as professing Christians is, "What makes a professing Christian desire to participate in these atrocities of ungodly injustice that are blatant and rebellious acts against the holy throne of Almighty God?"**

The only answer that would survive Biblical scrutiny is, "This blatant rejection of the holy throne of God could only be orchestrated by Satan, the prince of hatred, evilness, death, and deception." He often orchestrates his evil schemes through mesmerizing blindness targeting undiscerning believers. As earlier noted, Ephesians 6:12 states, *"For we do not wrestle against flesh and blood, but against principalities, against powers, against the rulers of the darkness of this age, against spiritual hosts of wickedness in the heavenly places."* **According to Biblical scripture, true believers in Christ are not fighting against humanity or those they oppose, but their battles are with the evil influence inside the human perpetrators who influence their acts of injustice, evilness, rebellion, and deception**.

---

When viewing graphic photographs of public lynchings and burnings of African Americans by evil-inspired White American mobs that are published, it is perplexing to see the expressions of satisfaction and joy on the faces of the perpetrators and others in attendance, including their children. Only Satan and his host of demons would expose innocent children to these gruesome and inhuman acts of ungodliness and receive joy and satisfaction for doing so. These acts are the epitome of satanic-induced evilness and clear-cut examples of demonic oppression and possession. Satan has exposed the powerlessness and inability of the institutional White church in the United States to combat his evilness. Even today, he continues to exert his humanity-given authority and evil influence throughout America's society and the deceived and undiscerning professing church of Christ across all races as it remains unaware.

---

Perhaps difficult to believe or understand, postcards and photographs of public lynchings and burnings of African Americans by White American mobs were often distributed as souvenirs and saved as mementos in many White family photo albums. Lynching postcards were in widespread production for more than fifty years in the United States and when mailed, were delivered by the U.S. Postal Service. After much opposition from outside influences, delivery by the U.S. Postal Service was eventually banned in 1908 (View *"Lynching Post Cards: Token of a Great Day"* online for more info).

---

Preceded by notifications, many of these documented lynchings were family affairs held on Sunday afternoons. The lynching of African Americans became known among many Southern Whites as a "picnic" ("pick-a-nigger-to lynch") as Whites would often share food, laughter, and celebrate. Even worse, the public burnings of African Americans became known among many Southern Whites as a "Negro barbecue." After the lynchings, parents would often pose for photos with their children in front of the hanging and sometimes burned corpse(s) of the lynched victim(s), as seen in many published pictures.

If White churches showed a relative indifference to lynching violence, there were some compelling reasons. The lynch mobs often included their parishioners. Many White pastors who opposed this ungodliness were afraid to address them publically from their church pulpits out of fear of backlash or persecution, as is common with many pastors today. We must never forget an important Biblical truth. **All servants of God who withhold God's truth will be held accountable for the results of doing so** (ref. Ezek. 3:18, 19).

When viewing these graphic photos, it is heartbreaking to see the number of innocent White children at those public lynchings and burnings with their parents still dressed in their Sunday attire. Apparently, there was little to no effort by White parents to shield their children from those atrocities as White parents, conservative White politicians, and conservative White-controlled school boards do today by suppressing this important and spiritual defining part of America's history and White culture.

Even more challenging to believe, it was noted that when a lynching would be held in some rural areas, some White schools would delay that day's scheduled activities until the children returned from viewing the lynched victim's corpse. **All parents and adults must be mindful that God will hold them accountable for their actions and inactions regarding the spiritual development of their innocent God-entrusted children.**

Parents are commanded by God to *"Train up a child in the way he should go, and when he is old, he will not depart from it"* (Prov. 22:6).

**Parental indoctrination into hatred and evilness is a primary reason that generational racism continued to plague race relations in the United States of America and the White racially segregated professing church of Christ throughout its history. This orchestrated evilness against innocent children reinforced the generational deception of Christianity among Christ's professing body of deceived and undiscerning believers.**

The following pictures are ceremonies by evil-inspired defiant White parents indoctrinating their innocent children into the racial hatred and evil ways of the Ku Klux Klan. This spiritually defiant act was fairly common among White parents throughout the Southern Bible Belt. This evilness was prioritized above obedience to God's parental command of training their children in the way of righteousness and how they should live, and modeling before them the unconditional interracial sacrificial love of Christ which is required for eternal salvation. This defiance was prevalent, even within the undiscerning body of White professing Christians.

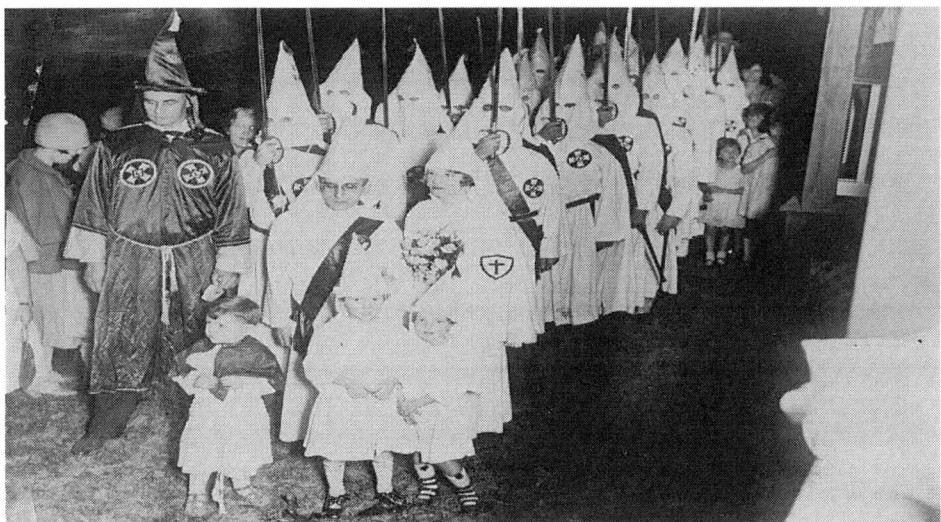

To those who doubt the reality of Satan, there is no greater proof that he is real and active in America's destruction through **racial strife with a focus on its children** (Note the deceptive and evil use of the cross of Christ in the second picture during a ceremony with innocent children before igniting it, and the deceptive evil use of a Christian symbol on the innocent older child in the last picture).

When Satan reveals himself and his evil strategies, as soldiers of the cross, God's faithful remnant must unite for battle under the blood-stained banner of Christ. Indeed, as was then, these are trying times. Merciful Father, please save Your innocent children from ongoing generational evilness, and in these final days, deliver Your spiritually floundering church from satanic control.

\*\*\*\*\*\*\*\*\*\*\*\*\*\*\*\*\*\*\*\*\*\*\*\*\*\*\*\*\*\*\*\*\*\*\*\*

Jesus instructed His disciples in Mark 10:14, *"Let the little children come to Me, and do not forbid them; for of such is the kingdom of God."* All parental actions in opposition to Jesus' instructions are of the kingdom of Satan. In Matthew 18:6 & 7, Jesus warns, *"But whoever causes one of these little ones who believe in Me to sin, it would be better for him if a millstone were hung around his neck, and he were drowned in the depth of the sea. Woe to the world because of offenses! For offenses must come, but* **woe to that man by whom the offense comes.***"*

As a **side note**, professing Christian parents should ask themselves, "What is my child learning from me regarding human justice and race relations?" Also, "As a professing Christian, have I truly modeled and taught Christ's sacrificial love for all humanity to my child *(or children)*?" Now is an excellent time to correct this area of ungodliness if it exists within your household or family. This spiritual correction should begin with a personal repentance for this omission before Almighty God and taking the lead role in correction.

Today, we may not be indoctrinating our children into the evil ways of the Ku Klux Klan. Still, just as foolish and as with many professing Christian parents in America, we may be keeping them from Jesus by allowing them to entertain the deceptive evilness and hatred of our society (ref. James 4:4-8).

**Parents must always beware of the deceptive evilness of Satan!**

\*\*\*\*\*\*\*\*\*\*\*\*\*\*\*\*\*\*\*\*\*\*\*\*\*\*\*\*\*\*\*\*\*\*\*

As we refocus our attention back on the lynching of African Americans in the United States, we will highlight other suppressed facts that are perhaps difficult to understand.

For instance, often, a body part from the lynched victim would be considered a prized souvenir, as was in the case of the lynching of Wylie McNeely in Leesburg, Texas, on October 11, 1921. He was lynched by a mob of 500 angry, demon-influenced White men. As reported in the "Baltimore Herald" dated October 19, 1921, **"The leaders of the mob drew lots for the part of the Negro's anatomy which they regarded as the choicest souvenir."** Also, as reported by the "New York World-Telegram" on December 8, 1933, regarding the lynching of David Gregory: **"Members of the mob of approximately 300, cut out the Negro's heart and sexual organs before casting it (corpse) to the flames."** As stated, these vile acts are inhuman and they are the epitome of satanic-induced evilness.

"More savage was the lynching of Mrs. Mary Turner and the murder of her unborn child, killed in Valdosta, Georgia for protesting her husband's lynching the day before (she was in her eighth month of pregnancy). Before a crowd of over 200 White witnesses that included women and children, Mrs. Turner was stripped, hung upside down by the ankles, soaked with gasoline, and set on fire. After burning, Mrs. Turner was still alive when a member of the White mob took a large hunting knife and cut open her swollen belly. Her unborn infant fell to the ground and cried. A member of the mob savagely killed the crying baby by crushing his head with his foot. After recognizing that Mrs. Turner was still alive, the demon-inspired White mob riddled her body with hundreds of bullets. There was a total of eleven lynchings of innocent African Americans related to this one vile incident.[6]

As with all of these atrocities held in public view, including women and children and witnessed in the presence of Almighty God, the perpetrators were known. It was reported that the perpetrators were well known, outstanding citizens of Valdosta. However, the racially segregated White churches and professing White Christians of Valdosta as throughout the U.S. demonstrated their complicity in these crimes by remaining silent, rather than being an outspoken voice of God for justice and righteousness. As was typical throughout the South regarding these racial atrocities, no one would be held accountable or, if so, they would be exonerated by all-white juries, without a recourse for justice. Also typical, the then all-white law enforcement throughout the South would seldom investigate these crimes. These atrocities remain as unresolved spiritual stains over America's religious landscape before Almighty God. The passing of time does not resolve or diminish sin before God, only repentance. However, consequences will remain.

"These lynchings weren't just vigilante punishments or, as the Equal Justice Initiative notes, 'celebratory acts of racial control and domination.' They were rituals. Specifically, they were rituals of Southern evangelicalism and its then-dogma of purity, literalism, and white supremacy. Many defenders of lynching understood their acts as a Christian duty, consecrated as God's will against racial transgression."[6]

There is now an effort of resistance to exposing White children and the public to this gruesome but important part of America's history to not give them a feeling of guilt (as seen in the governmental actions of suppression in the state of Florida and many other states nationwide).

**An important lesson to be learned for all children and adults is that there is no limit to the immorality and gruesome degradation that can occur when we enable Satan's deceptive presence in our lives. So we must always guard our hearts (ref. Prov. 4:23) with these historical examples of what can happen if we fail to do so in our life-long 'rearview mirrors.'**

Therefore, it is critically important that we do not suppress this spiritually vital part of America's history but keep it ever before us as a reminder of what can occur within our nation or any country when God is excluded and evilness is embraced and empowered through religion and politics.

---

Public information sources and religious historians have suppressed these and numerous other similar documented White initiated racial atrocities of institutional injustice. They are not included in the history books used in public education and educational material used in America's institutional churches. Therefore, many professing Christians in America remain uninformed regarding the primary cause of the historical spiritual divide between God and themselves. They do not realize that as long as the church-endorsed malignant spiritual stain of human injustice remains unaddressed before Almighty God, as spiritual descendants and generational beneficiaries, their labor for Christ is in vain. This partially explains the absence of God-ordained spiritual fruit and His presence in twenty-first-century religion (Note other causes that are highlighted in Chapter 16). The public has purposely been shielded from the knowledge of this important and spiritually defining aspect of America's White culture and history that has been evident since the initial violent European occupation of America. However, this suppression must end, and open and honest interracial dialog begins so racial healing and interracial oneness can become a reality according to God's eternal design. These are prerequisites for God to be glorified in America and true Biblical Christianity to be established before Jesus returns to receive His unspotted bride.

As this writing reveals, under the influence of evilness, White professing Christians and the racially segregated White institutional church played pivotal roles in many of these documented public lynchings and burnings and the demonically influenced effort to maintain White supremacy at all costs, including murder. **As noted, throughout America's history, very few White participants were ever convicted of these crimes in a human court of law. However, their participation and all those who condoned and suppressed these vile acts are recorded in God's "Book of Life" (Rev. 20:12).**

Also, as noted, the savagery, inhumanity, and depravity practiced by White participants would often be justified by the perceived mandate of preserving God's design for White supremacy, social order, and **Christianity**. **Regretfully, it has been Satan's distorted and deceptive version of Christianity that has been preserved and practiced throughout the history of the United States of America. This pseudo-Christianity remains void of eternal salvation for many deceived, undiscerning, and unsuspecting souls.**

---

Booker T. Washington, the founder of Tuskegee Institute, wrote a letter to the New York Tribune dated February 29, 1904, concerning these barbaric, demonic-inspired acts of White humanity. He stated:

*"These outrages take place in communities where there are Christian churches; in the midst of people who have their Sunday schools, their Christian Endeavor societies, and Young Men's Christian Associations; where collections are taken up for sending missionaries to Africa and China and the rest of the so-called heathen world. Is it not possible for the pulpit and press to speak out against these burnings in a manner that shall arouse a public sentiment that will compel the mob to cease insulting our courts, our Governors, and our legal authority, to cease bringing shame and ridicule upon our Christian civilization?"*[7]

******************************************

Currently, the passiveness of White Catholic and White Protestant professing Christians toward racial injustice is consistently exemplified by their absence and lack of meaningful support during the various movements by African Americans, Asian Americans, Native Americans, Hispanics, or Latinos for civil rights and human rights in America. More recently, their absence and lack of support were noted during the human rights protests following the brutal murders by racist, hate-filled White police officers of Alton Sterling, Breonna Taylor, Walter Scott, George Floyd, and a multitude of other innocent minorities in the U.S. Murders fueled by racial hatred from White police officers are all too commonplace throughout America and remain unabated while professing White Christians remain silent.

Their consistent absence and lack of meaningful support must be understood as condoning the racial injustice perpetrated by their evil-inspired White sisters and brothers in the United States. By and large, they fail to honor the Biblical requirement of taking a bold stand for God as entrusted representatives of His holy throne by speaking out and joining the front lines of opposition to all forms of injustice.

************************************

As another little-known and suppressed fact from America's history, it was primarily because of the support of conservative White professing Christians (Protestants and Catholics) that the Jim Crow laws existed and were aggressively enforced throughout the South for more than three-quarters of a century. Perhaps even more challenging to believe, these White church-supported laws existed during the time frame (documented in the 1950s) when, unlike today, a startling ninety-five percent of adult Americans professed Christianity, according to a Gallup poll. These unjust laws were state and local laws mockingly named after a Black minstrel show character. They were purposed to reinforce racial segregation and maintain White supremacy throughout the Southern Bible Belt. They were enacted after the Civil War and aggressively enforced in the early 19$^{th}$ and 20$^{th}$ centuries. Primarily, they were enforced until 1965. These laws directly opposed God's "Great Commandment" and were a direct attack orchestrated by Satan against the foundation of God's heavenly throne through willing White professing Christians and the racially segregated institutional White church. These unjust laws suppressed the rights of African Americans by denying them the right to vote, hold specific jobs, get a high-quality education, receive adequate health care, etc. Those who attempted to defy these laws often faced arrest, fines, jail sentences, violence, and death.

The following are actual Jim Crow laws from various states in the United States of America. They were reminiscent of the apartheid system of governmental laws that Europeans instituted after their invasions of South Africa, Australia, etc., and was reflective of a larger satanic-induced trend and strategy for worldwide control of God's creation:

## Miscegenation:

One law prohibited marriage between a White person and an African American who was more than 12% African American. Violating this law was a felony punishable by imprisonment in the state prison for up to five years.

One law made the Cohabitation of a White person and an African American without legal marriage a felony. The penalty for committing such an act resulted in imprisonment from one month to one year, with or without hard labor.

One law invalidated interracial marriages if the parties went to another legal power to get married.

One law barred intimate relations between Whites and African Americans. Failure to follow this law ended in fines up to $1,000, up to five years in prison, or both.

## Education:

One law called for separate public schools for the education of White and African American children.

One law gave all school district trustees the right to create separate schools for African American children.

One law required separate textbooks for White and African American school children.

One law made it unlawful for an African American child to attend a White school, and vice versa. No separate African American school was allowed to be located within 1 mile (1.6 km) of a separate White school. This law excluded schools in cities and towns but did not allow the schools in those areas within six hundred feet of the other.

One law made it unlawful to maintain or operate any college, school, or institution where persons of the White and African American races were both allowed to attend. The penalty for violating this law was a $1,000 fine.

One law barred state funds to non-racially segregated schools.

## Health Care:

One law mandated separate but equal accommodations for White and African Americans in nursing homes.

One law required separate tuberculosis hospitals for each race.

One law barred African American physicians and nurses from taking postgraduate courses in public hospitals.

Most Southern states mandated separate hospital facilities for African Americans and Whites. In most cases, racially segregated facilities for African Americans were substandard and underfunded which contributed to much unnecessary suffering and many unjust deaths.

Still as documented in the United States today, many unnecessary and unjust deaths of African Americans result from insufficient health care.

**Railroads and Streetcars**:

Most states required separate accommodations for White and African American passengers. Penalties for conductors who violated this law varied from state to state. Also, many states required separate waiting rooms for White and African American passengers, including bus terminals. Penalties for violation varied from state to state.

**Public Accommodations**:

One law barred African Americans and Whites from purchasing and consuming alcohol at the same location.

One law required all shows and tent exhibitions to provide two separate ticket offices with individual ticket sellers and two separate entrances to the performance.

Many state laws required that all public parks, recreation centers, playgrounds, restrooms, beaches, swimming pools, etc., be racially segregated.

Many state laws required racially segregated libraries.

Even today, many cemeteries for the burial of the dead remain racially segregated throughout the Southern Bible Belt.

*******************************************

These are just some of the racially-segregated White church-supported Jim Crow laws that were aggressively enforced throughout the Southern Bible Belt.

Even today, some previous Confederate states have legal remnants of these laws, still without opposition from professing White Christians in the Southern Bible Belt.

**Also, even today, Republican-controlled states throughout the Southern Bible Belt are still enacting laws of suppression and injustice against minority races, from unjust apportionments of government resources to voting district gerrymandering to diminish voting power and representation for minority races, still without meaningful opposition from White professing Christians.**

**There remains overwhelming support from professing White Christians throughout the South who elect the unjust lawmakers for this primary purpose. They are consciously choosing to disregard God's commands regarding human relations and are continuing in the 'footsteps' of their forefathers in rebelling against Almighty God, whom they openly, but falsely profess as Lord.**

**These are blatant acts of spiritual hypocrisy which is also reflected in the current desire to place the Ten Commandments of God in public schools (as reported in the state of Louisiana) while perpetrating these ongoing injustices in rebellion against God. Those who do so must realize that they will give an accounting to Almighty God for their role in enhancing the deception of Christianity in America through their self-focused support for injustice and unrighteousness.**

The unjust, White church-supported Jim Crow laws accounted for the unmerited deaths of thousands of African American citizens throughout the many years that they were openly and aggressively enforced. Many of the victimized African American citizens professed Christianity and, by God's design, were brothers and sisters in Christ to the White professing Christians who condoned and enforced these laws. This paradox is difficult to understand or accept by the rational God-fearing mind and is an affront to God Almighty.

This blatant rebellion reveals the unimaginable extent of satanic influence and its resulting spiritual blindness that only results in eternal damnation, which is Satan's eternal goal for all humanity. Embracing and empowering evilness for self-focused advantages has led to the ongoing ungodly division and spiritual destruction in the United States.

These unjust laws and the thousands of unwarranted African American deaths attributed to them could only have been orchestrated by Satan, the prince of death and the strategist of all rebellion against God's Divine order for human relations.

---

(As a **side note**, the Jim Crow era is documented at the Jim Crow Museum located in Big Rapids, Michigan. Virtual tours are available at JimCrowMuseum@Ferris.edu.)

Merciful God, *"He who has ears to hear, let him hear!"*

---

***"I have almost reached the regrettable conclusion that the Negro's great stumbling block in the stride toward freedom is not the White Citizens Council or the Ku Klux Klan but the white moderate who is more devoted to order than to justice; who prefers a negative peace which is the absence of tension to a positive peace which is the presence of justice."***

**- Dr. Martin Luther King, Jr. –**

\*\*\*\*\*\*\*\*\*\*\*\*\*\*\*\*\*\*\*\*\*\*\*\*\*\*\*\*\*\*\*\*\*\*\*\*\*\*

***We suggest that at this point, you take a break from this reading for a period of spiritual reflection, introspection, and fervent prayer for God's professing Christian church in the United States of America, and the spiritual state and direction of the United States as the Spirit of God leads you.***

***Request clarity for your role in God's resolution for the historical spiritual separation.***

\*\*\*\*\*\*\*\*\*\*\*\*\*\*\*\*\*\*\*\*\*\*\*\*\*\*\*\*\*\*\*\*\*\*\*\*\*\*

# Chapter 9

## Injustice Perpetrated Against Asian Americans

On May 28, 2021, President Joseph R. Biden, Jr. issued the "Executive Order on Advancing Equity, Justice, and Opportunity for Asian Americans, Native Hawaiians, and Pacific Islanders." This Executive Order was issued primarily to address the growing hatred and injustices perpetrated by White Americans towards the above-mentioned citizen groups of the United States of America.

Excerpts from this Executive Order:

"Asian American, Native Hawaiian, and Pacific Islander (AA and NPHI) individuals and communities are irrefutable sources of our Nation's strength. These communities have molded the American experience, and the achievements of AA and NHPI communities make the United States stronger and more vibrant. The richness of America's multicultural democracy is strengthened by the diversity of AA and NHPI communities and the many cultures and languages of AA and NHPI individuals in the United States."

"Asian American, Native Hawaiian, and Pacific Islander communities together constitute the fastest growing ethnic group in the United States and make rich contributions to our society, our economy, and our culture. Yet, for far too long, systemic barriers to equity, justice, and opportunity have put the American dream out of reach of many AA and NHPI communities. Many AA and NHPI individuals face persistent disparities in socioeconomic, health, and educational outcomes. Linguistic isolation and lack of access to language-assistance services continue to lock many AA and NHPI individuals out of opportunity. Too often, Federal data collection practices fail to measure, reflect, and disaggregate the diversity of AA and NHPI experiences. These practices contribute to often painful and enduring stereotypes about Asian Americans as a "model minority" and obscure disparities within AA and NHPI communities."

**"Our Nation has also seen again that anti-Asian bias, xenophobia, racism, and nativism have deep roots in our Nation.** Tragic acts of anti-Asian violence have increased during the COVID-19 pandemic, casting a shadow of fear and grief over many AA and NHPI Communities, in particular East Asian communities. Long before this pandemic, AA and NHPI communities in the United States – including South Asian and Southeast Asian communities – have faced persistent xenophobia, **religious discrimination**, racism, and violence. The Federal Government must provide the moral leadership, policies, and programs to address and end anti-Asian violence and discrimination, and advance inclusion and belonging for all AA and NHPI communities."

"At the same time, many AA and NHPI communities, and in particular Native Hawaiian and Pacific Islander communities, have also been disproportionately burdened by the COVID-19 public health crisis. Evidence suggests that Native Hawaiians and Pacific Islanders are three times more likely to contract COVID-19 compared to white people and nearly twice as likely to die from the disease. On top of these health inequities, many AA and NHPI families and small businesses have faced devastating economic losses during this crisis, which must be addressed."

---

President Biden made two important observations relevant to this writing. First, he noted, "Our Nation has also seen again that anti-Asian bias, xenophobia, racism, and nativism have deep roots in our Nation." Second, he noted that long before the COVID-19 pandemic, AA and NHPI communities in the United States had faced persistent religious discrimination.

So, as a nation that primarily identifies itself as "Christian," how did it become necessary for the President of the United States to issue this Executive Order to combat racial hatred, religious discrimination, and injustice against Asian Americans?

President Biden stated, "The Federal Government must provide the moral leadership." Why must it be necessary for the United States government to assume the role of the professing Christian church in America, the appointed representatives of God's holy throne? These are important questions that the White institutional church must address while the time is allowed for repentance and correction. Also, each individual must prepare to give an accounting of their actions and inactions as representatives of God's kingdom as they stand before God. What was their response to the "Great Commandment" of God and addressing the needs of all others, especially the "least" in our society?

---

Before we address these two observations of President Biden, we will review the background and origin of the Asian presence in America. This review in itself will partially address his first concern.

---

As Europeans came to America from a foreign continent (Europe), Asians also came to America from a foreign continent (mainly Asia). Though Europeans were first to come, they both came for similar reasons: economic opportunities (Europeans also claimed that their occupation of America was based on a desire for religious freedom, though the results of their forced, violent occupation, genocide, and enslavement of Native Americans did not reflect the defining tenets of Christianity, the religion they professed).

Europeans came first and established their occupation by overwhelming force in great numbers and superior weaponry. Their great numbers overwhelmed the original occupants, the Native Americans, by violence and enabled them to gain complete control (ref. chapter 6, "Injustice Perpetrated Against Native Americans"). They disregarded the rights of ownership, customs, and traditions of Native Americans and established unjust church-supported laws and regulations that would be applied for governance, maintaining control, and permanently securing the prosperity of their new land. These ever-changing laws and regulations were designed, and continue to be designed, to control and limit full inclusion and prosperity for every other race of people that would come into America after them.

---

"Asians have been in the U.S. for a long time. The history of Asians in the U.S. is the history of dreams, hard work, prejudice, discrimination, persistence, and triumph.

As presented in the excellent PBS documentary series "Ancestors in the Americas," the first Asians to come to the western hemisphere were Chinese Filipinos who settled in Mexico. Eventually, Filipino sailors were the first to settle in the U.S. around 1750 in what would later be Louisiana. Later around 1840, to make up for the shortage of slaves from Africa, the British and Spanish brought over slaves of "Coolies" from China, India, and the Philippines to islands in the Caribbean, Peru, Ecuador, and other countries in South America.

However, the first large-scale immigration of Asians into the U.S. didn't happen until 1848. Around that time, and as you may remember from your history classes, gold was discovered in America. Lured by tales and dreams of making it rich on "Gold Mountain" (which became the Chinese nickname for California), the Gold Rush was one of the **pull factors** that led many Chinese to come to the U.S. to find their fortune and return home rich and wealthy.

Most of these early Chinese workers were from the Guangdong (also called Canton) province in China. However, there were also **push** factors that drove many to want to leave China. The most important factor was economic hardship due to the growing British dominance over China after Britain defeated China in the Opium War of 1839-1842.

In addition to prospecting for gold in California, many Chinese also came as contract laborers to Hawaii to work in sugarcane plantations. While in California, Chinese miners experienced their first taste of discrimination in the form of the Foreign Miner Tax. This was supposed to be collected from every foreign miner, but in reality, it was only collected from the Chinese, despite the multitude of miners from European countries here as well.

When some Chinese miners objected and refused to pay the unfair tax, they were physically attacked and even murdered. Eventually, the Chinese tried to go to court to demand justice and equal treatment, but at the time, California's laws prevented Chinese immigrants from testifying against Whites in court. As a result, many murders went unsolved, and many murderers went free.

As portrayed in the excellent PBS documentary "Becoming American – The Chinese Experience," the Chinese also worked as small-time merchants, gardeners, domestics, laundry workers, farmers, and, starting in 1865, as railroad workers on the famous Transcontinental Railroad project. The project pitted the Union Pacific (working westward from Nebraska) and the Central Pacific (working eastward from Sacramento) against each other for each mile of railroad track laid.

At its peak, 9,000 to 12,000 Chinese worked for the Central Pacific in some of the dirtiest and most dangerous jobs (different sources have different estimates on exact numbers). Although there are no official records, some sources claim that up to 1,000 Chinese died during the project as a result of avalanche and explosive accidents as they carved their way through the Sierra Mountains (other sources claim much lower numbers of casualties).

Even though the Chinese workers performed virtually all of the hardest, dirtiest, and most dangerous jobs, they were only paid 60% of what European immigrant workers got paid. The Chinese workers actually went on strike for a few days and demanded that they get paid the same amount as the other ethnic groups. Officials of the Central Pacific were able to end the strike and force the Chinese workers back to work by cutting off their food supply and starving them into submission.

The project was completed on May 10, 1869, and a famous ceremony was staged where the two railroad lines met in Promontory Summit, Utah (about 20 miles north of Promontory Point). You might have seen the famous photograph where everybody posed in front of two train engines facing each other. Although a handful of Chinese workers were allowed to participate in the final ceremony and a small group was personally congratulated by Leland Stanford and his partners who financed the project, perhaps not too shocking, the Chinese workers were forbidden from appearing in the famous photograph of the ceremony, even though without their work and their lives, this project may never have been completed. Further, as Helen Zia points out in her excellent book *"Asian American Dreams: The Emergence of an American People,"* "The speeches congratulated European immigrant workers for their labor but never mentioned the Chinese. Instead, Chinese men were summarily fired and forced to walk the long distance back to San Francisco – forbidden to ride on the railroad they built.[2]"

\*\*\*\*\*\*\*\*\*\*\*\*\*\*\*\*\*\*\*\*\*\*\*\*\*\*\*\*\*\*\*\*\*\*\*\*\*\*

(As a **side note**, Leland Stanford, the founder of Stanford University in Palo Alto, California, served as the first Republican governor of California. After serving one term as governor, he became president of the Central Pacific Railroad and oversaw its construction. He owned many companies that supplied the required materials and expertise to build the railroad, accounting for his immense wealth.

He donated approximately 30 million dollars of land and funds for the startup of Stanford University. Regretfully, as was with many White institutions in America's history, this startup donation was stained with the human blood of injustice. Today, many ignore this deplorable fact.

While serving as president of the Central Pacific Railroad, Leland Stanford orchestrated many of the injustices against the Chinese workers. For example, because of his political influence, he was able to encourage the California legislature to pass taxes and unfair regulations that specifically targeted the Chinese. As noted, the Chinese workers he exploited to complete the railroad construction were unjustly treated in many ways. Sadly, as noted, many lost their lives while completing this task.

Today, Stanford University boasts a reported 36+ billion dollar endowment. Like many American institutions whose origin partly resulted from injustice perpetrated against minority races in this society, it is seemingly without remorse or meaningful plans for restitution.

Leland Stanford was also an emissary to the Mormons to secure their support and labor for the railroad's completion.[1])

\*\*\*\*\*\*\*\*\*\*\*\*\*\*\*\*\*\*\*\*\*\*\*\*\*\*\*\*\*\*\*\*\*\*\*\*\*

"After they returned to California, the Chinese increasingly became the targets of racial attacks and White church-supported discriminatory legislation because their labor was no longer needed, and Whites began seeing them as an economic threat.

This **anti-Chinese movement,** which was accompanied by numerous anti-Chinese riots, lynchings, and murders (including Tacoma, Washington, and most famously at Rock Springs, Wyoming), culminated with the **Chinese Exclusion Act** of 1882. This act barred virtually all immigration from China and prevented all Chinese already in the U.S. from becoming U.S. citizens, even their American-born children. For the first time in U.S. history, a specific ethnic group was singled out and forbidden to enter the U.S.

Because they were forbidden from owning land, intermarrying with Whites, owning homes, working in many occupations, getting an education, and living in certain parts of the city or entire cities, the Chinese basically had no other choice but to retreat into their own isolated communities as a matter of survival. These first **Chinatowns** at least allowed them to make a living among themselves. This is where the stereotypical image of Chinese restaurants, laundry shops, Japanese gardeners and produce stands, and Korean grocery stores began.

The point is that these did not begin out of any natural or instinctual desire on the part of Asian workers but as a response to prejudice, exclusion, and institutional discrimination - a situation that still continues in many respects today.

Nonetheless, even in the face of this hostile anti-Chinese climate, Chinese Americans fought for not only their rights, but also for their dignity and self-respect. Although they were forbidden to become citizens and, therefore, to vote, they consistently challenged their unequal treatment and the unjust laws directed at them by filing thousands of lawsuits at the local, state, and federal levels.

Even though much of their efforts would be unsuccessful, the actions demonstrated that, above all else, they wanted to become Americans and be treated just like any other American. Rather than accepting the demeaning stereotype of them as perpetual foreigners, Chinese Americans showed that they wanted to assimilate into American society and contribute to its growth, prosperity, and culture."[3]

---

This brief historical accounting of the Asian presence in America reveals a continuation of the ongoing ungodly pattern of injustice that was first revealed during the initial European occupation of this nation and persists to this day. The laws designed to suppress the full inclusion of Asians in America were similar to the White church-supported Jim Crow laws designed to suppress the full inclusion of African Americans in the South after slavery. Many unjust laws were designed to take full advantage of these minority groups as a labor force to build this country and its wealth, but deny them full inclusion in America's prosperity and way of life. The White institutional church in America presented little to no resistance but only support to the injustices and ungodliness revealed throughout the Asian presence in America.

**In fact, as was with all other minority groups in America, none of these historical injustices perpetrated against Asians would have been possible without the support and facilitating actions of the racially segregated White institutional church in America.**

After reviewing this historical accounting of the Asian presence in America, we now have clarity as to why President Biden wrote in his Executive Order, "Our nation has also seen again that anti-Asian bias, xenophobia, racism, and nativism have deep roots in our nation."

By writing, "Our nation has also seen again," he was referencing the alarming increase reflected in the most recent incidents of injustice and violence perpetrated against Asian Americans, primarily by Whites who despise their presence.

The divisive rhetoric of the preceding president of the United States, Donald J. Trump, exacerbated this increase by exploiting the fears and concerns of his two strongest supporters, conservative White professing Christians and White supremacy hate groups.

As a brief account of the rise of President Donald Trump as the banner carrier for racial division and hatred in America, we must go back to his candidacy for the office of President of the United States.

After announcing his candidacy, he was not a top contender. He was given little to no chance of being elected, primarily for being unqualified and for the many immoral attachments to his life. His floundering candidacy gained attention and support when he characteristically exploited the fears and concerns of many White Americans. He falsely claimed that Mexican officials were sending criminals and drug dealers into the United States through a poorly enforced southern border. He stated that his primary focus as president would be to secure the border by building a border wall, though he had no workable plan to do so. A commitment to build a border wall was not made by any other candidate, therefore he had the undivided attention of race fearful White Americans. Due to the increasing presence of minorities in the U.S., this commitment was seen as long overdue and was well received by hate-filled White supremacists and most conservative White professing Christians throughout the United States. They willingly overlooked his moral flaws and incompetence and immediately embraced him as the banner carrier for the maintenance of White supremacy in the United States. This false accusation and commitment was the turning point for his floundering candidacy. His candidacy disguised the underlying racist intent of his campaign to restore White supremacy in the United States by creating the slogan "Make America Great Again."

Almost immediately, conservative White professing Christians and White supremacy hate groups in America became his most prominent supporters (It is spiritually revealing and distressing to see the common interests of these two "should-be" spiritually opposing groups).

This fearful tactic of divisive and hateful rhetoric was the impetus that propelled him into office. Because of the election process (the Electoral College), he was elected even though he did not receive the majority of the cast votes and support from the majority of Americans. However, he received overwhelming support from conservative White professing Christians and White supremacists.

His presidency was characterized by a continuation of his successful strategy of divisive, hateful, and primarily false rhetoric against minority groups in America (the "least" in God's kingdom) and anyone not in agreement with him.

After the COVID-19 virus entered America, without proof, President Trump labeled the virus "Chinese Virus" and mockingly referred to it as the "Kung-flu." He reinforced this claim by ignoring the criticism that it was racist and anti-Chinese. However, he received no backlash from his supporting base. Because of their unwavering support and acceptance of his evil and divisive rhetoric (not openly opposing him as obedient representatives of God's holy throne), they remain complicit in the results of his divisive actions before Almighty God (ref. James 4:17).

Scott Kennedy, a China expert at the Center for Strategic and International Studies, stated, "The use of this term ("Chinese Virus") is not only corrosive vis-à-vis a global audience, including here at home, it is also fueling a narrative in China about a broader American hatred and fear of not just the Chinese Communist Party but of China and Chinese people in general."

Though his presidency was characterized by divisive rhetoric, false accusations, compromising foreign policy decisions that jeopardized national security, baseless fear tactics, scandals, securing more wealth for the wealthy, including himself, etc., he never lost the support of his two most significant supporting groups. Their loyal support was primarily because of his commitment to reducing the minority race groups' presence and influence in the United States and permanently securing the wealth, controlling power, and social status that Whites have enjoyed since their initial forced and violent occupation of this nation. The deception of Christianity in America was once again revealed and reinforced through his presidency and his spiritually confused supporting base.

Many religious leaders ignored the required foundation of Christianity (God's "Great Commandment" of unconditional, sacrificial love for all humanity). They confirmed their support by disregarding his lifestyle of immorality and incompetence. They firmly embraced his presidency and policies because they addressed their fear of losing their social and economic status and majority control. Many of his policies fulfilled their self-focused desire to reinforce White supremacy through the political process.

---

We have highlighted some of the documented injustices in the U.S. against Chinese Americans. Regretfully, they were condoned by the racially-segregated White church. In reviewing injustices perpetrated against Asian Americans, we will include injustice against Japanese Americans as well. Like every other racial minority group in America, Japanese Americans had to also endure systematic institutional injustices perpetrated by European (White) Americans.

When reviewing the historical presence of Japanese in the U.S. we see additional proof of institutional injustice and racism and how it became so deeply sewn into the fabric of America's spiritual makeup. Many White Americans and politicians today deny the existence of institutional racism and injustice in America. Their denial is a primary reason that America's history, which is saturated with institutional injustice and racism, must no longer be suppressed or whitewashed, but accurately recorded, analyzed spiritually, and become a learning tool for spiritual change. There have been numerous racial injustices against Japanese Americans, such as the injustice of their forced incarceration in temporary U.S. government-built internment camps throughout the U.S. between 1942 and 1946

As a brief review, on December 7, 1941, Japan launched a surprise military attack on the United States Naval Base at Pearl Harbor, Hawaii. In response to this attack, on February 19, 1942, President Franklin D. Roosevelt (**a life-long Episcopalian**) signed Executive Order 9066, which authorized the forced incarceration of Japanese Americans from the West Coast in internment camps inland. The targeted areas for Japanese residents included California, and portions of Washington, Oregon, and Arizona. The order was controversial and affected over 120,000 Japanese Americans (estimates are as high as 126,000). It was intended to prevent espionage on America's shore and was issued shortly after the bombing of Pearl Harbor. The war heightened racist attitudes and many White Americans feared that some Japanese Americans might be spies or saboteurs. Long-standing anti-Asian racism turned disastrous and deadly for innocent and unsuspecting Japanese Americans. At the beginning of the war, ten incarceration camps were insufficiently constructed throughout the United States in an expedited timeframe by the U.S. federal government. The camps were named Amache, Topaz, Manzanar, Tule Lake, Heart Mountain, Minidoka, Poston, Gila River, Rohwer, and Jerome.

The U.S. incarcerated innocent Japanese Americans and their families, including their children. Entire families were forced from their homes and unjustly incarcerated. The incarceration process took a devastating toll on Japanese Americans and their children. Many lost homes, businesses, and virtually everything that they had worked for decades to achieve. Families were confused and scared due to the uncertainty of their future. They were limited to taking only their personal possessions that they could physically carry. In their confinement behind barbed wire, they were forced to stand in long lines three times a day to get meals in crowded mess halls, use communal bathrooms and showers, and endure many other harsh living conditions. They lived in uninsulated barracks furnished only with cots and coal-burning stoves.

By the end of 1944, as America was winning the war, the U.S. government announced that incarcerated Japanese would soon be released to return to their homes on the West Coast. However, most had lost their homes, businesses, and everything that they owned mostly to opportunistic White Americans due to their unjust three-year incarceration. It was estimated that the incarcerated Japanese lost $400 million in property (estimated up to five billion dollars in today's value). During their incarceration, the U.S. government confiscated most of their land (estimated 200,000 acres) and made it available, along with its crops, mainly to European transplants. Most of the transplants were from Oklahoma and Arkansas. As many undeserving White Americans reaped long-term financial benefits and gains from this institutional governmental injustice, many Japanese families were devastated and never recovered from the emotional, physical, and financial toll of that forced and unjust ordeal. Many of the incarcerated Japanese Americans suffered lifelong illnesses and many died prematurely during the incarceration period. Many died due to inadequate medical care and insufficient living conditions. A few were killed by military guards for allegedly resisting orders. Mercifully, the last of the camps was closed in March, 1946.[4]

Two years after the camps' closure, the U.S. Congress provided a paltry total of $38 million in reparations in 1948. Forty years later, after much negative publicity, complaints from the remaining survivors and descendant family members of those who had been incarcerated, and pressure from human rights organizations, the U.S. government provided an additional $20,000 to each surviving individual who had been incarcerated in the camps. Regretfully, many of those who had been incarcerated were deceased and these minuscule amounts equated to a small fraction of the lifelong and life-altering misery endured. May church-supported U.S. governmental injustice never again be experienced by innocent American citizens.

---

In recent years, many hate crimes have been reported in America involving White Americans unjustly attacking innocent Asian Americans, exacerbated by conservative White church-condoned political rhetoric that has become all too commonplace (also reference Chapter 11).

A national survey conducted by Stop AAPI Hate and Edelman Data & Intelligence found that one in five Asian Americans and Pacific Islanders experienced a hate incident in the past two years (between March 2020 and March 2022).

"An elderly Thai immigrant died after being shoved to the ground. A Filipino-American was slashed in the face with a box cutter. A Chinese woman was slapped and then set on fire. Eight people were killed in a shooting rampage across three Asian spas in one night.

These are just examples of recent violent attacks on Asian Americans, part of a surge in abuse since the start of the pandemic.

From being spat on and verbally harassed to incidents of physical assault, there have been thousands of reported cases in recent months.[3]

As revealed in this chapter, these recent injustices perpetrated against Asian Americans are not a recent phenomenon. They are a continuation of the results of White America's desire to maintain White supremacy and complete control of all aspects of America's society through their historical display of hatred and suppression of minority race groups, which is antithetical to Biblical Christianity.

(Though this chapter highlighted a few of the injustices, refer to the *"Timeline of Systemic Racism Against AAPI"* @ https://exhibits.stanford.edu>feature for a more detailed report and timeline of injustice perpetrated against Asian Americans throughout their history in America by European (White) Americans and the racially-segregated White professing Christian church in America.)

Again, we must reiterate that these reported injustices were only successful because of the support and, oftentimes, orchestrated efforts of the then racially-segregated White institutional church in America.

America's White professing Christians have a long history of actively supporting policies that discriminated against Asian Americans on the basis of both race and religion. While some professing White Christians opposed Chinese exclusion, others supported it because they regarded Chinese people as heathens who threatened the racial and religious purity of the United States.[5]

In an article entitled "The long history of racism against Asian Americans in the U.S.," carried on PBS, the author stated, "In the United States, Asian Americans have long been considered as a threat to a nation that promoted a whites-only immigration policy. They were called a "yellow peril": unclean and unfit for citizenship in America."

As with every other minority race group in America, Asians were instrumental in building the wealth of White Americans and America's economy through forced and voluntary labor for limited and often substandard job opportunities. However, their presence was never desired or tolerated beyond that capacity.

Again, as a reminder, Jesus clarified His presence among humanity in Matthew 25, verse 40, ***"Assuredly, I say to you, inasmuch as you did it to one of the least of these My brethren, you did it to Me."***

The racially segregated White church's role in the historical injustices perpetrated against Asian Americans is well documented in America's history and, along with the many other documented racial injustices, has been instrumental in reinforcing the deception of Christianity in America.

*"Cursed is the one who perverts the justice due the stranger, the fatherless, and widow."*

**Deuteronomy 27:19**

*"Thus says the LORD: 'Execute judgment and righteousness, and deliver the plundered out of the hand of the oppressor. Do no wrong and do no violence to the stranger, the fatherless, or the widow, nor shed innocent blood in this place."*

**Jeremiah 22:3**

*"The people of the land have used oppressions, committed robbery, and mistreated the poor and needy; and they wrongfully oppress the stranger."*

**Ezekiel 22:29**

*"God stands in the congregation of the mighty; He judges among the gods.*
*How long will you judge unjustly and show partiality to the wicked?*
*Defend the poor and fatherless; Do justice to the afflicted and needy.*
*Deliver the poor and needy; Free them from the hand of the wicked."*

**Psalm 82:1-4**

*"When you face up to bad things in the past, the most important thing is not to allow them to happen today or in the future, and as storytellers, we must play our part in that."*

**- Michelle Yeoh -**

# Chapter 10

# Injustice Perpetrated Against Hispanics and Latinos

The refusal of the conservative White professing Christian Catholic and White Protestant church to act as God's representatives in ending injustice in America is seen in many actions and inactions throughout this nation's history, as revealed in this writing.

Another example is their acceptance of the relegation of needy Hispanic and Latino emigrants to a menial status of inequality as an economy-building and personal wealth-building labor pool. This acceptance has led to much pain, suffering, and death of needy Hispanic and Latino immigrants through White-initiated violence, racism, and other injustices. Since their initial forced occupation of this nation, their self-focused desire for complete control was without moral restraint and by any means necessary.

Historically, as seen throughout the world, the White race (Europeans) in America viewed minority races as expendable resources to expand and further develop their private, evil-inspired, "Whites only" utopia as envisioned in their home continent of Europe. As revealed throughout this writing, this utopia, or "heaven on earth," was grounded on immorality but falsely and deceptively disguised as "Christian." The lives of needy non-white immigrants were never considered equal as viewed through their Godless lens of self-considered superiority and their self-focused feeling of Divine entitlement.

As a sign of the lack of moral restraints, as previously noted, they frequently used the Holy Bible of God as a tool for manipulation and personal benefits rather than the roadmap for His guidance and spiritual development into His likeness. There has never been a large-scale desire by White professing Christians in the United States of America to honor God's salvation requirement for justice, righteousness, and sacrificial love toward the needs of all others, especially minority race groups. As was experienced by all other groups minority race groups within the U.S., this lack of love and desire for justice for God's entire human creation by White Americans was reflected through the injustices perpetrated against Hispanics and Latinos.

Before we continue, and because little effort has been made towards preserving their history in America, we will briefly review the early presence of Hispanics and Latinos in America and highlight some of the injustices they endured:

As noted, Hispanics and Latinos did not escape White Americans' ongoing, satanic-induced hatred and injustice perpetrated against all other minority race groups.

"Since the 1840s, anti-Latino prejudice has led to illegal deportations, school segregation, and even lynchings – often forgotten events that echo the civil rights violations of African Americans in the Jim Crow-era South.

The story of Latino American discrimination largely began in 1848, when the United States won the Mexican-American War. The Treaty of Guadalupe Hidalgo, which marked the war's end, granted 55 percent of Mexican territory to the United States. With that land came new citizens. The Mexicans who stayed in what was now U.S. territory were granted citizenship, and the country gained a considerable Mexican-American population.

As the 19$^{th}$ century wore on, political events in Mexico made emigration to the United States popular. This was welcome news to American employers like the Southern Pacific Railroad, which desperately needed cheap labor to help build new tracks. The railroad and other companies flouted existing immigration laws that banned importing contracted labor and sent recruiters into Mexico to convince Mexicans to emigrate.

Anti-Latino sentiment grew along with immigration. Latinos were barred from entry into Anglo establishments and segregated into urban barrios in poor areas. Though Latinos were critical to the U.S. economy and often were American citizens, everything from their language to the color of their skin to their countries of origin could be used as a pretext for discrimination. Anglo-Americans treated them as a foreign underclass and perpetuated stereotypes that those who spoke Spanish were lazy, stupid, and undeserving. In some cases, that prejudice turned fatal.

Mob violence against Spanish-speaking people was common in the late 19th and early 20th centuries, according to historians William D. Carrigan and Clive Webb. They estimate that the number of Latinos killed by mobs reached well into the thousands, though definitive documentation only exists for 547 cases. The violence began during California's Gold Rush just after California became part of the United States. At the time, white miners begrudged former Mexicans a share of the wealth yielded by Californian mines – and sometimes enacted vigilante justice.

In 1851, for example, a mob of vigilantes accused Josefa Segovia of murdering a white man. After a fake trial, they marched her through the streets and lynched her. Over 2,000 men gathered to watch, shouting racial slurs. Others were attacked on suspicion of fraternizing with white women or insulting white people.

Even children became the victims of this violence. In 1911, a mob of over 100 people hanged a 14-year-old boy, Antonio Gomez, after he was arrested for murder. Rather than let him serve time in jail, townspeople lynched him and dragged his body through the streets of Thorndale, Texas.

These and other acts of cruelty lasted until the 1920s, when the Mexican government began pressuring the United States to stop the violence. But though mob brutality eventually quelled, hatred of Spanish-speaking Americans did not.

In the late 1920s, anti-Mexican sentiment spiked as the Great Depression began. As the stock market tanked and unemployment grew, Anglo-Americans accused Mexicans and other foreigners of stealing American jobs. Mexican Americans were discouraged and even forbidden from accepting charitable aid. As fears about jobs and the economy spread, the United States forcibly removed up to 2 million people of Mexican descent from the country – up to 60 percent of whom were American citizens and many were professing Christians.

Euphemistically referred to as "repatriations," the removals were anything but voluntary. Sometimes, private employers drove their employees to the border and kicked them out. In other cases, local governments cut off relief, raided gathering places, or offered free train fare to Mexico. Colorado even ordered all of its "Mexicans" – in reality, anyone who spoke Spanish or seemed to be of Latin descent –– to leave the state in 1936 and blockaded its southern border to keep them from returning. Though no formal decree was ever issued by immigrations authorities, INS officials deported about 82,000 people.

The impact on Spanish-speaking communities was devastating. Some light-skinned Mexican-Americans attempted to pass themselves off as Spanish, not Mexican, in an attempt to evade enforcement. People with disabilities and active illnesses were removed from the hospitals and dumped at the border. As one victim of "repatriation" told Raymond Rodriguez, who wrote a history of the period, "Decade of Betrayal," "They might as well have sent us to Mars."

When deportations finally ended around 1936, up to 2 million Mexican Americans had been "repatriated." (Because many of the repatriation attempts were informal or conducted by private companies, it is nearly impossible to quantify the exact number of people who were deported.)

Around one-third of Los Angeles' Mexican population was deported, as was a third of Texas' Mexican-born population. Though both the state of California and the city of Los Angeles apologized for repatriation in the early 2000s, the deportations have largely faded from public memory. However, evil-induced history consistently repeats itself, as Satan simply repeats his successful schemes.

Though White church-supported U.S. government deportations ceased in 1936, today's Republican Party has made deportation of immigrants a key part of its political platform in response to the demands of conservative White professing Christians to maintain White supremacy in America. "It sounds like something only a crazed dictator would do. Not a democratic country, certainly not the U.S. But in fact, the U.S. has done it multiple times, and not just during wartime. The Trail of Tears, when President Andrew Jackson **(Presbyterian)** signed the 1830 Indian Removal Act to expel tens of thousands of Native Americans from their land. During the Depression, when the U.S. kicked out up to 1.8 million people of Mexican descent, half of them U.S. citizens, to preserve jobs for Whites. And Operation Wetback (yes, really), when President Dwight D. Eisenhower **(Presbyterian)** used the Border Patrol to truck over a million Mexican laborers back to Mexico. All of these actions were popular at the time, and all were seen in retrospect as shameful chapters in U.S. history. Yet here we are again. Studies show that deporting immigrants doesn't help the economy, it hurts it. Donald Trump says that if he's elected president, he will expel up to 20 million people, a figure far higher than the 11 million undocumented immigrants believed to be in the U.S. now. At the recent Republican convention (2024), attendees carried signs blaring "Mass Deportation Now" and chanted "Send them back!"[1] There was no consideration for the fact that many of the immigrants are professing Christians who are brothers and sisters in Christ to many of those desiring to deport them.

The largest group of supporters in today's Republican Party is conservative White professing Christians, in total disregard of the Republican Party's history of resistance to human justice for the oppressed and their ungodly policies in support of the financially wealthy at the expense of the poor and marginal. The Republican Party leadership realizes the reason for their unwavering support is primarily because of the immigration issue and the threat that their increasing population poses for majority control of the U.S government and America's economy due to the democratic process. This evil orchestrated and blatant rebellion against the holy throne of Almighty God reveals their hypocrisy which has shown to be a detriment to true evangelism and a stumbling block to salvation. White religious leaders were given a platform during the Republican convention, but they all ignored the "elephant in the room" (racism) and embraced the "Mass Deportation Now" platform, reinforcing the deception of Christianity in America.

---

Another little-remembered facet of anti-Latino discrimination in the United States is school segregation. Unlike the South, which had explicit laws barring African American children from white schools, segregation was not enshrined in the laws of the southwestern United States. Nevertheless, Latino people were excluded from restaurants, movie theaters, and schools.

Latino students were expected to attend separate "Mexican schools" throughout the southwest beginning in the 1870s. At first, the schools were set up to serve the children of Spanish-speaking laborers at rural ranches. Soon, they spread into cities, too. By the 1940s, as many as 80 percent of Latino children in places like Orange County, California, attended separate schools.

The bare-bones facilities offered to students lacked basic supplies and sufficient teachers. Many only provided vocational classes or did not offer a full 12 years of instruction. Children were arbitrarily forced to attend based on factors like their complexion and last name."[2]

As was with Native Americans, Africans, African Americans, and Asians, Hispanics, and Latinos suffered irreparable church-supported injustices from Whites in America. As so often seen throughout America's history, when their labor and services were required to advance White Americans economically, U.S. laws for foreign immigration into America were ignored or not enforced to secure their labor. When their labor and services were no longer needed, White Americans would disregard God's laws of sacrificial love and morality to rid America of their presence. As previously stated, none of these injustices would have happened without the support and, in far too many cases, the orchestrated activity of professing White Christians and the racially segregated White church in America.

Though these racial injustices were cruel, often fatal, and regretful by some, racial injustices perpetrated against Hispanics and Latinos did not end and are still experienced today throughout America.

More recently, conservative White professing Christians overwhelmingly supported building a wall along this country's southern border, a project that most Americans and professing Christians did not support on moral grounds. The reported national support for this project was 35-39%. However, the Pew Research Center reported the White evangelical (conservative White professing Christians) support at an overwhelming 75%. A 2018 Public Religion Research Institute survey concluded, "Among religious groups, White Christian groups, White evangelical protestants stand out as the group most in favor of building a wall." Jim Wallis of Sojourners Magazine stated in an article entitled, "Christians Can Stop Trump's Wall," "The wall was always a political appeal to a White base very susceptible and inclined toward racial politics."

"The border wall, promoted and endorsed by many, cuts deeper than simply serving as a national boundary. It is more than a physical wall between the United States, Mexico, and the rest of Latin America. The wall reflects and is symbolic of the fear many White Americans have toward Latino immigrants and, by extension, other Latinos living in the United States.

The accompanying public disdain and negative attitudes toward Latino immigrants affect the Latino population across our nation. Latino immigrants have gone into hiding once again, and the other Latinos who are not hiding experience suspicion and are often perceived and treated as unwelcome immigrants.

At the core of the anti-immigrant attitude and treatment is the sense of White superiority, fear of the foreigner, and how immigrants will change the culture of this nation. In other words, the fear of the minority becoming the ethnic majority fuels much of the actions and attitudes against immigrants and Latinos who bring with them their language and cultures. The wall is a symbol of fear and separation, a physical barrier that speaks volumes about how Latinos are perceived and treated. They are viewed as foreigners and, therefore, different; they do not belong here. The fear is that Latinos will change our communities and nation.

Such broad fear and pushback toward Latinos is an injustice, and it challenges the core values and beliefs of our Christian foundations.

Such attitudes and actions are not new. History reminds us of Manifest Destiny and how it led to the conquest of the Southwest and the grabbing of territory along the way, both Native and Hispanic, imposing White American culture, religion, and social-political structures. Manifest Destiny is solidly founded on the notion that the White American population was God's chosen people, called to conquer, populate and control the continent. Historically, Hispanics experienced lynching, racial oppression, segregation, and social/political marginalization.

The church was an integral part of Manifest Destiny as it bought into the notion that the populations encountered along the way were not only racially inferior, but their religions and cultures were as well. Roman Catholicism was defined as an inferior and ignorant religion, and thus it was important to convert the Latino population to Protestantism. Protestantism was brought into the conquered territories, first as a service to the Anglo population and then later as a mission to populations already here. Missionary work was meant to convert Hispanics and as a means of acculturation.

Churches are challenged by their history of racial and ethnic separation. Although language played an important role in developing separate structures and congregations, the church has been an integral player in white flight. Congregations fled their old neighborhoods, resulting in those neighborhoods becoming poor barrios *(poor Spanish-speaking communities)*.

Rather than embracing the new Latino arrivals, many churches simply ran away from the new population, seeking whiter areas in the suburbs. Instead of adjusting to the new realities of urban neighborhoods transitioning to more diversity, the church abandoned these areas and sought more compatible white areas.

Some suggest that such church action was not racist, nor were its members racists, but that the church was simply following the next generation of people who were moving to the suburbs. It was reconnecting families in an effort to survive. Conversion was perceived and promoted as part of the evangelization mandate."[3]

Racial politics and the preservation of the inequality of the status quo are the predominant focuses of conservative White professing Christians, as has been exemplified throughout their history in America.

---

**As a closing <u>side note</u>, in America today, structural racism affects Hispanics and Latinos as all other minority race groups. For example,**
**Within the criminal justice system, Latinos are 170% more likely to be killed by a police officer than a White person.**
*"Today, it is predicted that nationwide one in three black males and one in six Hispanic males will be incarcerated in their lifetime. We have come to accept this as natural. But why doesn't our discipleship inspire us to interrogate this belief?"*
- **Dominique DuBois Gilliard** -

---

*"Among most Hispanic origin groups, similar shares say they have experienced discrimination. Roughly half of Central Americans (57%), South Americans (56%), Mexicans (53%), and Puerto Ricans (52%) in the U.S. say they have experienced discrimination because of their race or ethnicity."*
- **Pew Research Center** -

# Chapter 11

## Injustice Perpetrated Through Politics

As noted, since the European occupation of this country, Satan has used Christianity as a deceptive covering for his evil and destructive strategies. Also, as noted, he has used its European occupants, the dominant racial group, as his primary vehicle to effect his deceptive schemes of injustice and rebellion against God's throne. This truth is no more evident than in America's White church-endorsed politics.

**Politics** are activities associated with governance, especially the debate or conflict among individuals or parties having or hoping to achieve and maintain power. Politics in America is basically an effective means to advance personal agendas, primarily at the expense of others who are vulnerable, less powerful, and less represented by human authority.

Most political leaders in America use religion for political purposes. It is a well-known and documented fact among politicians in America that to have lasting success in politics, one must have a religious affiliation, primarily one that is identified as "Christian."

Political leaders in America identify themselves as Christian at a rate that far exceeds the general population. According to the Pew Research Center, nearly nine-in-ten members of Congress identify as Christian (89%), compared with two-thirds of the general public (65%).

The Pew Research Center report stated, "When it comes to religious affiliation, the 117$^{th}$ U.S. Congress looks similar to the previous Congress but quite different from Americans overall.

While about a quarter (26%) of U.S. adults are religiously unaffiliated, describing themselves as atheist, agnostic, or "nothing in particular," just one member of the new Congress (Sen. Kyrsten Sinema, D-Arizona) identifies as religiously unaffiliated.

Congress is both more heavily Protestant (55% vs. 43%) and more heavily Catholic (30% vs. 20%) than the U.S. adult population overall.

Most members of the House and Senate are *(professing)* Christians, with the House just slightly more Christian than the Senate (88% vs. 87%). Both chambers have a Protestant majority; 55% of representatives are Protestant, as are 59% of senators.

The sole religiously unaffiliated member of Congress (Sinema) is in the Senate, and the only member in the "other" category (Huffman) is in the House."[1]

---

The highest elected official in America is the President of the United States. A historical review of this office reveals a similar pattern of religious affiliation.

Almost all of the nation's presidents have identified themselves as "Christian." Most have been Episcopalians or Presbyterians, with most of the rest belonging to other prominent Protestant denominations. Abraham Lincoln and Thomas Jefferson were the only presidents with no confirmed religious affiliation.

---

This same priority of religious affiliation, primarily Christian, is reflected throughout the United States in practically every level of government, even down to the state and local levels.

---

In chapter 3, we gave a Bible-based definition of "Christian." Since such a large percentage of elected officials throughout the United States identify themselves as "Christian," it would be helpful to restate the definition as a reminder before proceeding to give clarity to their claimed identity.

We stated that the Biblical character understanding of **a "Christian" is a person who manifests the quality and spirit of Jesus or someone who is "Christlike."** Another way that this was stated is "**a person whose life is an image of the character of Christ.**" The character of Christ is the aggregate of His beliefs, attributes, and traits that form His nature based on the sacrificial love of God.

Since such a large percentage of our elected officials throughout this nation identify themselves as "Christian" or "Christlike," the fruits of their labor should reflect the character of the One they claim as Lord. Their fruits should also reflect His priorities and the sacrificial love of God the Father. If not, then the affiliation that they claim is nothing more than deception and hypocrisy.

An important question comes to mind when we consider the different political party affiliations and how they interact. How can a Democratic Christian, a Republican Christian, or an Independent Christian, all under the same Spiritual umbrella and guided by the same Biblical principles, not be in agreement on political concerns or concerns that affect the welfare of humanity? The love of God mandates compassion for all others and is foundational for Christianity. Since Christians are guided by the Holy Spirit, the obvious question derived from this history of political division is, **"Is the Holy Spirit divided?"** The Biblical response is **"No."**

The apostle Paul stated in Ephesians 4:1-6, *"I, therefore, the prisoner of the Lord, beseech you to have a walk worthy of the calling with which you were called, with all lowliness and gentleness, with longsuffering, bearing with one another in love, endeavoring to keep the unity of the Spirit in the bond of peace. There is one body and one Spirit, just as you were called in one hope of your calling; one Lord, one faith, one baptism; one God and Father of all, who is above all, and through all, and in you all."*

In the body of Christ, there is unity through the bond of the Spirit of God with longsuffering and love for each other. Believers of Christ who serve humanity through politics must always *"endeavor to keep the unity of the Spirit in the bond of peace"* (Eph. 4:3, 1$^{st}$ Cor. 1:10). There cannot be persistent division among believers. *"Every kingdom divided against itself is brought to desolation, and every city or house divided against itself will not stand"* (Matthew 12:25). This is still a key Biblical truth, one that is actualized from the political divisiveness in America and the divisiveness in its religious institutions and society.

Smith Wigglesworth stated, "If there is any division, it is always outside of the Spirit. The spiritual life in the believer never has known dissension, because where the Spirit has perfect liberty, there is total agreement, and there is no schism in the body."

Persistent division can only exist outside the body of Christ. **The Holy Spirit is not divided!** The Bible clearly identifies the author of ungodly division as being Satan. He is the great deceiver and the father of lies and ungodly division [There is a Godly division (ref. Lk. 12:51-53)]. The twenty-first-century professing church of God and America's political leaders have ignored these Biblical truths.

Though professing to be "Christians," a careful review of the heart concerns and desires of the vast majority of our political leaders throughout the history of the United States government reveals a consistent pattern of hypocrisy, lies, deception, hateful rhetoric, and divisiveness. This pattern of evil-inspired behavior exists from the highest government office down to the state and local levels and reflects the historical divide and confusion within our society and professing Christian church.

Though professing "Christianity," a careful review of American history reveals that most of the U.S. presidents, from George Washington to Joe Biden (President at the time of this writing), have shown hypocrisy in their profession of faith. Its effect on their leadership and public influence has primarily been unnoticed by America's public but recognized by Almighty God.

In Chapters 5, 6, and 9, we discussed the spiritual stain of human slavery in America's history perpetrated by the European population of this nation and, in many instances, perpetrated by the racially segregated White institutional church to its financial benefit. We see a similar pattern of priorities when reviewing the lives of U.S. presidents throughout this nation's history. In opposition to the Biblical principles of justice and righteousness that are foundational to Christianity that they professed, twelve U.S. presidents owned African slaves and profited from this forced human misery of injustice that caused millions of unwarranted family separations and deaths of innocent Africans.

In opposition and rebellion to God's holy word, the following U.S. presidents, though professing Christianity, owned and profited from the labor and sale of African slaves. Forced ungodly human slavery was a primary source of their wealth.

1. George Washington **(Episcopalian)** - George Washington owned approximately six hundred slaves during and after his presidency.

2. Thomas Jefferson (Professed Christianity, but no formal religious affiliation) – Thomas Jefferson owned approximately six hundred slaves and was a lifelong slave owner. He fathered six children out of wedlock with one of his slaves named Sally Hemings.
3. John Tyler **(Episcopalian)** – John Tyler owned twenty-nine slaves. He consistently supported the slaveholder's rights and the expansion of African slavery.
4. Martin Van Buren **(Dutch Reformed)** – Martin Van Buren owned one slave.
5. Andrew Jackson **(Presbyterian)** – Andrew Jackson owned approximately two hundred slaves.
6. William Henry Harrison **(Episcopalian)** – William Henry Harrison owned eleven slaves.
7. James Monroe **(Episcopalian)** – James Monroe owned seventy-five slaves.
8. James Madison **(Episcopalian)** – James Madison owned approximately one hundred slaves.
9. Ulysses S. Grant **(Methodist)** – Ulysses S. Grant owned one slave.
10. James K. Polk **(Presbyterian)** – James K. Polk owned fifty-six slaves.
11. Andrew Johnson **(Christian)** – Andrew Johnson owned nine slaves.
12. Zachary Taylor **(Episcopalian)** – Zachary Taylor owned three hundred slaves.[2]

---

Eight of these twelve U.S. presidents owned and profited from African slavery while serving in office under the solemnly sworn oath of the presidency. They were George Washington, Thomas Jefferson, John Tyler, Andrew Jackson, James Monroe, James Madison, James K. Polk, and Zachary Taylor. Andrew Jackson was a slave trader. Many of the U.S. presidents who owned slaves are on record as condemning slavery, reflecting religious hypocrisy. Woodrow Wilson **(Presbyterian)** was the last president born into a household with slave labor. Eleven signers of the U.S. Constitution owned and profited from African slavery.

Historians and many theologians favorably view these honored political leaders as models for national pride and righteousness, disregarding their obvious life focus of immorality. In reality, these individuals, like so many others that we revere who professed Christianity [e.g., Alexander Hamilton **(Episcopalian)**, Patrick Henry **(Anglican)**, John Hancock **(Congregationalist)**, etc.], participated in the forceful destruction of many innocent African families through this nation's worst institution of sin, the sin of human slavery, and profited financially for doing so.

**As stated, human slavery, for most of them, was a primary source of their wealth. For example, though professing Christianity, Thomas Jefferson's wealth came mainly from the injustice of a factory he staffed with slave children. This was an ungodly wealth that was passed down through generations of his family lineage, perhaps the source of a long-standing curse over the lives of his inheritors (Deut. 27:19, Prov. 3:33). Likewise is the ungodly heritage of generational wealth of many White Americans and institutions today. It is generally stained with the immoral blood of injustice. Many of the successful White-owned businesses, churches, and grand mansions that we admire today throughout the South are examples and testimonies of the generational wealth gained from human slavery in America. Perhaps surprisingly to most, many remain under a curse. In addition to the innocent blood of Africans, the grounds of these developments are spiritually stained with the innocent blood of Native Americans, African Americans, and all other minority race groups in America's murderous history.**

### *** Side note ***

Though professing to be a Christian nation, the U.S. and its professing church of Christ have historically disregarded the immorality of its elected officials. Many of its historical honored political leaders who professed Christianity but openly rebelled against the holy throne of Almighty God through a life focus of injustice against the oppressed in America's society are still honored today, thus contributing to the deception of Christianity.

George Washington:  President's Day is honored every third Monday in February. It is a Federal holiday in honor of the birthday of George Washington. It was the first federal holiday to honor an American president. Also, his picture is featured on the $1 bill, with the controversial and perhaps hypocritical motto "In God We Trust" printed on the back.

Thomas Jefferson's picture is featured on the $2 bill.
Alexander Hamilton's picture is featured on the $10 bill.

Andrew Jackson's picture is featured on the $20 bill.
Ulysses S. Grant's picture is featured on the $50 bill.
James Madison's picture is featured on the $5,000 bill.

Statues have been erected in their honor. Buildings, streets, schools, and many professing Christians throughout America are named in honor of many of these historical leaders in total disregard of their life focus of immorality and their disregard for the foundation of the holy throne of God.

******************************************

Though viewed as political models of patriotism by historians, those who were unrepentant will be held accountable for their blatant sins against humanity at the end-time judgment. The hypocrisy of their lives must be viewed through Biblical reality, and their lives must be regarded as undesirable models of injustice and unrighteousness. We should learn from their mistakes and not continue to disregard them. We should correctly educate our children regarding America's history and its historical leaders, utilizing these leaders as examples of the spiritual blindness that often accompanies immorality.

As a child, I was taught a valuable lesson for discerning the legitimacy of the statements of others, a lesson that all professing believers should consider:

**"Don't listen to what people say. Look at what they do."**

As recognized by God, America must always be understood as a stolen land that was obtained, built, and maintained by injustice, a reality that should not be suppressed but openly acknowledged. However, those who were involved did a tremendously important thing in constructing the required U.S. Constitution, and we should continue to recognize their effort. However, when we consider their life focus of injustice and their obvious hypocrisy, spiritually, we must view them unfavorably as political leaders who used religion to enhance their political aspirations. When we genuinely use the Bible as our guide for discerning the legitimacy of their profession of Christianity, these individuals must not be considered examples of "Christlikeness" or righteousness they professed. Their hypocrisy must not be overlooked or disregarded. Their lives should be remembered as examples of the blinding persuasion of evilness that can reach all levels of humanity. No one is exempt from falling prey to this evil influence that is still present in our society that is successfully destroying innocent lives ($1^{st}$ Peter 5:8). It is enhancing a deceptive and false understanding of the importance of justice and righteousness as requirements for eternal salvation and validating ones professed belief in Jesus.

Immorality was a way of life for most of the U.S. presidents and founding fathers. Like most political leaders today, most of them deceptively professed "Christianity" or "Christlikeness." Regretfully, their lives were inspirations to many others throughout the following centuries who failed to see or admit their obvious hypocrisy. Many professing Christians still follow their lead of open rebellion against God's holy throne. Like most political leaders today, these individuals used religion as a strategy for public acceptance and political advantage. Also, like most political leaders today, they never understood what it truly meant to believe in Jesus or to submit to His Lordship. **As with most self-focused professing Christians in America today, they could not comprehend Jesus' sacrificial love for all humanity, nor indicate a willingness to reflect it through their deceptive, self-focused, and evil-inspired lives. This confusion is still evident.**

---

Though professing Christianity, Donald Trump, the 45th president, proved to be the embodiment of evilness. Evilness was seen in his immoral baggage which included, adultery, habitually lying, a life focused on divisive rhetoric for personal gain, illegal and questionable business practices, and he was found liable for sexual abuse and defamation. In addition, he was twice impeached.

Donald Trump's immorality reached an all-time low when he became the first former American president to be convicted of felony crimes. A New York jury of his peers found him guilty of 34 charges in a scheme to illegally influence the 2016 presidential election through a hush money payment to a porn star who said the two had sex. There was no limit to his willful immorality for self-focused gain and sensual pleasure. An independent survey of 154 presidential historians ranked Donald Trump as the worst U.S. president in U.S. history. Yet, though facing even more criminal charges and a testament to the blinding and mesmerizing persuasion of evilness, his supporters remained loyal.

Trump first identified as **Presbyterian** but changed his faith because of political advantage while in office. Though professing Christianity through most of his life, Trump rarely attended church before becoming president. He successfully used the strategy of many White politicians in America's ungodly history of injustice. He capitalized on the fragility of race-fearful White Americans for profit and power. By disregarding Trump's immorality and giving him their full support, he exposed the underlying evil tendencies and undiscerning spirits of many of America's White religious leaders. With all of Trump's immoral baggage and proven incompetence, his popularity remained strong among his supporting base because of his commitment to White supremacy and ridding America of its increasing racial minority presence and their potential for control through the democratic process, thus reinforcing the deception of Christianity in America. His loyal conservative White professing Christian and White supremacy base recognized him as their best hope to maintain their "evil-gotten" historical advantages, self-imposed superiority, and social status. Both groups with similar ungodly desires for maintaining White supremacy and its historical benefits embraced his presidency without reservation and consideration for justice and righteousness. They have even shown a willingness to overthrow the government of the U.S. if necessary to maintain their ungodly, self-focused advantages (e.g., 2021 insurrection). God ~~bless~~ '**change**' America. God will never bless evilness and rebellion.

---

Professing Christians of all races in the United States of America have traditionally ignored the immorality of public elected officials and supported them based on their policy commitments that addressed their self-focused interests. Someone once correctly said that voters in America do not vote their conscience but their pocketbooks. Historically, America has professed to be a Christian nation. However, for far too many registered voters, required Biblical principles of justice and righteousness seldom influence their voting priorities.

---

Our current president (during the time of this writing), Joe Biden, identifies as **Catholic**. His presidency has had many policy accomplishments and he will probably be remembered as one of America's more successful administrators and compassionate communicators, and for strengthening America's fragile democracy that was weakened by the previous administration. He restored confidence in the reliability of the U.S. within the NATO Alliance and many of America's longstanding partners. Indeed, his accomplishments are numerous. However, and regretfully, he endorses policies contrary to Christian and Catholic beliefs to remain aligned with the policies of his political party, reflecting his spiritual priority of political policy above God. For example, he is pro-abortion and pro-same-sex marriage, which are anti-Christian policies. Catholics are pro-life and stand firmly against the sin of same-sex marriage. (This statement must not be misunderstood as an endorsement of Catholicism as legitimate Christianity, but simply an example of religious rebellion, deception, and hypocrisy among U.S. presidents).

Arguably, Jimmy Carter, the 39th president **(Southern Baptist)**, was the only U.S. president who attempted to live out a legitimate Christian faith while serving as President of the United States. As expected, he encountered much resistance, even from within his own party. Contrary to the then-Democratic platform, he was anti-abortion and prioritized his Christian faith and beliefs in all of his executive decisions. He was the only Democratic president who was pro-life while serving in office. Though he was affiliated with a denomination with deep roots in White supremacy and racism, he rose beyond its historical evilness to share the love of God through his presidency. He eventually left the Southern Baptist denomination because of their spiritual hypocrisy and historical deception and his deep love for God. His presidency championed peace, human rights, and justice worldwide, and he was eventually awarded the Nobel Peace Prize for his efforts. His presidency was painted by many of his adversaries as weak, and was considered a national interest liability to a nation whose strength, prowess, and reputation were built and maintained on the worldly concept of "By any human means necessary." President Carter had many policy accomplishments but was not reelected to a second term. Though America has always considered itself a Christian nation, his "God-first" type of leadership was not what most White Americans desired or what America had ever experienced. As was with Jesus or anyone who espouses human justice, America's White professing Christian majority rejected him [It is revealing to note throughout America's history their continuous support for unjust political leadership. It is currently exemplified by their unyielding support for Donald Trump, the embodiment of self-focused unjust evilness, validating Abraham Lincoln's prophecy (page 100)]. However, perhaps in the annals of heaven, President Carter's presidency was noted as a spiritual ray of sunshine to an office with a long tradition of deceptive ungodliness, supporting, and capitalizing on human injustice.

Conservative White professing Christians' historical rebellion against the foundation of God's throne is still evident in America and was on display in the national political elections held in November 2022.

This election was considered to be one of the most important elections in the history of the United States of America, not only for determining the direction of its political future, but its stability as a democracy and the focus and direction of its spiritual future.

After a tumultuous recent history of increasing division and hatred perpetrated primarily by conservative political leaders who had primarily aligned themselves with many values, policies, and desires of White supremacy and hate groups in the United States, conservative White professing Christians passed up on a golden opportunity to turn from their past tendency of support for racial injustice and division. They passed on the opportunity to become a true reflection of God's heavenly throne and the foundational love of God's 'Great Commandment.'

This election presented an excellent opportunity for the professing church of God to come together across racial lines and other lines of division and reflect the oneness of Christ as brothers and sisters in Christ. It truly presented an opportunity for a new beginning and a new direction for the United States by reflecting the sacrificial love of God for all humanity. This much-needed coming together would have truly reflected, for the first time in the history of the United States, "One Nation under God, indivisible, with liberty and justice for all," as it proclaims. Instead, a careful review of the many political races across this nation reflected otherwise, even to some extent, a growing divide orchestrated by the author of ungodly division.

An example of the failure of conservative White professing Christians to truly represent God's throne was no more evident than in the U.S. Senate race for the state of Georgia. For the first time in the history of this state and perhaps this nation, two African American males represented the final candidates for the two major political parties vying for the same Senate seat. This Senate seat was critically important for determining the Senate majority party and the Senate-controlled direction of this nation.

Other than sharing the same race, the two opposing candidates were different in every area of concern and need for this Senate seat.

The incumbent, a Democrat, had a proven record of competence, political knowledge, and the required qualifications to hold the seat. Conversely, the challenger, the GOP-backed Republican, was unqualified, incompetent, and unknowledgeable about political and national concerns and world matters. Because of his past athletic accomplishments and popularity, he was chosen by the GOP as the best candidate to divide the African American vote and provide a better opportunity to secure the much-desired Senate seat for the GOP. With the endorsement of the conservative White professing Christian leadership in Georgia, the Georgia GOP leadership correctly assumed that even White supremacists and the remaining majority of their race-focused professing Christian base would vote for an African American who supported their deceptive, self-serving agenda. Walker was the ideal candidate because of his popularity and self-serving and self-advancing hunger. There was more concern within the GOP about advancing their desire for control of this nation's Senate than providing solutions for the more important historical spiritual evils of racial division and injustice in the United States by backing a morally competent, knowledgeable, and qualified candidate.

In a report in the 'Daily Beast' regarding this critical Senate race, the author noted that the race should never have been this close. The author wrote:

"From the moment Walker launched his campaign, it was obvious he was unqualified and unprepared, traits that only became more salient with every stop on the trail. Walker displayed not so much a lack of knowledge about basic topics as he did a surplus of incoherent and nonsensical theories on everything from climate change ("Don't we have enough trees around here?") to evolution ("Why are there still apes? Think about it!").

That distant relationship with facts and reality also showed up in Walker's seemingly inability to tell the truth, and his campaign shuttled from controversy to controversy as each fabrication became headline news. Lies about graduating college, a career in the military, and success in business were succeeded by revelations about three secret children, multiple allegations of having paid for abortions, and an alleged pattern of violent abuse of women. But Walker's backers stuck with him because he also helped push the lie that has come to define the MAGA Right, Donald Trump's deranged insistence that the presidency was stolen from him, despite nearly two years of evidence-gathering that proves that's not true.

GOP strategists were right in predicting their overwhelmingly white base would embrace a black candidate whom they saw as promoting their agenda, which is rooted in anti-blackness and revanchist white supremacy.

**It's also notable that a staggering 88 percent of white evangelicals, or nearly nine out of ten, cast their ballots not for Warnock, a true religious scholar who holds a doctorate in systematic theology and the pastor at one of Atlanta's oldest and most revered black Baptist churches, but instead chose Walker, whose naked hypocrisy in pursuit of political power is a shared trait.** It's likely that those same white conservative voters shrugged off Walker's moral failings, not just because it's politically convenient, but because it jibes with the racist views they already hold about black folks.

Sure, Warnock is progressive on issues that conservatives oppose, but the devil here is in details of race, a changing Georgia, white fears of status loss, and a black candidate who they entrust to do the GOP's white supremacist bidding. That's how we got here, despite Warnock being so much more qualified than Walker that it's maddening the comparison is even being voted on."[1]

Conservative White professing Christians preferred Herschel Walker, whose lifestyle and values resembled that of their preferred commander-in-chief, Donald Trump. Once again, Satan tapped into their greatest fears and concerns for status preservation and successfully utilized an age-old strategy to reinforce the deception of Christianity in America.

************************************

As a **side note**, there were noted paradoxes reflecting political and religious hypocrisy in these two candidates. Both reflected moral concerns that were in opposition to Biblical scripture.

Though Raphael Warnock was a **Baptist** pastor, like President Joe Biden and President Barack Obama, who both professed Christianity but supported their party's anti-Christian platform policies of pro-abortion and pro-same-sex marriage, he also supported those policies.

Their political leadership and public influence enhanced the deception of Christianity in America.

Though Herschel Walker had a history of utilizing abortions with past girlfriends to end unwanted pregnancies, he aligned himself with the GOP platform position of pro-life. [(This statement must not be misunderstood as an endorsement of the GOP). As revealed throughout this writing, both major political parties have a long history of satanic-induced open rebellion against God's Divine order. Primarily, the policies of the twenty-first-century GOP deceptively disguise their priorities, which are supporting the wealthy at the expense of the oppressed, maintaining wealth, social status, and White political control, and permanently securing the ill-gotten advantages of White Americans deceptively through the political process. Their policies generally avoid wealth sharing while reinforcing White supremacy. Though professing Christianity, their priorities are antithetical to Biblical tenets of Christianity, thus enhancing the deception of Christianity in America) (Deut. 15:11, Jm. 2:6, Prov. 14:31, 22:16, Ezek. 16:49, 1$^{st}$ Jn. 3:17)].

**************************************

This is just one of many recent examples that reflect the conservative White professing Christians' alignment and support for the White supremacy ideology of injustice in the United States. Though professing Christianity, there is still the rebelliousness seen in their forefathers against God's 'Great Commandment' of sacrificial love for all humanity, especially the minority races, the poor, and the least in our society.

---

Jackson, Mississippi, has been in the national news because of a shortage of clean water due to an antiquated and failing water system. More recently, it has drawn national news attention due to forced legislative actions by the conservative White professing Christian-supported majority-white Republican state legislature. They desire control of the Democratic and African American-controlled city. Jackson has African American leadership in city government but little statewide government support.

For those who may not know, Jackson is the capital of the state of Mississippi, and its population is majority African American. The state of Mississippi has the highest percentage of African Americans of any state in the United States. Yet, Mississippi did not have an African American serving in statewide government from 1894 until 1968, when Robert G. Clark, Jr. was elected by a narrow margin to serve in the state legislature. Due to unjust, White church-supported districting and gerrymandering by White legislators, African Americans in Mississippi and states throughout the Bible Belt have historically been under-represented in statewide government.

Mississippi law requires that all statewide office winners must receive more than 50% of the votes. If no one receives more than 50%, the legislature selects the winner, not the voters. Mississippi is a typical example of how the dominant conservative White professing Christian majority has used the political process to impose its will of injustice on minority groups. The checks and balances for equal representation in a governmental system of this nature must originate from the dominant racial group. They must be guided by the Christian principles of Biblical racial justice and sacrificial love, which have never existed within the majority of the White race or the majority of White professing Christians in the United States.

Though Jackson is the state's capital city, it has historically been denied adequate funding from the state of Mississippi to maintain basic services for the quality of life that should be evident throughout the U.S. The city's racial composition is the ongoing reason for the inadequate appropriation of state funds. Jackson has oversight by the historically proven race-focused and White professing Christian-supported White state government leadership. This form of governmental injustice and spiritual rebellion against the holy throne of God is prevalent throughout the United States of America to varying degrees.

For racial equality to be realized, the dominant racial group must serve as God's ambassadors of justice and righteousness, especially when the dominant group openly professes Christianity, as is the case throughout the Deep South Bible Belt. The majority of White professing Christians in Mississippi are a modern-day example of the failure of God's professing servants to honor their sacred obligation of justice and righteousness to humanity and God Almighty.

Could the reason for Mississippi's ranking as the nation's third worst state (behind New Mexico and Louisiana)[3] be directly related to its rebelliousness to God's principles of justice and righteousness? One study ranked Mississippi as the worst state in which to live in

2022.[4] Other studies ranked Mississippi as the poorest state, the hungriest state, and the unhealthiest state.[3] Indeed, these poor rankings reflect a lack of God's presence, favor, and oversight. It should be a major concern and impetus for major spiritual change within its spiritually deviant professing body of Christ and historically racist and unjust State Legislature.

**Throughout the history of the state of Mississippi and all other states in the union, as previously noted, none of these atrocities of injustice perpetrated against African Americans or any other vulnerable minority group could happen over a unified White professing Christian opposition.** The unjust political priorities of state elected officials throughout the Bible Belt stem from the self-focused and ungodly spiritual priorities of the institutional White church in the Bible Belt.

Perhaps these injustices continue for three reasons:

1. The professing White Christian supporters remain the beneficiaries of the results as documented throughout their history in America.
2. Many elected perpetrators of injustice and unrighteousness are friends, associates, church members, etc., and simply honor their supporters' wishes that they were elected to fulfill.
3. Self-focused ungodliness in the White professing church of God has traditionally been the accepted way of life. It exists without spiritual and verbal opposition from its self-appointed ungodly spiritual leadership, who will be held accountable for the dereliction of their sacred obligations by Almighty God.

*******************************************

These legislative injustices continue to happen while the deafening silence of White professing Christians continues to express their acceptance and support.

Their oppressed minority brothers and sisters cry out in their never-ending pain to the Lord, "When will the opposition to injustice from the dominant body of White professing Christians anticipating an eternity with Christ be realized?

Perhaps the response will be:
**"Their time is now or never!"**

## A Word of God to All Political Leaders

*"Fulfill my joy by being like-minded, having the same love, being of one accord, of one mind. Let nothing be done through selfish ambition or conceit, but in lowliness of mind let each esteem others better than himself. Let each of you look out not only for his own interests, but also for the interests of others."*
*(Philippians 2:2-4)*

---

## A Word of God to All Believers

*"Therefore I exhort first of all that supplications, prayers, intercessions, and giving of thanks be made for all men, for kings and all who are in authority, that we may lead a quiet and peaceable life in all godliness and reverence.*
*For this is good and acceptable in the sight of God our Savior, who desires all men to be saved and to come to the knowledge of the truth."*
*(1$^{st}$ Timothy 2:1-4)*

*"Power without love is reckless and abusive, and love without power is sentimental and anemic. Power at its best is love implementing the demands of justice, and justice at its best is power correcting everything that stands against love."*

- **Dr. Martin Luther King, Jr.**

---

*"I have one life and one chance to make it count for something. My faith demands that I do whatever I can, wherever I am, whenever I can, for as long as I can with whatever I have, to try to make a difference."*

- **President Jimmy Carter** -

---

*"Affirmatively advancing equity, civil rights, racial justice, and equal opportunity is the responsibility of the whole of our government."*

- **President Joe Biden** -

# Chapter 12

## Injustice, Deeply Rooted in America's Culture

Injustice by the racially segregated White institutional church in America's history was also exemplified by their desire to utilize their ill-gotten finances from the injustice of human slavery for self-serving purposes, securing advantages, and, unbelievably, glorifying God. These desires stemmed from spiritually-confused ungodly self-focused leadership and pride. Based on the implied requirement of God's "Great Commandment" of love, our resources are purposed for developing equality within His creation through voluntary sharing and personal sacrifice which is foundational for Christianity.

*\*\*\* In this Chapter the primary focus is on White professing Christians in the U.S. because of their dominance and historical control of the bulk of God's resources within the U.S., their historical, ungodly yet influential leadership in religion, and the unbiblical self-focused stewardship of the benefits gained from the blood of innocent humanity through their history of injustice\*\*\**

The pervasive self-focused priorities of White professing Christians throughout America's history included building grand cathedrals and monuments of worship to the loving and Almighty God Whom they rebelled against. Buildings still exist and remain as examples of unbiblical excesses funded by injustice. Rather than providing for the essential needs of God's hurting creation, the spiritual focus of God's White professing body of Christ was diverted by the mesmerizing evil influences of selfishness and pride.

Contrary to this historical trend, there is nowhere in the four gospels or the writings of Paul where believers are instructed to build grand cathedrals and monuments to the glory of God. However, Jesus clearly stated His requirement for believers to provide for the needs of the "least" in this world. In fact, one's obedience must be understood as a salvation requirement and a requirement for validating one's righteousness to Almighty God (ref. Matt. 25:46).

Jesus gave a sobering reminder to His church in Matthew 25:40. He said, *"Assuredly, I say to you, inasmuch as you did it to one of the least of these My brethren, you did it to Me."* Jesus' brethren include God's entire human creation. In verses 45 & 46, Jesus cautioned us regarding selfishness and disobedience in stewardship when he said, *"Inasmuch as you did **not** do it to one of the least of these, you did **not** do it to Me. <u>And these will go away into everlasting punishment, but the righteous into eternal life.</u>"*

Many poor countries do not possess the abundance of resources and finances that the financially wealthy religious institutions in the United States do. Many depend on the goodwill and the philanthropy of those who control this world's wealth to meet their dire needs.

By amassing wealth for self-focused desires, including prideful building desires and personal comforts and disregarding the needs of the "least," this historical and ongoing irresponsible stewardship and rebellion against God's "Great Commandment" of cross-centered, sacrificial love accounted for avoidable suffering and death worldwide.

## \*\*\*\* A <u>side-note</u> of revelation \*\*\*\*

Primarily, because of conservative White professing Christians' historical rebellion against God through their involvement and support, injustice is deeply rooted in America's European society and culture. As has been noted throughout world history, a fact that is perhaps difficult to believe by many professing Christians and historians, Europeans have been utilized since the end of the first-century Apostolic church to effect a direct strategic attack against the foundation of God's heavenly throne. This evil deceptive strategy of Satan first targeted the Roman Catholic Church and continued through both the Roman Catholic and Protestant churches after the Protestant Reformation Movement in the 1500s.

This group's public influence in the U.S., resulting from their deceptive profession of being "Christian" (or "Christlike"), resulted in a successful strategy of spiritual war orchestrated against God's kingdom to ensure that Biblical Christianity would never take root in the United States. **Regretfully, and perhaps to the surprise of many professing believers of Christ, as revealed throughout this writing, <u>it never did!</u>** (ref. *"The Fanaticism of Christian Discipleship"* for clarification of true Biblical Christianity as Christ ordained)

This successful strategy of demonically induced open rebellion placed in humanity's hearts against God's holy throne enabled Satan to firmly establish a pseudo-Christianity in the United States that deceived the professing body of Christ, even many of His elect. This pseudo-Christianity was built on the evil-induced values of selfishness, pride, and worldliness influenced by hatred and fear. The acceptance of the inept spirituality of this illegitimate Christianity, characterized by injustice and unrighteousness, has remained the accepted standard for Christianity throughout the history of America.

In this pseudo-Christianity, the operational role of the Holy Spirit was marginalized or disregarded altogether. As Satan realized, under a cloud of open rebellion, the Holy Spirit's presence and oversight would not be realized, and the reality of His existence would eventually be questioned among the undiscerning professing body of Christ. Satan then developed institutional religion in the U.S. without restrictions resulting from the Holy Spirit's presence, power, direct input, and required oversight. Therefore, institutional religion did not and still does not threaten his (Satan's) kingdom plan of deception in religion. This has resulted in religious and racial division and destruction in the United States and worldwide within those under the United States' spiritual umbrella. The damaging results of this strategy permeate every aspect of our society and world and are now an accepted way of life with far too many who could and should make a difference because of the love they profess.

In his development, Satan redefined Christian discipleship and authored many books reinforcing his deceptions during and after the timeframe of forced racial segregation in institutional religion. Due to the lack of discernment in spiritual leadership demonstrated by the inability to recognize his deceptions, many of his published resources are used throughout the worldwide institutional church system in discipleship training and spiritual development courses.

Without the required spiritual discernment, His body of professing believers has suffered from the results of many spiritual deceptions and bondages that are directly opposed and incompatible with God's Holy Spirit-guided kingdom design. It has been God's desire and eternal plan that His professing church body reflects His character to exert His power and authority over the forces of the evilness of this world. God desires that His servants reflect His sacrificial love in all areas of need, thereby glorifying Him and validating themselves.

This evil strategy perpetrated against God's people was successful only because God allowed it to happen, perhaps because of their persistent rebellion against His holy throne and Divine order. However, the professing body of believers can somewhat take comfort in knowing that Satan's evilness is limited to what God allows (ref. Job 1:12). At any time, Satan's strategies of evilness can be controlled, marginalized, or ended altogether. This will only result from our repentance, truly turning to God in obedience resulting in sacrificial, unconditional love for all humanity, living as His ambassadors of justice and righteousness, and accepting and trusting His sovereignty.

This evil strategy has accounted for America's Godlessness, hateful, and destructive nature since its European occupation. This strategy of open rebellion was not new but was the continuation of the strategy that was instituted by Satan at this world's creation. It was first perpetrated in the lives of Adam and Eve, the first humans created by God. It has been evident throughout the world since God created humanity and was revealed throughout the Bible for our edification and protection. God desires that His people live as one holy body in Christ and not be victimized by the forces of evilness.

This strategy was so successful that over 2,000 years after the birth of Jesus' church by the Holy Spirit, most of the professing body of Christ in America do not believe that the Holy Spirit is a living force (ref. 2009 Barna group survey below). However, we should not lose hope because a spiritual change of correction and restoration, starting with revelation, has begun and God is removing confusion. All are invited to join this God-initiated movement. Regretfully, most will decline and be forced to step aside.

##### \*\*\*\*\* A **side-note** of reference \*\*\*\*\*

The results of a Barna Group survey conducted in 2009 revealed that the majority of professing Christians in America do not believe that the Holy Spirit is a living force. This startling report stated, "Overall, 38% strongly agreed, and 20% agreed somewhat that the Holy Spirit is a symbol of God's power or presence but is not a living entity. Just one-third of Christians disagreed that the Holy Spirit is not a living force (9% disagreed somewhat, 25% disagreed strongly) while 9% were not sure." The report concluded that 58% of professing Christians in America either strongly agree or somewhat agree that the Holy Spirit is a symbol of God's power or presence but is not a living entity. This report also stated, "About half (49%) of those who agreed that the Holy Spirit is only a symbol but not a living entity also agreed that the Bible is totally accurate in all of the principles it teaches, even though the Bible clearly describes the Holy Spirit as more than a symbolic reference to God's power or presence."

Unsurprisingly, this same report revealed that nearly 60% of professing Christians in America either strongly agreed or somewhat agreed with the statement, "Satan is not a living being but is a symbol for evil."

The results of this survey present a troubling question for twenty-first-century church leadership, which requires a reality check. Could many of our professing churches of Christ in the United States be under Satan's influence or, even worse, his control? **With this understanding, the uncharacteristic historical injustices perpetrated by America's White professing institutional churches could be better understood.**

Accepting this understanding as reality should generate an urgent and unified desire for spiritual change that can only be realized under the guidance and empowerment of the Holy Spirit. Ironically, as just stated, the majority of professing Christians in America do not believe that the Holy Spirit is a living force. Only Satan could plan and successfully institute such a complex and devious strategy.

***********************************

It is truly alarming that in many instances in America's history, rather than 'standing in the gap' as a bulwark for the just treatment of the oppressed in the United States and worldwide, certain groups of the White professing body of Christ chose to profit from injustice (As noted and well-documented in America's history, White Protestant and Roman Catholic churches and many of their institutions owned, and profited from the labor and sale of enslaved Africans and Native Americans). **The spiritual blindness resulting from this open rebellion against God is not more evident than the acceptance of this ungodliness by professing White believers as being acceptable in Christianity, and thus, acceptable to God.**

They and their unrepentant spiritual leaders will be held accountable for the dereliction of their sacred obligations as entrusted representatives of God's holy throne. Ignorance will not be an acceptable excuse for the dereliction of these spiritual obligations. Regretfully, this sad reality of God's rebellious representatives in America's history is prevalent in many religious circles today. However, this rebellion against God's throne and kingdom order cannot continue and must be corrected while time is allowed. The salvation of many lost souls practicing a convincing deceptive and unbiblical form of religion who may erroneously consider themselves 'saved' hangs in the balance. Like their early fathers, most are in denial while rejecting God's 'Great Commandment' to their eternal demise. Throughout America's history, the racially segregated White institutional church was not willing to accept and model the total inclusiveness, sacrifice, and full scope of God's "Great Commandment" as clarified in chapter four. It boldly and openly rebelled against His heavenly throne.

Satan's deceptive strategy has accounted for the loss of eternal salvation for many unsuspecting souls who professed Christianity but unknowingly served him. **As with many of his strategies, those he utilizes for his evil purposes align themselves with many Biblical principles (e.g., anti-abortion, anti-LGBT, generally those that do not require wealth sharing or a diminishing of their historical and ongoing social status). While doing so, they secretly undermine God's will and His designed foundation for His kingdom, which is commonly reflected in efforts and support of policies against the "least" in God's kingdom (the poor, minority races, and the marginalized). They can consistently be identified by their rebellion against justice and righteousness for all humanity and their consistent lack of meaningful support for the needs of the "least" in God's kingdom.** To unsuspecting converts and seasoned but undiscerning professing Christians, these alignments with certain Biblical principles disguise the inherent and more damning self-focused ungodliness that undermines the foundation for Christianity.

All historical and current works of darkness will be revealed in this end-time season of revelation, correction, and restoration. The exposure of the strategies of evilness is necessary as God prepares His sons (and daughters) for end-time spiritual warfare to finally establish His kingdom in the United States and worldwide. This revelation is good news and a reason for joyous celebration. Hallelujah! To God be the glory!

# Chapter 13

## Biblical Justice vs. Social Justice

As a nonbiblical understanding, human justice is divided into two categories: Biblical and social justice (Social justice is the view that everyone deserves equal economic, political, and social rights and opportunities which is foundational for God's "Great Commandment" and true Biblical Christianity). The acceptance of this understanding by the professing church of God is another example of the deception of self-focused worldliness in twenty-first-century religion. The Bible does not make this distinction.

Many who accept the worldview of two distinct categories of human justice believe and teach that Biblical justice and social justice are not the same. In contrast, many others teach that, in Biblical understanding, they are one and the same. This argument has historically been debated and has proven to be a dividing issue within the professing body of Christ, mainly along racial, moral, and economic lines of interest.

As discerning believers in Christ, we must always be mindful of the identity of the author of all division and spiritual confusion. As Christ's body, we must not fall prey to Satan's deceptive strategy of illegitimate, fruitless, and divisive debates. Professing Christians should always resolve differences through the revealing lens of God's 'Great Commandment,' with all resolutions prioritizing the needs of the least (those in need) in God's kingdom.

The view of the two as existing and being different reflects a fundamental lack of understanding or a blatant refusal to accept the inclusiveness of Biblical justice. As stated, there is no Biblical basis for accepting the worldview of social justice as unique from Biblical justice. Many professing believers have demonstrated a willingness to do so, perhaps because it gives an inner peace when not being responsive to the injustice of what is identified as a social justice issue.

**Christianity must be understood as all-inclusive when referencing human justice. There are no exclusions.**

---

As a **side note**, it is important to note that conservative White professing Christians in America have traditionally supported this distinction for obvious reasons. What we identify as social injustices generally require wealth-sharing and wealth redistribution, which is also a primary implication of God's "Great Commandment." It is primarily because of this underlying implication that they have traditionally rejected His "Great Commandment" and true Biblical Christianity.

---

In opposition to the unbiblical view of the two as existing and being different, there was an excellent observation in an article ("Social Justice and Biblical Justice Are Actually One and the Same") published in "Christianity Today" on October 6, 2021.[1] As from the title, the writer stated, "Social justice and Biblical justice are actually one and the same." The writer also said, " 'Justice' and the 'gospel' have somehow been pitted against each other within the white evangelical church, and you cannot have one without the other." This article was well-written, 'on point,' and Biblically sound. It should be well-received as a ray of light and hope within the professing body of Christ and to the many innocent victims of social injustice. It is a valid Biblical point for universal acceptance.

It is perplexing that this debate even persists since both are referencing the ungodly ills of this world. All ills of injustice are an offense to God and must remain an offense to His servants. Human justice in all forms is a foundational focus of the gospel of Christ, and our involvement is a factor in determining our 'Christlikeness.'

In reference to this topic, the sixteenth-century reformer Martin Luther stated, "The church that preaches the gospel in all its fullness, except as it applies to the great social ills of the day, is failing to preach the gospel."

John Wesley stated, "The gospel of Christ knows no religion but social; no holiness, but social holiness."

As a **side-note** of reference, for better clarity, we recommend the following books addressing these topics:

"White Too Long," by Robert P. Jones
"Social Justice Jesus," by Edward S. Georgeson
"Confronting Injustice Without Compromising Truth,"
By Thaddeus J. Williams

---

There are many varying published lists of social justice issues in America. Yeshiva University of New York, NY, published a list of America's nine greatest social justice issues of 2020 with which we agree (They must all be considered Biblical injustice since there is no difference). They were listed in the following order. Some include our observations and recommendations to assist the twenty-first-century church in establishing its priorities for involvement:

**Voting rights:** As a continuation of an ungodly American tradition, voter suppression, as was legalized in the White church-supported Jim Crow laws, is an ongoing reality. Unjust redistricting and gerrymandering to gain advantage must end, and all unjust voting districts justly redrawn. All erected barriers for the disenfranchised must be removed.

**Climate justice:** We must strengthen opposition to the causes of climate change. Climate change can put a strain on resources and impact the well-being of entire communities. As an example of environmental racism and a point of concern, industrial pollution sites are often located in poor and minority communities.

**Health care:** More minorities die because of insufficient health care in America than White Americans. All obstacles to universal health care must be abolished. Reliable, affordable, and equal health care should be prioritized and made available to everyone.

**Refugee crisis:** Compassion must be shown, and doors must be opened for those in need who desire a better life in this country. Unjust obstacles to citizenship which are purposed to maintain the status quo must be eliminated. Except for the Native

Americans, we are a country of immigrants, and all immigrants should be welcome.

**Racial injustice:** Racism has a long history in America, not only among nonbelievers of Christ but even within certain groups of the professing body of Christ. Restoration and healing require individual and corporate confession, repentance, and restitution.

**Income gap:** America's income gap between the rich and poor is the largest it has ever been, exacerbated by the sin of greed. Legal unjust advantages afforded only to the rich to gain and maintain wealth must be abolished.

**Gun violence**: The rate of gun violence in America is the highest among developed nations, compounded by growing resentment and easy access to firearms. America has the highest rate of civilian gun ownership globally. As with many institutional ills in our society, minorities are impacted most. Strict gun laws are required, which should include a ban on assault rifles and military type weapons.

**Hunger & food insecurity**: It is estimated that 37 million people in America regularly face hunger, and 38 million live in poverty. Hunger and food insecurity should not exist anywhere on earth, especially in the world's wealthiest nation.

**Equality:** Whether related to finances, access to resources, property acquisition, the brutality or inequity of law enforcement by white officers toward minorities, incarceration, or severity of punishment rates, inequality in America and worldwide is as great as ever before. Recent trends within our society reflect an alarming increase.

***********************************

**Historically, these injustices have remained as spiritual stains in America's religious landscape. They remain because their solutions generally require wealth sharing, and professing White Christians have never voiced meaningful, large-scale opposition, thus enhancing the deception of Christianity in America.**

\*\*\*\*\*\*\*\*\*\*\*\*\*\*\*\*\*\*\*\*\*\*\*\*\*\*\*\*\*\*\*\*\*\*\*\*\*

[Though Yeshiva University considers this list as the greatest social justice issues, we believe that the sin of **abortion** should be included since injustice, from the Biblical perspective, includes all forms of injustice. From Genesis to Revelation, the Bible reminds us that every life is precious to God. In agreement with the word of God, we believe that life begins at conception, is formed by God, and is sacred to Him, even those who may have been conceived in sin. **The Bible condones a woman's right to choose. However, if her choice to have sex results in pregnancy, priority must always be given to the unborn, fully human baby who cannot speak for itself.** We believe that every unborn baby should justly be allowed the God-given right to life and the God-given right to share in the benefits of God's kingdom on earth. God is the giver of all life. Humanity does not have His authority to end it by abortion or any other form of murder (ref. Exodus 20:13, Job 31:15, Psalm 139:13, Isaiah 49:1, Jeremiah 1:5, Luke 1:41). The National Right to Life Committee (NRLC), the nation's oldest pro-life organization, estimates that 63,459,781 abortions (at the time of this writing) have occurred since Roe v. Wade legalized abortions in 1973. The Pew Research Center reported that sixty percent of Americans support abortion rights. Unfortunately, this sixty percent includes many professing Christians, which reflects the spiritual confusion that exists within the body of Christ.

By association with God and honoring His holy word, true believers are pro-life. They must stand against this injustice against the unborn, who cannot speak for or protect themselves, as representatives of God's holy and righteous throne. We must pray for the many mothers who have selected this option, the many who are contemplating it, and the many unborn at risk. Also, we must pray for our many brothers and sisters who are disregarding the sanctity of life as revealed in the word of God. They have aligned themselves with the self-focused values of this world, as opposed to God's will, by condoning this gross immorality.]

As a **side-note** of religious hypocrisy, most White professing Christians in America profess to be pro-life, but in opposition to

God's "Great Commandment" of love and Jesus' new commandment of love (John 13:34,35), they wickedly support all obstacles to citizenship and full inclusion in the United States for desperate minority races fleeing persecution and severe poverty in their countries of origin, thus enhancing the deception of Christianity in America. Many of those desperately seeking entrance into the United States are professing Christians and by God's design are brothers and sisters in Christ to those who stand in opposition to their full inclusion, including elected officials.

---

Injustice in any form is unacceptable in God's kingdom and must never be allowed to continue in order to establish and maintain oneness with God. As entrusted representatives of God's holy throne of justice and righteousness, professing Christians must be on the frontlines of every battle for justice in America and abroad. They must at all times model the sacrificial love of God toward all humanity by living sacrificially and sharing their advantages so that others who are hurting and in desperate need may also live and justly experience the benefits and prosperity of God's kingdom.

We are commanded to:

*"Defend the poor and fatherless; Do justice to the afflicted and needy. Deliver the poor and needy; free them from the hand of the wicked."*

**(Psalm 82:3,4)**

*The wicked plots against the just, and gnashes at him with his teeth. The Lord laughs at him, for He sees that his day is coming. The wicked have drawn the sword and have bent their bow, to cast down the poor and needy, to slay those who are of upright conduct. Their sword shall enter their own heart, and their bows shall be broken."*

**(Psalm 37:12-15 NKJV)**

# Chapter 14

## European (White) Americans for Racial Justice

In the first chapter of this book, we briefly highlighted the story of John Howard Griffin, a White **Roman Catholic** novelist who took a bold and unusual step of faith for racial justice in America. He went against the overwhelming tide of White racism in the Deep South Bible Belt. He and his family paid a huge price for his actions. However, his life was forever changed after gaining understanding by personally experiencing the plight of African Americans in the Deep South. From that experience, he developed a burning desire for racial justice and dedicated his life to that cause. In all fairness, many White "unsung heroes," religious leaders, and institutions have opposed the injustices that most White groups, White Protestant and Catholic churches, White citizens, and institutions condoned or perpetrated.

In reviewing video recordings of civil rights marches of the 1960s, we invariably see Whites marching alongside the African American demonstrators. Many bold and fearless Whites demonstrated their support for the cause of racial equality, justice, and righteousness by actively participating in demonstrations. Regretfully, their efforts to "stem the tide" of the overwhelming majority of Southern Whites were rarely successful, and many of them paid a hefty price. Some paid with their lives as martyred servants of Almighty God who will be rewarded in Heaven (Rev. 6:9-11). God knows who they were in America's history and those who are doing so today. As noted, God always maintains a remnant of true believers to represent His heavenly throne and maintain His kingdom on earth (Those who have a passion and sacrificial heart for human justice and are willing to "pay the price," no matter the cost). We pray that God will richly reward them for their efforts at the time of accountability and rewards given for works done.

Even more regretful, many caring Whites who opposed these injustices remained silent so as not to "rock the boat" or risk persecution. As earlier noted, in the Biblical perspective, silence equates to agreement, which is sin (ref. Ephesians 5:11, James 4:17).

We also pray for them because we strongly feel that those who remain unrepentant for their inaction will also be justly judged at the time of accountability. In God's kingdom, there is no neutral position. Either we are for Him or against Him. If we are for Him, we must be actively involved in His causes.

---

Though rarely acknowledged in history recordings, many members of the White race participated and played active roles in many of the struggles for racial justice for minority race groups throughout America's history. One example was those caring Whites who were instrumental in developing the African Free School.

The African Free School (founded November 2, 1787) was founded by members of the New York Manumission Society to provide education to children of slaves and free people of color. Though comprised of all influential White men, mostly **Quakers**, this unique society fought against slavery and promoted the gradual abolition of African slavery in the state of New York. Many of the students of the African Free School excelled and became leaders in the African American community in New York.

Established in 1794, the first school was a one-room schoolhouse that held about 40 students. Originally, the Manumission Society hired only White teachers, but it eventually employed Black teachers as well. By 1835, when the schools ended their run as privately supported institutions, the African Free School had seven buildings in different neighborhoods, and it had educated thousands of girls and boys. At that time, the African Free School and its facilities were integrated into the public school system. This was several years after New York freed the last adult slaves under its gradual abolition law.[3]

---

As was a rare occurrence, the story of John Brown made it into many history books in America and beyond.

"**John Brown** (1800-1859), a **Calvinist**, was an ardent abolitionist who worked with the Underground Railroad and worked to inspire a slave insurrection at Harpers Ferry, West Virginia. He was a White man willing to die to end slavery. As a 12-year-old boy traveling through Michigan, Brown witnessed an enslaved African American boy being beaten, which haunted him for years to come and formed his own abolitionism. In 1855, Brown moved to Kansas, and with the passing of the Kansas-Nebraska Act of 1854, there was conflict over whether the territory would be a free or slave state. Brown, who believed in using violent means to end slavery, became involved in the conflict; in 1856, he and several of his men killed five pro-slavery settlers in a retaliatory attack at Pottawatomie Creek. With the intent of inspiring a slave insurrection, he eventually led an unsuccessful raid on the Harpers Ferry federal armory on October 16, 1859, holding dozens of men hostage. Brown's forces held out for two days; they were eventually defeated by military forces led by Robert E. Lee. Many of Brown's men were killed, including two of his sons, and he was captured. Brown went to trial and was executed on December 2, 1859."[3] (Though we highlighted the life of John Brown, this must not be misunderstood as condoning violence to address racial injustice. We condemn all forms of violence. We strongly believe that love will conquer hate and justice and righteousness will ultimately prevail.)

---

As was in the early days of the aftermath of African slavery, as already noted, more recent history reveals that many White Americans played active roles in civil rights struggles for minorities in America. White Americans were instrumental in all aspects of the movements for racial equality, such as volunteering to be included with the Freedom Riders.

"Freedom Riders were groups of White and African American civil rights activists who participated in Freedom Rides, bus trips through the American South in 1961 to protest segregated bus terminals. Freedom Riders tried to use "Whites only" restrooms and lunch counters at bus stations in Alabama, South Carolina, and other Southern states. The groups were confronted by arresting police officers – as well as horrific violence from White protestors – along their routes but also drew international attention to the civil rights movement."[1] Freedom Riders, as was the case with the original group, often faced violence from racist members of the White community who were determined to thwart all efforts for racial integration.

The original group of 13 Freedom Riders was seven African Americans and six White Americans. They left Washington, D.C., on a Greyhound bus on May 4, 1961. Their plan was to reach New Orleans, Louisiana, on May 17 to commemorate the seventh anniversary of the Supreme Court's Brown v. Board of Education decision, which ruled that segregation of the nation's public schools was unconstitutional. In Atlanta, Georgia, some of the riders split off onto a Trailways bus.

On May 14, 1961, the Greyhound bus was the first to arrive in Anniston, Alabama, where an angry mob of about 200 White people surrounded the bus, causing the driver to continue past the bus station. The angry mob followed the bus in automobiles, and when the tires of the bus blew out, someone threw a bomb into the bus. The Freedom Riders escaped the bus as it burst into flames, only to be brutally beaten by members of the surrounding mob as pictured.

The second bus, a Trailways vehicle, traveled to Birmingham, Alabama, and those riders were also beaten by an angry white mob.[1] Indeed, as members of the Freedom Riders, the Whites were victimized for their participation by their own church-supported White society, as were the African American participants. Because of their passion for racial equality and righteousness, they were viewed by the angry and opposing White racist members of their society as traitors and were derogatorily labeled "Nigger lovers."

(The documented history of the Freedom Riders is displayed at the Freedom Rides Museum in Montgomery, Alabama.)

---

"During the Civil Rights movement, having White Americans in powerful positions supporting the cause was invaluable. Walter Reuther **(Judaism)**, the former president and leader of the United Automobile Workers Union, was instrumental in helping ensure African Americans were heard. Respected as one of the most powerful people in Detroit at the time, he took full advantage of his position and spoke in support of African American causes and equality. Most notable was Reuther's speech at the 1963 March on Washington, D.C., the same march we remember for Martin Luther King Jr.'s "I Have a Dream" speech, in which he challenged Congress to enact civil rights legislation immediately."[2]

Many in America are familiar with Ruby Bridges. She was one of the four African American children to first attend an all-white school in the Southern Bible Belt in New Orleans, Louisiana in November 1960, each at the tender age of six years old. The other three were Leona Tate, Tessie Prevost, and Gail Etienne who together attended McDonogh 19 Elementary School at the same time that Ruby Bridges attended William Frantz Elementary School alone.

However, we are missing one of the more important parts of the Ruby Bridges story if we fail to include the story of a loving and caring woman named Barbara Henry. Barbara Henry was a White woman who had moved to New Orleans from Boston, Massachusetts. She agreed to teach young Bridges even though she was ostracized by the school and the local community for doing so. Unsurprisingly, all of the other White teachers in the school refused to teach young Bridges. In order to minimize the effect on the entire school, Barbara Henry taught Bridges one-on-one for an entire school year, despite facing heavy criticism, hatred, and even death threats. Throughout the demonic orchestrated chaos of evilness surrounding this historic event, Mrs. Henry relied on her unwavering faith in God as she demonstrated His eternal salvation requirement of unconditional, sacrificial love for all humanity and loving all others as oneself.

The spiritually defiant White community was in an uproar with daily riots in front of the school. This threat to the child's safety from racist White adults who desired to harm her necessitated armed federal protection throughout each day from U.S. Federal Marshals.

Unbelievably, a coffin carrying a black doll was displayed by the rioters to frighten the young child and further incite the angry mob. Some rioters carried signs falsely stating God's displeasure with racial integration and His desire to maintain racial segregation.

When viewing footage of the riots, it is heartbreaking to see the number of White parents who brought their innocent children with them to participate in the daily display of racial hatred. Apparently, it was their desire for their children to experience and maintain their legacy of racial hatred and White supremacy. As earlier noted, this evil-influenced, irresponsible parenting only enhances the generational hatred that is still plaguing race relations in the U.S. As expected and as was orchestrated by Satan, most White parents took their children out of William Frantz Elementary School now that, incredibly, an African American child was learning in the same building. However, it is encouraging to see that a few White parents allowed their children (four were documented) to remain and ultimately associate and play with young Bridges. Their picture reflected the image of childhood innocence and the racial oneness of God's kingdom design (Matthew 18:3,4, 1st Corinthians 14:20).

Since the European occupation of America, many White Americans have erroneously identified God as the author of racial division and White supremacy. Without remorse, many are still promoting this lie during the current evil orchestrated resurgence of hate in the U.S. This was clearly seen in the religious statement of belief adopted by the Ku Klux Klan as revealed in chapter 8. The Holy Bible has often been misquoted and held hostage by evilness and used out of context to validate deception, even by many well-respected White religious leaders today in a less obvious manner.

When viewing actual pictures of race riots in America, invariably, you will see White rioters carrying signs falsely stating God's approval and involvement. To varying degrees, this satanic-originated Protestant nationalism is still evident today among many religious circles in America. America's rebellion against the cross of Christ, which expresses the sacrificial love of God for all humanity, is still on display throughout religion in America, thus contributing to the deception of Christianity. May God help the blind to see, and enable Jesus to return to a spiritually-delivered and unspotted bride.

When considering the many ungodly racial events of evilness and hatred of America's past, one must continually question the role of the then predominant racially segregated White institutional church and its spiritual focus and impact on the White society. Obviously, there was little to no institutional spiritual resistance to this orchestrated evilness, seemingly, only support. Indeed, an unbiased, scripturally based analysis is needed to better understand the primary contributing cause for the spiritual divide between God and twenty-first-century religion in America. The spiritual sores of America's past sins remain as open and untreated wounds before Almighty God.

Kind, daring, and righteous gestures such as those displayed by Mrs. Barbara Henry continued to give concerned, prayerful people of all colors and faiths, hope for America's future in its struggle for the Biblical mandates of human rights, justice, and equality.[2]

---

Immediately following the Civil Rights movement and the assassination of Martin Luther King, Jr., there was still a tremendous amount of work that needed to be done for the African American community in its struggle for justice and equality. Morris Dees **(Baptist)** recognized this and co-founded the Southern Poverty Law Center.

Despite understanding the repercussions he would face defending the rights of the African American community, he pressed forward. The lawsuits he originally filed were lawsuits to open public employment, integrate the Alabama state trooper force, and dismantle hate groups such as the Ku Klux Klan.

Because of his efforts and the efforts of people like him, remarkable strides were made in the movement toward equality for all.

Having powerful people support the dream Dr. King spoke of made it more likely for it to become a reality.[2] Regretfully, over a half-century after Dr. King was assassinated, key portions of his dream are still not realized in the United States, with much work still to be done by God's people of faith.

---

We will briefly highlight the lives of other White Americans who boldly renounced the racist, wicked ways of the majority of their race and their racially segregated, hate-inspired religious institutions. They chose to take a stand for racial justice and righteousness as obedient representatives of God's heavenly throne. Though swimming against the overpowering waves of institutional racism and injustice perpetrated by the majority of their race, they made a tremendous difference in obtaining God-ordained justice for African Americans:

**Jessie Daniel Ames** (1883-1972), a lifelong **Methodist** and civil rights leader from Austin, Texas, fought against racism in the then racially segregated Methodist church. After being confronted with the horrors of African American lynchings, she helped create the anti-lynching movement in America's South. She founded the "Association of Southern Women for the Prevention of Lynching." She was one of the first Southern White women to speak out and work publicly against the lynching of African Americans.

She fought to dispel the widely accepted myth that White women needed protection from African American men. She pointed out that the rape of White women by African American men, which was the supposed justification for lynching, seldom occurred and that the true motives for lynchings were rooted in racial hatred. Despite risks to her personal safety, Ames stood up to the perpetrators and led organized efforts by White women to protest lynchings. Her efforts led to a decline in these murders in the 1930s and 1940s.[4]

"**Anne McCarty Braden** (1924-2006), a devout **Episcopalian**, was a journalist and community organizer from Louisville, Kentucky. She defied racist real estate practices and the House Un-American Activities Committee and organized White Southerners to support the civil rights movement.

She is best known for purchasing a home in a White suburb in Louisville, Kentucky, in 1954 for a Black colleague, Andrew Wade IV, and his family. Unknown assailants dynamited the house. However, no one was hurt in the blast. The police made no arrests, but Anne and her husband Carl, as well as five other Whites, were charged with sedition for inciting unrest with their purchase of the house. Carl was sentenced to 15 years of prison time. This verdict was overturned in 1956 after Carl had served seven months. Anne's case never went to trial. She and her husband were banned from jobs, threatened, and reviled by their fellow White Southerners for what they did. Despite these charges and community disapproval, Anne continued her work in social activism.

She wrote a book about her sedition trial, *"The Wall Between,"* which was nominated for the National Book Award. She worked closely with Rosa Parks and Ela Baker, and was mentioned in Dr. King's *"Letter from a Birmingham Jail."*[5]

**Jonathan Daniels** (1939-1965) of Keene, New Hampshire, was valedictorian of the 1961 class of the Virginia Military Institute. At age 26, he was a seminary student at Harvard University, **Episcopal** Divinity School in 1965, when he responded to Dr. King's call for clergy of all faiths to come to Selma, Alabama, to support the voting rights marchers. He went to Selma in response to Dr. King's call. He stayed after the march to work on the integration of churches and voting rights.

Jonathan was one of 30 jailed for picketing white stores in Fort Deposit, Alabama. A week later, after leaving jail in Haynesville, Daniels, Father Morrisroe, and two African American teens attempted to enter a nearby grocery store to buy a soda. Tom Coleman, a part-time deputy, emerged from the store with a shotgun and threatened the group. Jonathan pushed the teenagers out of the way, and the gun went off. Father Morrisroe was critically injured; Jonathan was killed instantly.

After his death, Stokely Carmichael, an African American activist, said, "He had an abundance of strength that comes from the inside that he could give to people. The people of Lowndes County realized that with the strength they got from Jon Daniels, they had to carry on, they had to carry on."[6]

**Rev. Joseph Ellwanger** (born 1934) was raised in Selma, Alabama. He was one of the few White pastors in Alabama to actively participate in the African American civil rights movement. He fought on the frontlines of the movement in the 1960s. He was part of the 1960s steering committee of the Southern Christian Leadership Conference (SCLC), a group led by the Rev. Martin Luther King Jr., and he played a leadership role in several key civil rights activities in Alabama. Ellwanger faced challenges to his involvement in the Movement. That's because he served the **Lutheran** Church's Missouri Synod (LCMS), a conservative denomination that resisted getting involved in activities connected to politics and social activism. Rev. Ellwanger said, "I had to overcome my own conservative theological background and my conservative fellow members of the Lutheran Church in order to take this position. In fact, I was critiqued and censored a couple of times by what would have been the president of the district. He was, so to speak, my boss and definitely reprimanded me and threatened me for getting involved." He noted that "other preachers, White and some Black, hesitated to join the Movement, and some received pushback from their congregations for daring to even bring up civil rights." Rev. Ellwanger went on to say, "Participating in the Movement, I told my peers, 'is what I see God calling me to do at this time.' This is calling the larger community to simply treat people as human beings. If that is not the real solid basic Gospel, then they have been misreading the Bible and misreading the Gospel over the years."

Rev. Ellwanger sees voting rights as an ongoing struggle. He recently said, "The pushback to suppress the vote and make it more difficult for people to vote is what happens after there is some real progress in the quest for justice. Once a victory is won, the opposition finds a way to try to get back at it. That's exactly what is happening, of course, at the present time."[7]

**Andrew Goodman** (1943-1964) **and Michael Schwerner** (1939-1964)**,** two Jewish **(Judaism)** men from New York, traveled to Mississippi in 1964 to help register African Americans to vote. They and James Chaney **(Catholic)**, an African American from Meridian, Mississippi, were associated with the Council of Federated Organizations (COFO) and its member organization, the Congress of Racial Equality (CORE). Since 1890 and through the turn of the century, southern states had systematically disenfranchised most black voters by discrimination in voter registration and voting.

The three men traveled from Meridian to the community of Longdale to talk with congregation members at a black church that had been burned. The church had been a center of community organization. The three were arrested following a traffic stop for speeding outside of Philadelphia, Mississippi. They were escorted to the local jail and held for a number of hours. As the three left town in their car, they were followed by law enforcement and other Ku Klux Klan members. Before leaving Neshoba County, their car was pulled over. The three were abducted, driven to another location, and shot to death at close range. The bodies of the three men were taken to an earthen dam built on the property of one of the Klansmen, where they were buried.

During the investigation of their murder, it emerged that members of the local White Knights of the Ku Klux Klan, the Neshoba County Sheriff's Office, and the Philadelphia Police Department were involved in the crime. After the Mississippi state government refused to prosecute for murder, the United States federal government charged eighteen individuals with civil rights violations. Seven were convicted and received relatively minor sentences for their actions.

Forty-one years after the murders took place, a Ku Klux Klan organizer, Edgar Ray Killen, was convicted of manslaughter. Killen was a local White ordained **Baptist** preacher who orchestrated the murders. He was charged by the state of Mississippi for his part in the crime and was said to have recruited the mob that carried out his murderous plan. The bodies of the three victims were found within walking distance of Killen's house. In 2005 he was convicted of three counts of manslaughter and was given a 60-year sentence. He died in prison in 2018 at the age of 92, still hateful and unrepentant.[8]

It was due to the involvement of Dick Gregory, an African American civil rights activist/comedian, that the three bodies were eventually found and the suspects charged. He offered a Hugh Hefner-donated $25,000 reward for information on the location of the murdered victim's bodies. From that offer, he received an anonymous tip in the form of a letter giving the location of their bodies.[9]

**Viola Fauver Liuzzo** (1925-1965), a **Unitarian Universalist**, was a housewife and mother from Detroit, Michigan, who heeded the call of Dr. Martin Luther King and traveled to Selma, Alabama, in the wake of the "Bloody Sunday" attack. She participated in Selma to Montgomery marches and helped with coordinating logistics. She was fatally hit by bullets fired from a pursuing car of Ku Klux Klan members in Lowndesboro, Alabama, while giving a ride to a 19-year-old black man, Leroy Moton, a civil rights marcher (Her car is pictured). The four men, which included an F.B.I. informant, in the pursuing car from which the shots were fired, were charged with her murder. However, as was common during that era, an all-white, all-male jury acquitted all four men of Liuzzo's murder. Eventually, three were sentenced to 10 years in prison for violating Liuzzo's civil rights. The fourth, the F.B.I. informant, was not convicted after being granted immunity.

Her murder became international news. Her name has been inscribed on civil rights memorials throughout the United States. However, racist White people had far less sympathy for Liuzzo when she was murdered. Hate mail flooded her family's Detroit home, accusing her of being a deranged communist. Ku Klux Klan crosses were burned in front of her home. Her husband, Anthony Liuzzo Sr., had to hire armed guards to protect his family. His wife's murder took a physical and mental toll on him, from which he never recovered. A Ladies' Home Journal magazine suggested that she had brought death on herself by leaving home – and 55% of its readers agreed. White people called her a White whore and a Nigger lover. Even her daughter Sally did not escape the White wrath. Students threw rocks at her and taunted her on the way to school. Her family suffered and paid a tremendous cost for her activism and death. Viola Liuzzo's murder sparked the passage of the Voting Rights Act.[10]

**Rev. James Joseph Reeb** (1927-1965) was a White **Unitarian** minister from Boston who was martyred for the civil rights cause of African Americans. He died on March 11, 1965, in Selma, Alabama. While in Boston, Rev. Reeb grew outraged while watching television reportings of the brutal "Bloody Sunday" attack by police against marchers in Selma. He immediately traveled to Selma to support the civil rights movement following "Bloody Sunday." An angry mob of White supremacists physically attacked him for participating in the march. He died of head injuries in the hospital two days after being severely beaten. Three men were tried for Rev. Reeb's murder, but as was common during that era, they were acquitted by an all-white jury. No one was ever convicted for his murder. He left behind his wife and four children.

**James Zwerg (United Church of Christ)** was born in Appleton, Wisconsin, on November 28, 1938. His father was a dentist who provided free dental care to the poor one day per month. His parents were professing Christians who taught him that all humans are created equal. His first time in a classroom with a black student was when he went to Beloit College to study sociology. While there, he developed an interest in civil rights after reading the Martin Luther King book, *"Stride Toward Freedom: The Montgomery Story."* The book was given to him by his roommate, Robert Carter, who was an African American from Alabama. He later recalled how he witnessed prejudice against his African American roommate. He valued his roommate's friendship. Zwerg decided to sign on for an exchange semester at the predominately black Fisk University in Nashville, Tennessee. After arriving, he signed up for a workshop on non-violence provided by James Lawson. This workshop gave him the opportunity to mirror the experiences of his roommate at Beloit.

Zwerg met John Lewis at Fisk, who was active in the civil rights movement. He was impressed by John Lewis's commitment and zeal for civil rights.

In October 1960, Lewis and students involved in civil rights established the Student Nonviolent Coordinating Committee (SNCC). The organization adopted the Gandhian theory of nonviolent direct action. Zwerg joined the SNCC, and his first demonstration was at a "Whites only" movie house. During this demonstration, Zwerg was hit with a monkey wrench, knocked out cold, and dragged to the edge of the sidewalk.[11]

**Rev. Robert Graetz** (1928-2020) was a **Lutheran** pastor from Ohio who moved to Montgomery, Alabama in the 1950s to pastor a predominately Black congregation. Some Lutheran authorities worried that Graetz might become ensnarled in the developing racial unrest in Montgomery. "He had to promise he would not start trouble," his wife Jeannie Graetz recalled in a 2019 interview with NPR. "Well, he did not start the trouble. He just joined the trouble."

A few months after Graetz and Jeannie arrived in Montgomery, Rosa Parks and other local leaders, including Dr. Martin Luther King, Jr., launched a bus boycott to protest segregated seating in city buses. Graetz was acquainted with Parks because the local NAACP youth council, which Parks directed, met in Graetz's church.

The call to boycott the bus system was problematic for many Black workers in Montgomery because they depended on bus transportation to get to and from their jobs. Graetz immediately began organizing carpools to assist with their transportation needs and spent three hours each morning driving people to work in his own car.

In Montgomery in 1955, that was enough to make Graetz a target of the racist White church-supported Ku Klux Klan. Twice, his home was firebombed. Neither he nor his wife nor their young children were injured, but a third bomb thrown at their house was enough to kill them all. Fortunately, it did not detonate.

Graetz and his wife also faced death threats directed at them and their three children, one of them a toddler. FBI agents urged them to leave Montgomery, but they stayed, encouraged in large part by the support they received from their African American friends and neighbors.

"We felt that the Lord had put a circle of love around us," Jeannie Graetz said, "There were people who hated us, but that hate could not get through to us because of the Lord's protection."

Graetz and his wife left Montgomery in 1958 and continued their social justice work in locations around the country.[12]

---

Dr. Martin Luther King, Jr. called attention to the tireless works of Whites in the struggle for civil rights for African Americans in his 1963 *"Letter From a Birmingham Jail."* He wrote:

"I am thankful, however, that some of our white brothers in the South have grasped the meaning of this social revolution and committed themselves to it. They are still all too few in quantity, but they are big in quality. Some, such as Ralph McGill, Lillian Smith, Harry Golden, James McBride Dabbs, Ann Braden, and Sarah Patton Boyle have written about our struggle in eloquent and prophetic terms. Others have marched with us down nameless streets of the South. They have languished in filthy, roach-infested jails, suffering the abuse and brutality of policemen who view them as "dirty nigger lovers." Unlike so many of their moderate brothers and sisters, they have recognized the urgency of the moment and sensed the need for powerful "action" antidotes to combat the disease of segregation."

---

There are many other God-fearing White Americans who chose to take a stand against the destructive wave of evil-inspired hatred and injustice perpetrated by their fellow race members against innocent minorities throughout America's history. There are many unknown White heroes who are doing so today. Moved by compassion for the oppressed, many of them committed their lives and were persecuted. Many paid the ultimate price as martyrs for righteousness. Many of their stories will never be told or accurately documented in history books. However, their stories will be accurately documented in God's *"Book of Life"* (Rev. 20:12) and His eternal recognition given.

---

*"A man dies when he refuses to stand up for that which is right. A man dies when he refuses to stand up for justice."*
— Dr. Martin Luther King, Jr. -

# **Chapter 15**

# **The Biblical Response to Injustice by the Oppressed**

There may be no greater pain for humanity than the pain of experiencing injustice, suffering for something you did not do or deserve, and tolerating a lack of fairness. The lifelong impact of injustice can be traumatic. If not correctly handled with the understanding and attitude of Christ, the results can often be disastrous or, even worse, fatal.

If you have experienced injustice, you may feel as Job felt in the Bible. Job said, ***"If I cry out concerning wrong, I am not heard. If I cry aloud, there is no justice"*** (Job 19:7). However, as Job eventually realized, ***"The LORD executes righteousness and justice for all who are oppressed"*** (Ps. 103:6).

When experiencing injustice, one can sometimes feel as if no one cares or understands. It can often lead to a feeling of despair and hopelessness. Regardless of your background, social status, or religious beliefs, as human beings in a fallen society, we are not exempt from injustice. Injustice permeates our society and is sewn into the fabric of its spiritual existence. We live in a fallen society that is under the influence of evil, where the ungodly strong prey on the weak and vulnerable. This truth applies to the animal kingdom (minus the God association) as well as the earthly kingdom of Godless humanity.

**Evilness thrives on selfishness, and selfishness is the root cause of injustice.** Just being poor, the wrong color, the wrong gender, being in the wrong place at the wrong time, or associating with the wrong people can quickly lead to a life-altering encounter of injustice.

Many people are incarcerated and serving time for crimes they did not commit. Many people are homeless and without basic shelter through no fault of their own. Many children are suffering the hunger pains of neglect. Many people are working long hours and are underpaid. Many people are consistently disregarded because of the color of their skin. Many people are denied fair housing. Many women are working the same jobs as men but receiving less pay. Many women are living in fear in an abusive relationship and are afraid to seek help. Many refugees are fleeing dangerous living conditions and seeking a better life for their families, with no place to go. Their presence may not be desired or tolerated, even in prosperous countries as witnessed in the United States. Many children are afraid to attend school because of bullying, and the list goes on.

We are living in a society where injustice is a way of life for far too many. This sad reality of life is in opposition to God's design for His kingdom on earth. **God is a God of justice.** Psalm 33:5 states, *"He loves righteousness and justice."* God desires justice for His entire creation. However, as stated, we live in a fallen society characterized by ungodliness, and ungodliness is a forerunner to injustice.

---

There are important truths to be noted when experiencing injustice and fighting for elusive justice. It is important first to understand that God hates injustice. Second, you cannot protect yourself from or correct institutional injustice on your own strength and wisdom. Only God can provide the protective covering and open the doors of justice in an unjust society. Only God can provide the strength and protection needed to endure life's injustices. The Bible offers hope for those experiencing the pains of injustice. It gives assurance that God hears your cries for justice. So, what are we to do?

*********************************
## We must not seek revenge but leave that to God's righteous judgment.
*********************************

The natural human and worldly tendency and desire is to "get even" with the perpetrators of the injustice, those who are causing us harm or facilitating the suffering that we may be enduring. We must resist the urge to make them feel the pain and suffering they have caused. We must bear in mind that God knows and feels our pain and suffering. He is not indifferent to what we are experiencing. Those who love Him and have committed their lives to His care must trust His sovereignty.

We are instructed in Romans 12:19-21, *"Beloved, do not avenge yourselves, but rather give place to wrath, for it is written, "Vengeance is Mine, I will repay," says the Lord. Therefore "If your enemy is hungry, feed him; If he is thirsty, give him a drink; For in so doing you will heap coals of fire on his head." Do not be overcome by evil, but overcome evil with good."*

---

We must love those who perpetrate acts of injustice against us and treat them with kindness, trusting God's oversight. Though difficult to do with our own ability, we must pray for God to strengthen us to do so. We must pray for their deliverance and salvation, for they are influenced by evilness.

Jesus instructs us in Matthew 5:44, *"But I say to you, love your enemies, bless those who curse you, do good to those who hate you, and pray for those who spitefully use you and persecute you."*

---

God has committed His care to those who love Him. If you have not committed your life to God and placed your concerns in His care, now is an excellent time to do so. If you are willing to turn from the evilness of this world, repent of your sins, receive Jesus as your Lord and Savior, and follow Him in obedience and complete faith in His sovereignty, the promises of God's care are for you. You can be assured that:

*"The LORD also will be a refuge for the oppressed* (yourself)*, a refuge in times of trouble"* (Psalm 9:9).

*"Because of the oppression of the weak and the groaning of the needy, I will now arise, says the LORD. I will protect them from those who malign them"* (Psalm 12:5).

However, committing your life to God will not exempt you from injustice. Thankfully, it will place you under His loving care, and God will strengthen you in your times of need. God is faithful to his promises. God assures His people, *"He will not leave you or forsake you"* (Deut. 31:8). God says to His people in Isaiah 41:10, *"Fear not, for I am with you; Be not dismayed, for I am your God. I will strengthen you. Yes, I will uphold you with My righteous right hand."* Though you may experience injustice, God will always be with you and keep you in His care. The Lord is concerned with that which concerns you. Psalm 138:8 states, *"The LORD will perfect that which concerns me."*

If you have already committed your life to God and are experiencing injustice, the wisdom of the Holy Spirit can help you deal with injustice now. Dealing with injustice now involves spiritually discerning what to do and what not to do, when to go and when not to go, where to go and where not to go, what to say and what not to say, who to trust and who not to trust, and the list of uncertainties go on. In other words, as believers in Christ and servants of God, we can depend on the Holy Spirit to guide us through the many life-altering uncertainties of life and give comfort throughout the journey, for He is our guide and comforter (ref. 2$^{nd}$ Cor. 1:3).

If you have committed your life to God and are experiencing injustice, it can give you comfort to know that you are not alone in your suffering. There is a great cloud of witnesses who have gone before you whose testimonies of faith in God should serve as your motivation. They would understand what you are going through.

The writer of Hebrews reminds us, *"Therefore we also, since we are surrounded by so great a cloud of witnesses, let us lay aside every weight, and the sin which so easily ensnares us, and let us run with endurance the race that is set before us, looking unto Jesus, the author and finisher of our faith, who for the joy that was set before Him endured the cross, despising the shame, and has sat down at the right hand of the throne of God* (Hebrews 12:1, 2).

This great cloud of witnesses refers to the people of faith that were noted in the previous chapter. We must not see them as spectators who are watching us from the sidelines, but we must see their lives as witnessing and testifying to us regarding the faithfulness of God and the power of having faith in Him and placing our lives in His care. We should gain inspiration from their lives. Like many of us, they experienced the evilness of this world, but they did not allow the injustices of this evil world to hinder the completion of the race that God had set before them. The weight that they would lay aside was anything of this world that obstructed their ability to run effectively for the completion of God's will for their lives.

Jesus and all of the apostles of the Bible experienced injustice. However, they did not allow injustice to hinder the fulfillment of their kingdom calling, their God-given purpose. The apostles ran with endurance the race that God set before them, looking unto Jesus, the author and finisher of their faith.

The apostle Paul gained strength from the many injustices he experienced for the glory of God. As in each of them, he witnessed the faithfulness of God that sustained him and enabled him to persevere. He grew stronger in his times of trials.

In $2^{nd}$ Corinthians 11:24-28, Paul gave his testimony of injustices he encountered in living for the Lord. He said, *"From the Jews five times I received forty stripes minus one. Three times I was beaten with rods; once I was stoned; three times I was shipwrecked; a night and a day I have been in the deep; in journeys often, in perils of waters, in perils of robbers, in perils of my own countrymen, in perils of the Gentiles, in perils in the city, in perils in the wilderness, in perils in the sea. In perils among false brethren; in weariness and toil, in sleeplessness often, in hunger and thirst, in fastings often, in cold and nakedness – besides the other things, what comes upon me daily; my deep concern for all the churches."*

Though Paul's experiences of injustice were numerous, his attitude was always one of thankfulness and joy. Like all rational humans, Paul did not desire to suffer, however, he considered it an honor to suffer for Christ. As Christ had set the example and model before him, Paul could now run his race with Christ as his model and inspiration. Christ did not focus on the suffering but on the crown. Paul always kept in his remembrance the injustices that Jesus incurred for him. Indeed, throughout his trials, Paul found God to be faithful as he reminded the Corinthians in $1^{st}$ Corinthians 1:9, *"God is faithful, by whom you were called into the fellowship of His Son, Jesus Christ our Lord."* He also assured the Thessalonians in $2^{nd}$ Thessalonians 3:3, *"But the Lord is faithful, who will establish you and guard you from the evil one."*

If we are unjustly treated in this life, as servants of God, we can find comfort in knowing that we are abiding under His protective shelter (Psalm 91) and His faithfulness is everlasting. He does not change. Hebrews 13:8 reminds us of this eternal truth, *"Jesus Christ is the same yesterday, today, and forever."*

Despite all of the injustices that Paul experienced, God faithfully kept him and saw him through each crisis, enabling him to complete his God-given mission for the glory of God's kingdom. After all of life's considerations, completing our God-given mission should be our life-long focus and goal.

As stated, all of the apostles of Christ experienced injustice simply because they committed their lives to Christ. Indeed, we are surrounded by a cloud of witnesses who know from experience what we are going through. We can gain strength in realizing what they knew, that God is with us through the injustices of life. He is faithful and will always honor His word and provide for the needs of His own.

With this assurance, as believers in Christ, we do not respond to injustice as the world does but as faith-living servants of our faithful, omnipotent (having unlimited power), and omniscient (having all knowledge; God knows everything) God. **Nothing escapes His awareness or exists beyond His ability to resolve.** What a mighty God we serve.

Injustice should not be seen as an end of our joy, pleasure, happiness, and fulfillment of purpose in life, but a new beginning to faithfully and joyfully living in Christ, who, for the joy (the reward, the crown, knowing that His servants will live with Him throughout eternity) that was set before Him endured, the injustice of the cross, despising the shame. Hallelujah! To God be the glory!

---

*"For if you forgive men their trespasses, your heavenly Father will also forgive you.*
*But if you do not forgive men their trespasses, neither will your Father forgive your trespasses."*
**Matthew 6:14, 15**

---

# **Chapter 16**

## **The Cost of Restoration**

White church-supported injustice presents enormous challenges for God's kingdom, and most of the challenges require wealth sharing, which stems from agape love and should flow automatically. Agape love is the highest form of love. It is the love of God for humanity, expressed through humanity's sacrificial relationship with each other, considering the needs of all others before our own. This is Christianity expressed to God as revealed through Christ.

To the servants of God who serve as faithful stewards of His resources, meeting the needs of others is not just a focused Biblical requirement but also an inexpressible joy.

When considering this underlying implication for human justice and Christian discipleship, obviously, the ones controlling the most wealth are more impacted. Though everyone is required to sacrifice, those holding more wealth are required to make the greater sacrifice to realize God's designed kingdom order. In God's designed order, there should be no lack. We should not be satisfied until all are brought into equal standing of sufficiency, which is the underlying implication of God's 'Great Commandment.'

As a reminder of a central Biblical kingdom requirement, Jesus stated in Luke 12:48, *"for unto whomsoever much is given, of him shall be much required."* In other words, those whom God has entrusted with more of His resources are held to a higher degree of expectation for sharing and providing for the needs of all others as Christian stewards.

**These issues of injustice in America will end only when White professing Christians (the dominant, most prosperous, and influential race group in America) take the lead role in**

**opposing them and leading by sacrificial example, reflecting the character and heart of Christ.**

Resistance to human justice and true sacrificial Biblical love is prevalent in the lives of many who claim the title of "Christian" but remain unconverted and do not possess God's love in their hearts. As noted, the correct Biblical meaning of Christian is "Christlike," or having the character of Jesus, developed on the foundation of God's sacrificial love for all others regardless of their differences.

This widespread confusion among professing Christians reflects a fundamental lack of understanding of God and Biblical Christianity. Those exhibiting this confusion should cease identifying themselves as "Christian" (Christlike). In reality, through them, Satan is undermining the foundation of God's kingdom and jeopardizing their eternal salvation.

If we are in a spiritual environment that condones this attitude, we should repent of our personal errors, which can easily result from incorrect, self-focused teachings on Christian financial stewardship and Christian discipleship, and prayerfully consider a change. Most twenty-first-century teachings on Christian financial stewardship are self-focused rather than sacrificial cross-focused (ref. *"The Fanaticism of Christian Discipleship"* for more information).

In essence, resistance to any form of justice is a repudiation of God's foundation for Christianity. It must also be understood as a repudiation of God, for God is love (1st John 4:16), and as previously noted, justice and righteousness are the foundations of God's holy throne.

---

So, what does God require of His servants? Micah 6:8 states, *"And what doth the LORD require of thee, but **to do justly**, and to love mercy, and to walk humbly with thy God."* As a people of faith, we must prioritize honoring God's requirements, especially His requirement for justice, a vital portion of the foundation of His heavenly throne.

Proverbs 29:7 states, *"The righteous care about justice for the poor, but the wicked have no such concern."*

It is important to note that in terms of Biblical scripture, those who care about justice for the poor are considered righteous, and those with no such concern are considered wicked. This understanding may be a startling and fearful revelation to some because the Bible is clear regarding the eternal destination for the righteous and the wicked (Ps. 9:16,17, 11:5-7, 32:10, 37:17, 20).

As a reminder to the wise, 1st John 3:7 states, *"Little children, let no man deceive you: he that doeth righteousness is righteous, even as he is righteous."* 1st John 3:10 states, *"In this the children of God are manifest, and the children of the devil: whosoever doeth not righteousness is not of God, neither he that loveth not his brother."* In other words, a righteous character expresses itself in righteous conduct. Being righteous will truly do righteousness.

God's judgment will be harshest on those who resist justice and providing for the needs of the oppressed. James 2:13 states, *"For there will be no mercy to those who have shown no mercy. But if you have been merciful, then God's mercy toward you will win out over his judgment against you"* (The Living Bible) (also ref. Matthew 5:7).

Matthew 7, verses 21-23 state, *"Not everyone that saith unto me, Lord, Lord, shall enter into the kingdom of heaven; but he that doeth the will of my Father which is in heaven. Many will say to me in that day, Lord, Lord, have we not prophesied in thy name? and in thy name have cast out devils? And in thy name done many wonderful works? And then will I profess unto them, I never knew you: depart from me, ye that work iniquity "*(KJV).

The historical ills of injustice perpetrated by America's European society and its racially segregated professing church of God have been veiled under the cloak of being a Christian nation. Many firmly believed that God ordained their privileged existence. Sorrowfully, this self-initiated crowning to glory had to come through the unjust and forced sacrifice of others, who, Biblically, many are considered their brothers and sisters who have equal rights to the prosperity of God's earthly kingdom.

Throughout the ages, it has been selfishly desired that this supposed God-ordained privileged existence be maintained at all costs, even to the point of giving Satan access to high governmental and ecclesiastical leadership positions and following his lead. This self-focused action is simply a determined effort to maintain the historical inequalities and specialized treatments that Whites have enjoyed since their initial violent and unjust occupation of America. His governmental and ecclesiastical leadership access has served to reinforce the demonic chaos of this nation in conjunction with delegitimizing Christianity.

On the front cover of the book entitled *"100 Years of Lynchings,"* the author chose to use the outline of the United States covered in blood. This cover best summarizes the spiritual state of America as it currently stands before God's throne. No part of this nation is exempt from its atrocities of injustice. Commencing with the initial European occupation, this entire nation stands guilty before the Lord because of the historical atrocities of the dominant racial group of this nation and the complicity of the White professing conservative body of Christ toward the "least" and vulnerable ones of this nation.

The entire history of this nation's professing church of God in Christ, including the twenty-first-century church, stands in rebellion against the cross of Christ and the holy throne of God, but assumes an unvalidated righteousness.

As previously noted, in Matthew 25:40 Jesus said, *"inasmuch as you did it to one of the least of these My brethren, you did it to Me*." And in verses 45 and 46, Jesus said, *"inasmuch as you did not do it to one of the least of these, you did not do it to Me. **And these will go away into everlasting punishment, but the righteous into eternal life.**"*

**Many White professing Christians in America today will admit that these injustices did happen and will sincerely be regretful. They will often say that these injustices happened before their time and had nothing to do with them; therefore, they will claim innocence because they were not personally involved. Many will find peace in this reasoning, but regretfully, it results from an unbiblical understanding.**

**This understanding is void of a critical spiritual truth. If we are benefiting from current injustices or the injustices of our forefathers, then the innocence we proclaim is invalid as long as we are reaping the benefits. Until we repent before the Lord, which must include restitution, our acts of worship and**

sacrifices will not be honored. Our lives and lifestyles will remain as examples of an inequality provided through generational ties of unjust gains. Therefore, the hypocrisy reflected through our lives of unjust prosperity will continue to serve as a detriment to evangelism and Biblical Christianity. Those with discernment whom we attempt to evangelize will only see our hypocrisy rather than focus on our erroneous testimonies of the goodness and blessings of God. The testimonies are erroneous because many of the blessings we claim were not from God but inheritances from historical unjust gains orchestrated by Satan. They resulted from the sinful history of the forefathers of the White race and are maintained by evil-inspired, ungodly selfishness, which also opposes God's "Great Commandment" of love.

This longstanding hypocrisy that exists within the lives of most White professing Christians in America has only reinforced the deception of Christianity in America.

*******************************

As attested by Biblical scripture, Christianity in America is, and always has been, a covering for evilness, a secretly and undetected designed strategy of Satan, developed on injustice, lies, and deceptions.

As noted, this strategy targeted and was instituted by Satan through the deceived dominant White race in our society. The intricate design of this evil strategy even deceived most of the elect of God until this end-time season of revelation.

*******************************

Contrary to widespread acceptance, minority races in America's unjust society live each day under the painful weight of White-initiated, institutional racism. Contrary to God's design for equality, minorities will never fully receive the benefits and fruits of the prosperity of God's kingdom, as they remain in the possession and control of the self-focused and rebellious White recipients (primarily through self-advancing governmental policies orchestrated through the democratic process, which is controlled by the White religious majority). The true message of the sacrificial cross of Christ has failed to penetrate the formidable, self-focused walls of the

White institutional church in America. It is an extension of the ungodliness reflected throughout our worldly-focused atheistic society.

---

So, the most important question at this point of our writing is, "What is the result of the historical church-supported injustices in America?" The regretful answer is given to us in the fourth chapter of the book of Genesis, the twenty-sixth chapter of Isaiah, and Proverbs 3.

As was with the blood of Abel, the voices of the blood of millions of innocent victims of injustice have been crying out to the Lord from the ground of this nation where their blood is absorbed (ref. Genesis 4:9-11, Isaiah 26:21-27:1). These innocent victims include Native Americans, Africans, African Americans, Asians, Hispanics, Latinos, aborted babies, the poor, and all others of the "least" in this society who are victims of church-supported injustice. Many were professing Christians who were martyred as servants of Almighty God. The land of America is saturated with the blood of injustice.

The lands that our homes, churches, communities, cities, and institutions of spiritual development are built upon were unjustly and, in many instances, violently taken from the Native Americans by White Americans. The lands were developed and maintained by injustice against every minority race in America. This ungodly act of self-considered Divine entitlement resulted in the slaughter, rape, and forced slavery of millions of innocent Native Americans, Africans, Asians, Hispanics, and Latinos. As noted, many of the victims were professing Christians. They were martyred after being targeted by Satan. <u>As a result, there remains a curse over America and the lives of those benefiting from the many current and historical wicked injustices perpetrated by the professing church of God in Christ, both Protestant and Catholic.</u> They benefited economically and socially while deceptively and erroneously identifying as "Christian" or "Christlike," to God's detriment. Proverbs 3:33 states, *"<u>The curse of the LORD is on the house of the wicked. But He blesses the habitation of the just</u>"* (ref. Deut. 27:19, Ps. 37:28, Matt. 25:41, Rom. 1:18, Col. 3:5,6, Gal 1:8,9). The foundation for

Christianity in America was formed on injustice, unrepented sin, deception, and lies.

The current effort by America's White society and institutional church to "whitewash" (ref. Acts 23:3) the sad reality of White church-supported institutional injustice throughout America's history is orchestrated by Satan. He desires to maintain control of the illegitimate church system that he developed through America's European fathers that still exists today. His church is currently maintained by his obedient army of strategically placed chosen vessels of undiscerning deceptive religious leaders disguised as servants of God. Their end shall be according to their works of deception (ref. $2^{nd}$ Cor. 11:13-15). They can be found throughout America, from the rural pulpits to the famous, world-renowned televangelists who have gained personal wealth at the expense of the sacrificial cross of Christ. They are those whose deceptive leadership and teachings focus attention away from the foundation of God's throne and the historical and ongoing injustices of the professing Christian church in America, its main stumbling block.

Indeed, this is a difficult reality for many to accept. As a society and professing church of God in Christ, we are now in the end-time season of reckoning. As previously stated, all current and historical strategies of evil deception will be exposed, and God's true sons (and daughters) will be revealed. The daily scenes of hate-inspired national and world chaos are evidence of Satan's long-standing strategies and influence. Indeed, these are serious times that demand serious spiritual action before the long-awaited and soon coming return of Jesus.

White Protestants and White Catholics in America must no longer ignore or deny their historic and ongoing role in this country's spiritual deception while the time is allowed for repentance. They can no longer participate in or remain in support of injustice in America and worldwide. They must accept responsibility, confess, and repent before Almighty God of their role in undermining God's foundation for His heavenly throne. Wherever applicable, they must make restitution (Restoring what has been lost, damaged, or stolen to the person or people to whom it belongs). They must become vocal and take a leadership role in every battle for justice as repented representatives of God's heavenly throne. They can no longer remain silent or passive. Along with all professing people of God in Christ, they must realize a key Biblical truth, as earlier noted: silence equates to agreement, which is sin (Eph. 5:11, James 4:17).

There can be no spiritual healing without direct, focused confrontation. A cancer cannot be cured by pretending it is not there. To have lasting spiritual healing and to align with the heart and will of God, White professing Christians in America must confess their historical and ongoing injustices perpetrated against minority races in the U.S. and abroad, their discomfort with people who are different from them, their ongoing desire to perpetuate the historical lie that they are chosen by God and superior to every other race, their willingness to take things that are not theirs and keep things they did not rightfully earn, their profound desire to lie about themselves and distort and white-wash their ungodly history throughout America and the world, their longstanding willingness to do violence to get what they want, and their willingness to ignore and turn away from involvement to secure justice for the oppressed when members of their race do violence and injustice to others because it benefits them.[1] In general, they must learn to love all others as they love themselves, a proof of one's professed belief in Jesus and God's requirement for eternal salvation.

---

This wake-up call is issued primarily to White Protestants and White Catholics. However, in addition to the moral failures of the White institutional church in America and Vatican City, the remaining church body across racial lines must also realize their involvement in reinforcing the deception of Christianity in America.

Across racial lines, it must also be noted that the universal church in America has rebelled against God and refused to prioritize and obey His kingdom's requirement of sacrificial love for all humanity as its foundation, as established in God's 'Great Commandment,' and modeled by Jesus.

It has been primarily noted in this writing that the foundational love of Biblical Christianity for minority races has rarely been evident throughout the history of the White professing Christian church in America. However, it must also be noted that this foundational requirement of Christianity has seldom been revealed throughout all races of the professing Christian body in America. Though erroneously disguised as Christianity, religion in America was developed primarily on a nonbiblical self-focused ideology.

The liberal acceptance of self-focused immorality among the entire institutional church body has only reinforced the deception of Christianity in America.

---

This writing primarily focuses on the role that injustice has played in developing and maintaining a deceptive pseudo-Christianity throughout America's history. However, for the edification of the body of Christ, we will also briefly highlight other causes that have reinforced the spiritual divide between God and the professing church of Christ and enhanced the deception of Christianity in America.

---

A longstanding spiritual problem that exists within the professing body of Christ is priests, pastors, and other church leaders preying on their vulnerable parishioners for self-satisfaction and personal gain. When people struggle with their faith and destructive issues in their personal lives, Godly spiritual leaders are needed to counsel and pray for them, reflecting the love and compassion of Christ. Christian leaders must consider the needs of all others before their own. However, a tragic reason why many people struggle with Christianity has emerged in the legal courts throughout the world, reflected in a record increase in lawsuits because of sexual abuse within the professing church of Christ. The lawsuits result from the betrayal by priests, pastors, and other church leaders who preyed on their parishioners instead of praying for them. Sexual abuse of women and children by priests, pastors, and other church leaders is of epidemic proportion in institutional churches throughout America.

The Catholic Church has received the most notoriety for this spiritual stain within the professing body of Christ, which has resulted in many parishes filing bankruptcy due to the associated legal expenses. However, as recently seen in the alarming increase of sexual abuse scandals throughout America's churches, there are no religious or denominational boundaries. This epidemic has now been documented extensively in virtually all religious communities.[2]

When confronted with allegations of sexual abuse, time and again, the church's hierarchy refused to acknowledge an awareness that these spiritual stains existed, thus making them complicit before Almighty God. When denial became impossible because of evidence, church leaders would often remove abusers and reassign them to other ministerial appointments. Church documents have revealed with clarity in both the Catholic and Protestant churches across America that, all too often, the hierarchy was more concerned with avoiding scandal and negative publicity than it was with protecting the abused. Investigative findings have proved a depraved, systemic failure of many in institutional church leadership to protect the most vulnerable under their care.

As noted, the institutional denial and cover-up of sins of sexual abuse is widespread and has existed since the end of the first-century church of the Apostles of Christ. Also, as noted, allegations of sexual misconduct are now widespread throughout all religious groups in America.

For example, the Southern Baptist Convention has recently admitted to these abuses after investigative reports determined that their leadership knew and would cover up allegations and move offenders to other communities, all while facing some of their own claims of indecency. The reports revealed a longstanding pattern of abuse cover-ups by hierarchy and their methods of covering the abusers over many decades. The hierarchy would often silence or discredit the abusers, thus bringing disgrace to God's kingdom and enhancing the deception of Christianity in America.

---

Another spiritual stain in God's kingdom is practicing homosexuals, and others practicing sexual sins are now accepted in membership in many churches throughout America. Many churches are not just receiving them into their fellowship but are ordaining practicing homosexuals as pastors and church leaders. Many churches throughout America have decided to be more accepting of unrepentant sinners as a commitment to be more inclusive. **Sin must never become an allowable or acceptable behavior within the body of Christ. Sin brings forth death** (ref. James 1:15) **and God's wrath** (Romans 1:18)!

Paul addressed this concern that was recognized in the church at Corinth. He wrote in 1st Corinthians 5:9-13, *"I wrote to you in my epistle not to keep company with sexually immoral people. Yet I certainly did not mean with the sexually immoral people of this world, or with the covetous, or extortioners, or idolaters, since then you would need to go out of the world.* **But now I have written to you not to keep company with anyone named a brother, who is sexually immoral,** *or covetous, or an idolater, or a reviler, or a drunkard, or an extortioner –* **not even to eat with such a person.** *For what have I to do with judging those also who are outside? Do you not judge those who are inside? But those who are outside, God judges.* **Therefore put away from yourselves the evil person."*

Homosexual desires are not of God and must be treated as deliverance issues. Homosexual relationships should be viewed in the larger context of the Bible's stance on sexual sin. **In summary, all sexual relationships outside of the bond of a *one-time marriage between a man and a woman are forbidden.** The Bible condemns homosexuality because it is rebellion against God's created order of male-female marriage (Romans 1:18-32) which is God's ordained design and requirement for bringing forth new life.

Currently, this intrusion of fleshly ungodliness within the professing body of Christ primarily resulted from the absence of God-anointed deliverance ministry in America's institutional churches. **The absence of the ministries of healing and deliverance also reflects an absence of the Holy Spirit.** The absence is a result of a longstanding strategy of Satan to remove all obstacles that would hinder his ability to further weaken the body of Christ. Deliverance ministry must be restored as one of the required three ministries of every church; **preaching, healing, and deliverance** (ref. Luke 4:18 and *"The Fanaticism of Christian*

*Discipleship"* for more information). Every 'true' church of God in Christ will have the required anointed threefold ministry of Christ. If you are presently involved with a religious institution that lacks any of these ministries, we suggest that you prayerfully consider a change.

[As another form of deception throughout America's churches, the lack of God's required threefold ministry is often disguised by increased fervency and theatrics from the pulpits. This deception is prevalent across all race groups, but can more often be witnessed in African American churches.]

*As a **side note**, the Bible does not condone divorce and remarriage (ref. *"The Fanaticism of Christian Discipleship"*)

---

This growing acceptance of sinful relationships within the body of Christ is a satanic strategy designed to counter God's required holiness within His church body. Many religious institutions are being further divided by this acceptance, which was never an issue of concern historically. But now that we have allowed worldliness and its values inside the once formidable and holy walls of God's first-century church model, we are saddled with the difficult task of developing God's Bible-based church amid an ever-increasing tide of satanic resistance. The Biblically bona fide church of God in Christ is characterized by holiness, justice, and righteousness and must be built on a renewed foundation of passionate, sacrificial, and unconditional love for all humanity under the guidance of the Holy Spirit.

Because of ungodliness, the floundering institutional church in America has not been able to mount a Holy Spirit-empowered response to Satan and his orchestrated battles of spiritual warfare. Through his string of victories, he has successfully thwarted all attempts at Biblical Christianity taking root in America. As earlier noted, in its place he has successfully instituted a convincing pseudo-Christianity that, to the unsuspecting believers, has similarities to true Biblical Christianity. However, it remains void of the operational role of the Holy Spirit and eternal salvation, which every professing Christian desires and anticipates. As believers in Christ, we must stand against sexual immorality at every opportunity but honor the God-given rights of everyone

(Lev. 18:22, 20:13, Deut. 5:17, 1st Cor. 6:9-10, 18, 1st Thess. 4:3-5, 1st Tim. 1:10, Rom. 1:26-27). Indeed, we are to love and minister to those who are practicing sexual sin, but according to the Bible, and contrary to a growing trend in religion in America, we should not receive them into fellowship within the body of Christ before repentance.

---

Also, as earlier noted, the "pro-choice" movement is gaining traction within the body of Christ. The sin of abortion is simply the killing of innocent babies in the mother's womb. Potential mothers are now killing their babies at an alarming rate in America. Godly mothers have historically been protective of their babies at all costs and considered them blessings from God (Ps. 127:3). The Bible is clear on all forms of murder. God commanded in Exodus 20:13, ***"Thou shalt not kill."*** The sanctity of life is revealed throughout the Bible, and by association with God, all Christians are under His spiritual umbrella and are pro-life.

**"The Sanctity of Life: Created in His image:** God places special value on human life (Gen. 1:26, 27; Ps. 8:4-6). Human life is sacred because man and woman alone were created in the image of God, and that life deserves protection. God commands His people to protect and defend innocent human life (Ezek. 16:20, 21, 36, 38). Under the Mosaic Law, the murder of another person deserved punishment by death because of the value of the life that was destroyed (Gen. 9:6; Ex. 20:13).

Scripture extends this special status and protection to human life in every stage of development and need (Is. 46:3, 4). The unborn child shares in God's image (Ps. 139:13-16). Believers are exhorted to defend and care for the sick, the elderly, and the poor (Lev. 19:32; Deut. 15:7, 8). No one is excluded from protection and care.

Throughout history, this Biblical view of the sanctity of all human life has faced opposition – most notably from those who advocate a "quality of life" viewpoint, suggesting that human life must possess certain qualities and abilities before it can be considered truly valuable and worthy of life sustenance. According to this distorted humanistic view, if the unborn child, the handicapped infant, or the elderly person does not possess these qualities, that individual is not entitled to the protection that Scripture or the Law would give.

The Bible rejects this "quality of life" view. The value of human life does not depend upon the person's functional abilities or independent viability but is assured because of the image of God, which is found in every human life. God does not measure the quality of a human being before He bestows His image. God calls upon us to extend our care and compassion to every life He has created, in every stage of development and in every need."[3]

The grisly, demonic-initiated, sin of murdering innocent babies in the mother's womb is justified by the ungodly understanding that a woman has the right to choose. A woman's body is not her own. It belongs to God and all choices regarding her body must honor God, especially the nourishing of new life. 1st Corinthians 6:19-20 states, *"Do you not know that your bodies are temples of the Holy Spirit, who is in you, whom you have received from God? You are not your own, you were bought at a price. Therefore honor God with your bodies."* The horribleness of murdering unborn babies is deceptively made acceptable in America under the medical heading of "reproductive health care." We must ask, "Why aren't America's spiritual leaders more outraged and vocal regarding the growing acceptance of the killing of the unborn. All servants of God are required to be a voice for the voiceless, those who can't speak for themselves. Only Satan and his servants would remain silent regarding sin. May God have mercy on America and protect His innocent unborn. Believers beware!

---

Another growing acceptance within the professing body of Christ that opposes His holy word is the acceptance of members of secret society organizations into Christian fellowship. This problem is prevalent throughout the twenty-first-century institutional church system and is another example of the intrusion of worldliness and its values inside the professing body of Christ.

Today, members of secret societies are represented throughout all levels of church involvement. The Bible forbids the yoking of believers with unbelievers through vows or all other means. Paul addressed this concern when he wrote in 2nd Corinthians 6:14-18, *"Do not be unequally yoked together with unbelievers. For what* *fellowship has righteousness with lawlessness? And what communion has light with darkness? And what accord has Christ with Belial? Or what part has a believer with an unbeliever? And what agreement has the temple of God with idols? For you are the temple of the living God. As God has said: "I will dwell in them and walk among them. I will be their God and they shall be My people." Therefore "Come out from among them and be separate, says the Lord. Do not touch what is unclean, **and I will receive you**." "I will be a Father to you, and you shall be My sons and daughters, Says the LORD Almighty."*

Except for marriage (1st Corinthians 7:12-14), in the Biblical perspective, anyone yoked with an unbeliever is considered an unbeliever and is not received by God. This is a startling revelation to most professing Christians as it must also have been to the church at Corinth. For the Lord clearly says in this writing by Paul, when we come out from among them and touch not what is unclean, **He will receive us.**

Our early church fathers, in agreement with God's holy word, forbade this acceptance. Members of secret society organizations were not accepted into fellowship until they had renounced their vows and membership and repented of this sin.

There is only one valid association in the kingdom of God, the universal body (brotherhood and sisterhood) of Christ, united under His precious blood as one body. Even though other organizations may openly profess Christianity, all secret society relationships are unscriptural and forbidden.

There are many available resources that give clarity to this sensitive, confusing, and deceptive topic. Recommended resources:

*"The True Alpha and Omega,"* by Minister Jerrod Smith & Brother Clifton Lucas
*"Coming Apart at the Seams,"* by Minister Fred Hatchett
(This book can be downloaded @ DontGoGreek.com)
*"College Fraternities,"* by David & Donna Carrico
*"Freemasonry,"* by Jack Harris
*"Free From Freemasonry,"* by Ron G. Campbell

Another acceptance that has enhanced the deception of Christianity is honoring pagan-initiated traditions and celebrations, such as Easter, Christmas, Valentine's Day, birthdays, etc. The celebration of Christmas and Easter was a masterful strategy of Satan instituted through the Roman Catholic church as a strategy to attract new converts by 'Christianizing' their pagan traditions. The first-century church, our Biblical model, forbade these celebrations because of their pagan association and their opposition to God's holy word. God commands us to *"Learn not the way of the heathen"* (Jer. 10:2). **To live consecrated to God, professing believers must not honor any celebrations of pagan origin. Though seemingly honoring Jesus, there are hidden demonic strategies embedded in each one against God's kingdom. Believers beware!** Though not allowed by the first-century Apostolic church leadership, these celebrations are now widely accepted and considered the two most popular events of the Christian calendar. These celebrations were instituted with an awareness of their pagan origins but an unawareness of their opposition to God's holy word. **All pagan-initiated celebrations maintain pagan components that dishonor God and secretly glorify the kingdom of darkness.** Though difficult to accept by most professing Christians, the Bible does not condone these traditional, humanity-conceived celebrations.

Technically, observing these celebrations are acts of disobedience. God clearly commanded in Deuteronomy 12:32, *"Whatever I command you, be careful to observe it; **you shall not add to it** nor take away from it"* (Also: Deut. 4:2, Prov. 30:6, Eccles. 3:14, and Rev. 22:18, 19). There is nowhere in the Bible where God allows believers to honor any pagan-initiated celebrations. Again, believers beware!

(Recommended resources for clarification are available at: www.eternalcog.org, TomorrowsWorld.org, fwa@faithfulword.com, and radiomissions.org.)

---

As Satan has realized from His days in God's kingdom before the creation of this world and humanity, God is a God of order. He does not accept anything outside of His designed order. Since the first-century Apostolic church, Satan has focused his schemes on creating spiritual disorder within Christ's church body. He has had much success because of little to no united, organized resistance from the confused and generally misled body of Christ. We will conclude by briefly highlighting one of his other strategies that has been tremendously successful for his kingdom.

---

God designed different ministry roles for men and women within His church body reflective of His order of creation. He clarified those roles in His holy word. His order was not to be altered. Contrary to the twenty-first-century trend within many religious groups, women were never to serve in leadership positions of bishops, elders, evangelists, or pastors. God strictly reserved those roles for men within His Divine order for ministry (ref. Deut. 4:2, 1$^{st}$ Cor. 11:3,8-9, 14:33-35, 1$^{st}$ Tim. 2:9-3:13, 3:1-13, 1$^{st}$ Tit. 1:5-9). Women ministering in roles of final authority are out of God's order.

In a worldly strategy of rebellion that was launched in the twentieth century, women in America sought equality in all areas of life. Women expressed their desire to serve in the same capacity as men in everything from the corporate boardroom to politics to the military to law enforcement. This women's equality movement spilled over into the professing church of Christ. Many religious organizations began ordaining women in leadership roles contrary to God's ministry design. This movement gained momentum during the "Women's Liberation Movement" in America in the 1960s and 1970s. This national movement sought equal rights, opportunities, and greater personal freedom for women in America. Satan's kingdom realized much success from this deceptive strategy as more religious groups yielded to his organized and compelling efforts. Their desire was to not offend women and remain in alignment with society rather than being an obedient, God-approved, model for required Biblical principles.

As proof of his strategy's success, many religious groups and institutions are being torn apart by this debate as it further divides the body of Christ and enhances his overall spiritual disorder strategy (Also exemplified by denominationalism). Also, many renowned theological seminaries are openly and boldly rebelling against God's Divine order. Perhaps, in some instances, for the purpose of receiving a needed financial gain, they are preparing women for unbiblical leadership roles in ministry that God will never approve. The primary purpose of theological seminaries is to educate students in scripture and theology and prepare them for their God-given ministry calling. If seminaries are faltering on this major ministry concern regarding the Biblical instructions of the role of Women in ministry, it creates a cloud of doubt over all else that they teach and proclaim. It brings into question their legitimacy as God-ordained institutions of Biblical knowledge and spiritual development. **Students beware!** (ref. *"The Fanaticism of Christian Discipleship"* for more deceptive strategies orchestrated by Satan reinforcing the deception of Christianity in America.)

We realize there will be much opposition to this sensitive subject as Satan develops counter-strategies that always result after Biblical revelations and spiritual corrections. We briefly highlight this strategy in this writing, realizing that there will be many questions to be addressed. We suggest the following resources for more detail:

*"Leadership For Women in The Church"*
By: Susan Hunt and Peggy Hutcheson

*"Evangelistic Women: A Study of Women's Ministries"*
By: Pamela Stewart

*"Women in the Ministry?"* By: Dr. Russell K. Tardo
(This booklet can be obtained at www.faithfulword.com)

(Tony Evans, the senior pastor of the Oak Cliff Bible Fellowship in Dallas, Texas, has an excellent twenty-seven-minute presentation that can be viewed on You Tube: *"The Importance of Women's Gifts in Ministry."* Also, John MacArthur, the pastor of Grace Community Church in Sun Valley, California, has an excellent presentation on You Tube entitled *"Does the Bible Permit a Woman to Preach?"*)

Women serving in male-ordained ministry leadership positions feel strongly that God called them to do so, though the Word of God does not permit it, and there are no examples in the Bible to validate their feelings. **God never allows anything in opposition to His holy word. Satan is the great deceiver.**

In this end-time season of revelation, spiritual correction, and restoration, women who are serving in ministry leadership roles outside of God's design must cease doing so, repent of their error, and accept God's Divine order for ministry leadership. God's Divine order will be restored in this end-time season within His obedient remnant. **Regretfully, out of pride and/or Biblical confusion, many will continue to oppose Him.** Again, we must be thankful that God is allowing an opportunity for correction and repentance before Jesus returns to earth.

We must have a Biblical basis for doing the things we do. When we do things in opposition to God's holy word, even though they are intended to glorify Him, we allow access for Satan to enter our lives and those under our spiritual umbrellas. Twenty-first-century professing Christians must pray for discernment and honor God's holy word at all costs. They must adopt the first-century church's policy and model of not doing anything that dishonors God.

*****************************************

**Because of their dominance, the White Protestant church in America and the Roman Catholic church of Vatican City have exerted tremendous influence through religion worldwide.**

**The overwhelming majority of resource material and church-related information used throughout the worldwide church body primarily are direct or indirect products of these two leading institutions. Many of their published products disguise hidden deceptive schemes orchestrated by Satan that have steered their ungodly courses of action since the first-century Apostolic church (Especially their publications that address Christian discipleship and Christian financial stewardship).**

**Satan's evil and deceptive schemes are purposed to marginalize or prevent the required operational role of the Holy Spirit and distort the body of Christ's understanding of Biblical Christianity and the level of faith, holiness, obedience, and sacrificial love that it demands and that pleases God. (Prov. 3:5,6, Mk. 12:30,31, Heb. 11:6, 1st Cor. 13, Phil 2:8)**

The book of Acts is a model picture of God's church. It is His required model for His faithful servants to receive His available empowerment for spiritual wholeness through the indwelling presence of the Holy Spirit. God's empowerment is required to counter Satan's deceptions effectively and reveal God's true character to this unbelieving world. The twenty-first-century church must return to God's Biblical model and diligently hold true to it. It must purge itself of all satanic schemes that have confused and "derailed" the body of Christ spiritually since the first-century Apostolic church. Regretfully, Satan's convincing schemes have been tremendously successful in deceiving even many of the elect of God throughout the following centuries. Thankfully, Satan's schemes are now being revealed for the restoration of Christ's professing body on earth before the long-awaited and soon coming return of Jesus. (Reference the companion resource, *"The Fanaticism of Christian Discipleship,"* for more revelatory information and clarification of Christian consecration and God's required empowerment.)

************************************

Demonically induced deception and human rebellion against God have been prevalent within God's creation since its beginning, starting with the demonically induced rebellion of Adam and Eve. The rebellion revealed throughout America's history by those who professed Christianity was also seen in the lives of the children of Israel throughout the Old Testament. They continually rebelled against God and sought restoration after experiencing the results of His anger.

**The universal church in America must end all forms of rebellion against God and His Divine kingdom order and prioritize Holy Spirit-guided spiritual change during this end-time season of revelation, spiritual correction, and restoration. Failure to do so may result in an undesirable, fearful, and unexpected eternal separation from God.**

Regardless of your religious affiliation or beliefs, Jesus still requires His character within each member of His church body, as clarified in Biblical scriptures. **Without faith, love, holiness, and obedience, all else is vanity, and in spite of sincerity, no one**

**living in opposition to His character will see Him** (ref. Heb. 5:9, 12:14, 1st Cor. 13:3, 1st Pet. 1:14-16).

Restoration must begin with individual and united fervent prayer in humility for revelation and the required guidance of the Holy Spirit. It requires a personal and nationwide church effort of confession, repentance, and restitution (ref. 2nd Chron. 7:14).

---

**Holy and most merciful Father,**
*"He who has an ear, let him hear what the Spirit says to the churches"* **(Rev. 2:29).**

---

*"We have sinned with our fathers, we have committed iniquity, we have done wickedly."*
**Psalm 106:6**

---

### Words of God to the Twenty-first-century church:

*"Yet from the days of your fathers you have gone away from My ordinances and have not kept them. Return to Me, and I will return to you," Says the LORD of hosts."*
**Malachi 3:7**

*"So you, by the help of your God, return; Observe mercy and justice, and wait on your God continually."*
**Hosea 12:6**

*"Let us search out and examine our ways, and turn back to the LORD."*
**Lamentations 3:40**

*"Draw near to God and He will draw near to you. Cleanse your hands, you sinners; and purify your hearts, you double-minded."*

**James 4:8**

*"Therefore say to them, 'Thus says the LORD of hosts: "Return to Me," says the LORD of hosts, "and I will return to you," says the LORD of hosts."*

**Zechariah 1:3**

*"Let the wicked forsake his way, And the unrighteous man his thoughts; Let him return to the LORD, And He will have mercy on him; And to our God, For He will abundantly pardon.*
*'For My thoughts are not your thoughts, nor are your ways My ways,' says the LORD."*

**Isaiah 55:7, 8**

*"If my people, which are called by my name, shall humble themselves, and pray, and seek my face, and turn from their wicked ways; then will I hear from heaven, and will forgive their sin, and heal their land."*

**2nd Chronicles 7:14**

*"For, as I have often told you before and now say again even with tears, many live as enemies of the cross of Christ. Their destiny is destruction, their god is their stomach, and their glory is in their shame. Their mind is on earthly things. But our citizenship is in heaven. And we eagerly await a Savior from there, the Lord Jesus Christ."*

**Philippians 3:18-20**

# Chapter 17

## Conclusion

Many discerning believers are praying for a better day for this nation and world. The salvation of the many lost souls who profess Christianity but remain unconverted must become a spiritual priority for those who are spiritually enlightened about God's heart and kingdom priorities. Many who do not deny this nation's ungodly history feel that it has made much improvement from its documented history of racial injustice and hatred toward the 'least' in our society. However, recent events reveal that there is still much work to be done before this country may be considered a "Christian" nation. Major spiritual changes are required, which must begin with the professing people of God, primarily the dominant White Protestant and White Catholic churches in America. **Sadly, throughout its history in America, the White institutional church has practiced a deceptive, demonically induced pseudo-Christianity, oblivious of its true spiritual status before Almighty God.**

In this writing on justice, we have revealed many anti-Christian acts that have traditionally been condoned and, in many instances, orchestrated by the White institutional church in America and Vatican City. Instead of being on the front lines of opposition to Satan's long-standing strategies of death, theft, and destruction (ref. John 10:10), in agreement with their forefathers, many have instead chosen to oppose God and His kingdom's design of unconditional, sacrificial love for all humanity. This was the revealed model of God's kingdom through the sacrificial life and death of Jesus. He must not just remain our Lord and Savior for eternal salvation but our model for how we are to live and love all others sacrificially.

The spiritual battle lines are drawn, and everyone who professes Christianity must now decide whether they will stand for human justice as representatives of God's throne or the historical evils of injustice revealed throughout American and world history. A new day is dawning as the world prepares for the return of Jesus. In this end-time season, the light of God will be revealed through His sons and daughters, His remnant of empowered, dedicated servants. As earlier noted, the eternal salvation for many lost souls whom Satan is deceiving "hangs in the balance."

Injustice in any form is unacceptable to God and must remain unacceptable to His servants. Accepting injustice in any form is a blatant misrepresentation of God's throne. Human justice must remain a priority for every professing believer in Christ. They must be ready to make the required sacrifices to uplift the oppressed to a state of wholeness and shared prosperity in all life matters, at home and abroad. They must strive to be found on the 'front lines' of every battle for justice as representatives of God's throne.

Regardless of your past experiences or ancestral ties, we pray that you now see the true light illuminating from God and feel an urgency within your heart to become more involved with human justice as a representative of His heavenly throne. However, if you are not physically able to do so, we recommend that you consider supporting those who are on the 'front lines' with your prayers and finances.

We suggest that you consider the following agency for prayer and financial support:

The Equal Justice Initiative (eji.org)

As previously noted, God's professing but wayward church body has entered a life-altering and world-changing period of revelation, spiritual correction, and restoration. The long-anticipated day of eternal reckoning is on the horizon. All spiritually rebellious professing Christians in America must boldly turn from their sinful ways and the demonically induced evilness of injustice. As noted, this evilness began with the European occupation of this country. It was systematically reinforced by deceptive demonic strategies that primarily targeted the dominant White professing church of Christ throughout America's existence, who must now become gatekeepers of righteousness as repented and faithful ambassadors of God's heavenly throne. Those who prioritize and honor this mandate of God will be included in His end-time remnant of obedient servants, His end-time army, which is currently being developed.

---

In the appendix of this book, we gave a pictorial example and review of the historical injustices of this nation. This example of White church-supported injustice throughout the Bible Belt, and to varying extents, throughout America, highlights the hypocrisy that has existed in Christianity throughout America's history. Though we highlighted the historical injustice in public education that has not been well-documented and, in far too many instances, whitewashed, injustice to varying extents has been reflected in every aspect of our American society.

The professing White church in America has traditionally chosen to downplay or overlook the seriousness of its involvement in American injustice and its willing participation in Satan's orchestrated attacks against God's throne. **As a result, all else that has seemingly been accomplished under the banner of "Christianity" has only been an orchestrated smoke screen disguising the wide and enticing gate to damnation for far too many unsuspecting souls.**

The apostle Paul clearly stated in 1$^{st}$ Corinthians 13:1-3, *"Though I speak with the tongues of men and of angels, but have not love, I have become as sounding brass or a clanging cymbal.*

*And though I have the gift of prophecy, and understand all mysteries and all knowledge, and though I have all faith, so that I could remove mountains, but have not love, I am nothing.*

*And though I bestow all my goods to feed the poor, and though I give my body to be burned, but have not love, it profits me nothing."*

**In summary, Paul simply says that without love, anything that we do in the kingdom of God profits us nothing and is of no esteem in God's sight.**

Because of self-focused motives and deceptive spiritual leadership, many professing Christians in America have missed the narrow gate leading to eternal salvation.

---

We will conclude this writing with a seldom-discussed but eternally important warning issued by Jesus that is applicable to this writing and all professing believers of Christ. This warning is given to the universal church at large.

Jesus stated in Matthew 7:13-14, *"Enter ye in at the strait gate; for wide is the gate and broad is the way, that leadeth to destruction, and many there be which go in thereat:*

*Because strait is the gate, and narrow is the way, which leadeth unto life, and few there be that find it."* (KJV)

In opposition to the wide gate of salvation that, by and large, twenty-first-century religion professes, Matthew Henry stated in his commentary regarding Jesus' warning;

"The account that is given is of the bad way of sin and the good way of holiness. There are but two ways, right and wrong, good and evil, the way to heaven, and the way to hell; in the one of which all of us walk: no middle place hereafter, no middle way now: the distinction of the children of men into saints and sinners, godly and ungodly, will swallow up all to eternity.

Here, an account is given to us of the way of sin and sinners, both what is the best and what is the worst of it.

That which allures multitudes into it and keeps them in it; *the gate is wide, and the way broad,* and there are many travelers in that way. First, you will have an abundance of liberty in that way; the gate is wide, and stands wide open to tempt those that go right on their way. You may go in at this gate with all your lusts about you; it gives no check to your appetites, to your passions: you may walk in the way of your heart and in the sight of your eyes; that gives room enough. It is a broad way, for there is nothing to hedge in those that walk in it, but they wander endlessly; a broad way, for there are many paths in it; there is a choice of sinful ways, contrary to each other, but all paths are in this broad way. Secondly, you will have an abundance of company in that way; many there be that go in at this gate and walk in this way. If we follow the multitude, it will be to do evil; if we go with the crowd, it will be the wrong way. It is natural for us to be inclined to go down the stream and do as most do, but it is too great a compliment to be willing to be damned for company, and to go to hell with them, because they will not go to heaven with us: if many perish, we should be the more cautious.

That which should affright us all from it is that it leads to destruction. Death, eternal death, is at the end of it (and the way of sin tends to it), everlasting destruction from the presence of the Lord. **Whether it be the high way of open profaneness <u>or the back way of close hypocrisy</u>, if it be a way of sin, it will be our ruin if we repent not.**

Here is an account given to us of the way of holiness.

What there is in it that frightens many from it; let us know the worst of it, that we may sit down and count the cost. Christ deals faithfully with us and tells us, first, that the gate is straight.

Conversion and regeneration are the gate by which we enter into this way, in which we begin a life of faith and serious godliness; out of a state of sin into a state of grace, we must pass by the new birth (Jn. 3:3,5). This is a strait gate, hard to find, and hard to get through; like a passage between two rocks (1$^{st}$ Sam. 14:4). **There must be a new heart, and a new spirit, and old things must pass away. The bent of the soul must be changed, corrupt habits and customs broken off; what we have been doing all our days must be undone. We must swim against the stream; much opposition must be struggled with and broken through, from without and from within.** It is easier to set a man against all the world than against himself, and yet this must be in conversion. It is a strait gate, for we must stoop, or we cannot go in at it; we must become as little children; high thoughts must be brought down; nay, we must strip, must deny ourselves, put off the world, put off the old man; **we must be willing to forsake all for our interest in Christ.** The gate is strait to all, but to some straighter than others, as to the rich, to some that have been long prejudiced against religion. The gate is straight; blessed be God, it is not shut up, nor locked against us, nor kept with a flaming sword, as it will be shortly (Matt 25:10).

Secondly, the way is narrow. We are not in heaven as soon as we have gotten through the strait gate, nor in Canaan as soon as we have gotten through the Red Sea; no, we must go through a wilderness, must travel a narrow way, **hedged in by the divine law,** which is exceedingly broad, and that makes the way narrow; self must be denied, the body kept under, corruptions mortified, that is as a right eye and a right hand; daily temptations must be resisted; duties must be done that are against our inclination. We must endure hardness, must wrestle and be in agony, must watch in all things, and walk with care and circumspection. We must go through much tribulation. It is an afflicted way, a way hedged about with thorns blessed be God; it is not hedged up. The bodies we carry about with us and the corruptions remaining in us make the way of our duty difficult, but as the understanding grows more and more sound, it will open and enlarge and grow more and more pleasant.

Thirdly, the gate being so straight and the way so narrow, it is not strange that there are but few that find it, and choose it. Many pass it by, through carelessness they will not be at the pains to find it; they are well as they are, and see no need to change their way. Others look upon it, but shun it; they like not to be so limited and restrained. Those that are going to heaven are but few, compared to those that are going to hell; a remnant, a little flock like the grape-gleanings of the vintage; as the eight that were saved in the ark (1$^{st}$ Pet. 3:20). This discourages many; they are loth to be singular, to be solitary; but instead of stumbling at this, say rather, 'If so few are going to heaven, there shall be one the more for me.'

Let us see what there is in this way, which, notwithstanding this, should invite us all to it; it leads to life, to present comfort in the favor of God, which is the life of the soul; to eternal bliss, the hope of which, at the end of our way, should reconcile us to all the difficulties and inconveniences of the road. Life and godliness are put together (2$^{nd}$ Pet. 1:3); the gate is straight and the way narrow and uphill, but one hour in heaven will make amends for it.

The great concern and duty of every one of us, in consideration of all this; ***Enter ye in at the strait gate.*** The matter is fairly stated; life and death, good and evil, are set before us; both the ways, and both the ends: now let the matter be taken entirely and considered impartially, and then choose you this day which you will walk in; Nay, the matter determines itself, and will not admit of a debate. No man, in his wits, would choose to go to the gallows because it is a smooth, pleasant way to it, nor refuse the offer of a palace and a throne, because it is a rough, dirty way to it; yet such absurdities as these are men guilty of, in the concerns of their souls. Delay not, therefore; deliberate not any longer, but enter ye in at the strait gate; knock at it by sincere and constant prayers and endeavors, and it shall be opened; nay, a wide door shall be opened, and an effectual one. It is true, we can neither go in, nor go on, without the assistance of divine grace, but it is as true, that grace is freely offered, and shall not be wanting to those that seek it, and submit to it. Conversion is hard work, but it is needful, and blessed be God, it is not impossible if we strive.[2]

---

Regarding this challenging statement of Jesus, Smith Wigglesworth stated, "Yes, beloved, this means you will have to work for it because your own nature will interfere with you; your friends will often stand in the way. Your position will many times almost bring you to a place where you will be doomed if you take that stand.

Strive to enter in. Seek to be worthy to enter in. Let God be honored by your leaving behind the things that you know are taking your life, hindering your progress, blighting your prospects, and ruining your mind, for nothing will dull the mind's perceptions like touching earthly things that are not clean. Those who are entering in are judging themselves so that they will not be condemned with the world (1st Cor. 11:32).

Oh, that God the Holy Spirit will have a choice with us today, that we will judge ourselves so that we are not condemned with the world! *"For if we would judge ourselves, we would not be judged" (v. 31).* What is it to judge yourself? If the Lord speaks, if He says, "Let it go," no matter if it is as dear as your right eye, you must let it go. If it is as costly as your right foot, you must let it go. It is far better to let it go. Strive to enter in."[3]

The apostle Paul stated in Acts 24:16, *"So I strive always to keep my conscience clear before God and man."*

---

Jesus was asked the question, *"Lord, are there few who are saved?"* Jesus replied,

***"Strive to enter through the narrow gate, for many, I say to you, will seek to enter and shall not be able.***

***When once the Master of the house has risen up and shut the door, and you begin to stand outside and knock at the door, saying, 'Lord, Lord, open for us,' and He will answer and say to you, 'I do not know you, where you are from,' then you will begin to say, 'We ate and drank in Your presence, and You taught in our streets.'***

***But He will say, 'I tell you I do not know you, where you are from. Depart from Me, all you workers of iniquity.'***

***There will be weeping and gnashing of teeth, when you see Abraham and Isaac and Jacob and all the prophets in the kingdom of God, and yourselves thrust out*** (ref. Lk. 16:19-31).

***They will come from the east and the west, from the north and the south, and sit down in the kingdom of God.***

***<u>And indeed, there are last who will be first, and there are first who will be last."</u>*** (Lk. 13:24-30, KJV)

Since the European occupation of this nation, far too many professing Christians have assumed the sufficiency of God's grace without living as His chosen ambassadors for justice and righteousness. Disregarding Jesus' warning, most professing White Christians throughout America's history have prioritized the White race as being first in God's kingdom at the expense of all minority races in America (also ref. James 5:1-6). Many have lived nonchalantly or, in far too many instances, in opposition to human justice and righteousness. If we are in that number, we may be sadly disappointed throughout eternity. Satan is a master of religious deception. He constructs his gate so that it will look like the door to heaven, and the institutional church in America has, throughout the history of this nation, shown to be a willing participant in promoting his deceptions.

*If we are not warriors for justice and righteousness, there is no greater proof that we have not received Jesus as Lord.*

As the apostle Paul reminded the Thessalonians, ***"He (Jesus) will punish those who do not know God and do not obey the gospel of our Lord Jesus. They will be punished with everlasting destruction and shut out from the presence of the Lord and from the majesty of his power on the day he comes to be glorified in his holy people and to be marveled at among all those who have believed."*** (2$^{nd}$ Thess. 1:8-10, NIV)

Regretfully, we can do nothing for the many who have perished in rebellion against God's holy throne and His sacrificial commandments for human relations as stated in His holy word due to misinformation, greed, spiritual blindness, and/or hard-heartedness. However, we can determine our eternal destiny today by renouncing all evilness, fully turning to God, living as ambassadors of His heavenly throne, and reflecting Christ's sacrificial love to all humanity.

*Now is the time of new beginnings, which begin with repentance. Share the news of hope!*

## **As a closing commitment:**

*"Now therefore, fear the LORD, serve Him in sincerity and in truth, and put away the gods which your fathers served on the other side of the River and in Egypt, Serve the LORD!*
*And if it seems evil to you to serve the LORD, choose for yourselves this day whom you will serve, whether the gods which your fathers served that were on the other side of the River, or the gods of the Amorites, in whose land you dwell.*
*But as for me and my house, we will serve the LORD."*

**Joshua 24:14, 15**

---

*"True peace is not merely the absence of tension; it is the presence of justice."*

*"We will not be satisfied until justice rolls down like waters."*

**- Dr. Martin Luther King, Jr. -**

---

*"Seek justice for all, or all else is for naught."*

**- Walter B. Pennington -**

---

# **Concluding Prayer**

Father God, I ask that You fully open my eyes and heart to the needs of Your hurting world, especially those near me. Forgive me for my selfishness and not being responsive to those needs in the past. Forgive me for all acts of injustice in my past life and my family lineage.

Omniscient (all-knowing) Father, I ask that You reveal any wrongfully received advantages in my life through my actions or family lineage. I ask that You do so that I may renounce them according to the leading of Your Holy Spirit. Wherever possible, enable me to resolve any hurt, loss, or inconvenience I have caused to others and restore to the rightful owner(s) anything in my possession as an act of restitution (ref. Lev. 6:1-5, Num. 5:5-7, Lk. 19:8).

My omnipotent Father (all-powerful), I ask that You break all legal rights of generational spirits operating behind a curse throughout my family lineage and myself. Please, Father, deliver me from all evil influences and strongholds in my life. Thank you for the revelation of the foundation of Your heavenly throne. Thank You for awakening me from my uncaring spiritual stupor and enabling me to see Your heart's concerns and the light of salvation. Thank You for reminding me of the need to be a reflection of Your light by displaying Your sacrificial love to all humanity.

Father God, I ask that You entrust me with the additional resources to fulfill every need of the oppressed that You present to me in my lifetime here on earth. I truly desire to bring everyone to an equal status of existence in Your kingdom here on earth in obedience to Your "Great Commandment" and Jesus' new commandment for Christian discipleship (Jn. 13:34), regardless of our differences.

Enable me to love everyone sacrificially as Jesus loves me. Truly empower me for the task ahead as an anointed representative of Your heavenly throne.

I ask this for Your glory, in the name of Jesus. Amen.

# Epilogue
## *(and prophecy*, Isa. 58 and 59*)*

White professing Christians standing united against injustice as repented representatives of God's holy throne would finally end the demonic-induced nightmare of injustice in America. It would enable professing Christians to truly realize the will of God regarding human relations for the first time in American history. Also, it would lay the foundation for establishing Biblical Christianity in America, validated by God's presence, power, and oversight.

In breaking the historical curse over America, God's presence and oversight would make His peace and unity evident from shore to shore (Prov. 3:33). America would truly become *"One nation under God, indivisible* (inseparable from God and each other)*, with liberty and justice for all."*

Without its current evil-induced religious deception and hypocrisy, America would become a "shining light on a hill," revealing the glory of God to the world. *"But the path of the just is as the shining light, that shineth more and more unto the perfect day"* (Prov. 4:18, KJV).

With God's presence and oversight, every false religion would be exposed under His ever-revealing light, and *"every tongue would confess that Jesus Christ is Lord, to the glory of God the Father"* (Phil. 2:11). Jesus could then joyfully return to receive a repented, glorious and unspotted bride.

As one church body united under the sacrificial cross of Christ, let us join in prayer and dedicated action for this heavenly desire to become a reality. Through our unified effort, God will truly be glorified in America.

*Merciful Father, may "Your will be done on earth as it is in heaven." Amen.*

(Two separate and unequal school systems)

# Appendix

(A pictorial review and example of the segregated White church-supported racial injustices in the southern Bible Belt of America public school systems. Though this example was in the state of Mississippi, these injustices were typical throughout the Bible Belt, leading to the Brown vs. Board of Education ruling by the United States Supreme Court in 1954, mandating public school integration.)

## **Cruger White school main exterior – 1950s**

This well-built school facility was equipped with the modern conveniences of that era. The need for the federally-forced school integration mandate can easily be understood when comparing the Cruger and Tchula White schools with the African American schools in those towns and all other facilities in the state.

After federally-forced integration, this public school facility was converted to the private Cruger-Tchula Academy in 1965 to maintain racial segregation. How the conversion from public to private happened is uncertain. But what is certain is that a newly-constructed gymnasium for this private academy was built on land that a local segregated White denominational Church previously owned. It did not accept African American students after the conversion to a private academy. It closed down in 2001.

This was the first segregated academy in Mississippi. Whites in many other towns followed their lead.

## **Cruger White school east view – 1950s**

This view highlights the modern masonry-constructed details of this building, with plenty of windows for natural interior lighting and manicured open space for outside activities.

This school was fully equipped with comfortable, well-lighted classrooms, a cafeteria and hot lunch program, modern indoor bathroom facilities, and cold water fountains, as was found in practically every other racially segregated White school throughout Mississippi. Every necessary convenience missing in the African American schools could be found in the White schools.

## **Cruger White school teacherage – 1950s**

A school teacherage was a house or other residential building designed to house one or more school teachers or administrators and their families. They were usually located on or near the school grounds for convenience and ease of access. These were comfortable accommodations provided to White teachers and White school administrators by the Holmes County school board. These were prevalent with the White schools throughout Holmes County, Mississippi.

No such housing was provided for African American teachers or school administrators in the county.

## Cruger White school auditorium – 1950s

This auditorium was typical of the auditoriums in White schools throughout Holmes County, Mississippi. They were usually equipped with comfortable seating, pianos, and custom-designed draperies, as seen in this picture, and the décor was appropriate for maximizing the spacing and comfort for large gatherings.

None of the African American schools in Holmes County had this level of quality or space for mass gatherings of the student body.

## **Cruger African American school exterior – 1950s**

It may be hard to believe that this was the actual public school facility for African Americans in Cruger. The contrast between this facility and the White facility in Cruger was extreme. This picture does not reveal the complete story of insufficiency. The exterior sides of the building were only partially covered with roof felt. Therefore, the interior was not adequately protected from unfavorable weather conditions. There was no plumbing or running water in this school and no cafeteria or hot lunch program. Students and teachers had to bring lunch from home. There was no auditorium or area for mass gatherings. Off to the right of this picture, not seen, were two crude outhouse structures used for bathrooms: one for boys and one for girls (pictured on the next page). Obviously, the all-white Mississippi Board of Health had no concern for the hygiene and well-being of African Americans.

## **Typical outhouse (bathroom) facility**

Though no pictures could be found of the actual outhouses of the African American school in Cruger, Mississippi, the above image closely resembles them.

Two outhouses located behind the school facility were used for bathrooms: one for boys and one for girls. These were simple structures comprised of a single toilet seat carved from wood. The toilets were situated over a dug-out pit for collecting the waste material. There were no running water or face bowls for hand washing or mechanisms for treating or disposing of waste material. To avoid using them, the teachers would drive to Mrs. Amy Thurmond's house (a teacher) when necessary.

Odious outhouses were commonly used at rural African American schools throughout Holmes County before the 1960s. No White schools were required to endure these unsanitary and unjust conditions.

## **Cruger African American school interior – 1950s**

This classroom was typical for African American schools in Holmes County, Mississippi. The use of a single coal-burning heater was common. There were no safeguards between the students and the heaters. Smoke was a common nuisance in the building because of inadequate smoke ventilation. Notice the one light bulb hanging from an unprotected electrical wire from the dilapidated ceiling and the crude bookshelf on the left wall. Annually, the floors would be mopped with motor oil to preserve the wood, so the students and teachers were constantly exposed to the hazardous fumes. After many decades, I still remember the sickening smell of the oil-mopped floors. The all-white school board's disdain for African Americans was reflected in these atrocities. Teachers complaining would often result in dismissal.

## **Cruger African American school exterior – 1950s**

The overall conditions of this school were deplorable. The small room to the left in this picture was an actual classroom. It was unheated in the cold winter months. The students who sat in the back row had to crawl across desks to get to their seats. There was no room for an aisle to allow passage. Rev. Walter B. Pennington, Sr. briefly served as the school principal and taught classes in this room until resigning to devote full time to God's ministry in Nettleton, Mississippi. Mrs. Pennington succeeded him as the school principal.

The dilapidated basketball goal pictured was actually one end of the basketball court. Unlike the White schools with indoor gymnasiums and comfortable stadium-type seating, spectators had to bring chairs, stand, or sit on the ground during basketball games.

## Cruger African American school interior – 1950s

Curtains were commonly used in African American schools to separate classrooms. Each classroom in the Cruger school was comprised of three different grade levels. Noise between the classes was a common distraction. The one chair out front was the teacher's only work area. None of these deplorable inadequacies were found in the White schools in Holmes County. These deplorable conditions were the result of a White church-supported, all-white racist school board that had little regard for the welfare of African Americans. I am familiar with this particular school because I attended there through the fourth grade.

## Tchula White school main building – 1950s

This building was one of six facilities for the White school in Tchula, Mississippi. After federally forced integration, the student body and administration abandoned this facility, and the White citizens formed the Cruger-Tchula private academy in Cruger to maintain racial segregation. The student body and administration changed overnight from White to African American. As a backlash to this change, there was much White resistance to African Americans utilizing this facility and coming into the White community.

An arson fire destroyed this beautiful, modern-constructed building on August 15, 1969. To this day, no one has been charged with this crime.

## **Tchula White school main exterior – 1950s**

This picture reveals the front entrance to the main building, which was destroyed by an arson fire after federally forced integration. As previously stated, the all-white fire department did not save the burning building. It is puzzling that with the widespread design of the building, none of it was saved. It is uncertain if the fire department even responded to the fire. This picture also reveals the unique architectural design of this impressive masonry-constructed building. This design was unusual for public schools of that era, especially in Holmes County, the poorest county in Mississippi. As can be easily seen from these pictures, all-white school board-approved expenditures for White schools in Holmes County, as throughout the Bible Belt, far exceeded those for African American schools.

## **Tchula White school gymnasium – 1950s**

After an arson fire destroyed the main building in August 1969, this gymnasium was used for classrooms. The news of this adjustment was not well-received by the surrounding White community. An arson fire destroyed this building on December 12, 1969. There is no record of anyone being charged with this crime. After this second burning, the African American student body was relocated away from this racist, all-white community to a much safer location. Mrs. Susie Pennington was the principal of this school during those turbulent times until it was officially closed. Thankfully, she was Divinely protected throughout this ordeal of overt White church-supported racism.

## Tchula White school vocational building – 1950s

Vocational buildings were not typical in the Holmes County school system but could be found at some White schools. These buildings were provided for students to learn how to do a job that required special skills. This was one of several means for White students' advantage in the job market and career options before and after high school graduation. No African American school in the county had school board-supported vocational training for students.

## **Tchula White school principal's home – 1950s**

School-provided housing for principals in Holmes County was only provided for White school principals. This beautifully designed home was never allowed to be utilized for that purpose after Whites vacated this school facility because of federally forced school integration.

## Tchula White school teacherage – 1950s

[See explanation for Cruger White school teacherage]

## Tchula White school auditorium – 1950s

Like the White school auditorium at Cruger, this beautiful auditorium was well-equipped for that era with custom-designed draperies and comfortable seating. No expense was spared in the White schools in Holmes County. Holmes County has traditionally been one of the poorest counties in Mississippi. However, it was not uncommon to find grand pianos in White public school auditoriums, as pictured above. There was no comparison between this all-white school and the African American school in Tchula, with no auditorium or adequate mass gathering space. This auditorium was located in the main building and was destroyed in the hate-inspired arson fire on August 15, 1969, after public school integration.

## **Tchula White school 1st grade – 1950s**

    Notice the contrast between this Tchula White school 1st-grade class and the Tchula African American school 1st-grade class on the next page. Notice the quality of students' desks with adequate storage space, ideal classroom spacing for learning, large classroom size reflecting more building planning and construction detail, and plentiful supply of updated learning resources, including charts, graphs, and a classroom piano. As you notice these items and conditions, notice the lack of them in the Tchula African American school.

    These contrasts were typical throughout the Holmes County school system and public schools throughout the southern Bible Belt to varying degrees. This classroom was destroyed in the arson fire in August 1969.

## **Tchula African American school 1<sup>st</sup> grade –1950s**

Again, as was typical in African American schools, notice the lack of learning resources in contrast to the picture of the Tchula White school 1<sup>st</sup>-grade class. Usually, textbooks and learning resources in African American schools were bought new and used as resources in the White schools. They were provided to the African American schools after the learning resources in the White schools were updated. Many of the used books and materials would be marred with markings and missing pages. Usually, there were not enough books or resources for all of the students in African American schools. Students were often required to share books and other learning resources. Notice the only two textbooks on the table to be shared compared to the Tchula White school 1<sup>st</sup>-grade class.

## Tchula African American school 6th and 7th grades – 1950s

This picture of two classrooms in the African American school in Tchula was typical of the African American schools in Holmes County, Mississippi. Many classes were overcrowded and included multiple grades. As noted in the Cruger African American school, curtains were commonly used to separate classes, and a single light bulb hanging from the dilapidated ceiling on an unprotected wire provided the primary lighting. This was common for most African American schools. Needless to say, the lighting and resource materials were inadequate for reading and learning. Notice the shameful conditions of this classroom setting and the lack of books and learning resources. African American teachers had to be very creative in overcoming these unjust obstacles.

## Tchula African American school building - 1950s

This was the one school building for African American students in Tchula, Mississippi, compared to the six-building facility for the White school. Though overcrowded, inadequately furnished, and equipped, it was used for classrooms and all other school functions. The White school was comprised of the main building for classrooms and administration, a separate vocational building, a modern gymnasium, a teacherage, a principal's house, and a sixth building (Its use is uncertain). In addition to being paid less than White teachers and principals, no housing was provided for African American teachers or principals.

## Tchula African American school north view 1950s

This side view of the African American school in Tchula, Mississippi, reveals the much-needed building addition to the rear of the original school building. Though a recent addition, notice the exhaust chimney reflecting the outdated heating source.

# **Appendix Summary**

The unjust, ungodly disparity between African American and White schools in Holmes County, Mississippi, was typical of public schools throughout the Southern Bible Belt before the Brown vs. Board of Education ruling by the United States Supreme Court in 1954.

After viewing these pictorial examples of White church-supported racial injustice in the Holmes County public school system, it becomes easier to see the importance of this Supreme Court ruling for equality in public school education in the United States. If left to the various racist, church-supported, all-white school boards and lawmakers throughout the South, the required changes necessary for equality would not have been realized.

It was somewhat comforting to know that the 1954 U.S. Supreme Court, comprised of all White men, ruled in favor of justice and righteousness during that turbulent time of overt racial hostility and religious rebellion throughout the U.S. Unlike the current U.S. Supreme Court that is influenced by political priorities and public opinion, the integrity of the 1954 U.S. Supreme Court, reflected in their commitment to the solemn oath made before God Almighty, was paramount. It factored into this unpopular ruling for justice and righteousness. They expected and received much public backlash from Whites who felt betrayed but were not deterred from honoring their sacred oath. As shown in this writing, that era was characterized by widespread racial hatred, White church-supported injustice, White supremacy, and White church rebellion against God's designed order for human relations. It also enhanced the hope among Christ's remnant of true believers, seeing that the spiritual evilness and confusion shown in race relations throughout the South's Bible Belt were not as prevalent in some areas of America's White society, as proven by this all-white Supreme Court.

(As a **side note**, the composition of the U.S. Supreme Court was all White males until the appointment of Thurgood Marshall, an African American civil rights lawyer, in 1967.)

After much contentious debate, this landmark decision ruled that U.S. state laws establishing racial segregation in public schools were unconstitutional. It signaled the end of legalized racial segregation in public schools throughout the United States. It overruled the separate but equal principle set forth in the 1896 Plessy v. Ferguson Supreme Court decision. The Plessy v. Ferguson ruling stated that racial segregation laws did not violate the U.S. Constitution as long as the facilities for each race were equal in quality. This doctrine came to be known as "separate but equal." Obviously, the "separate but equal" principle was not honored in Holmes County, Mississippi, and throughout the Southern Bible Belt.

Though this Supreme Court ruling was a landmark decision, it did not address all of the racial injustices in public schools of that era. For example, it did not address the racial pay disparity among school system employees. White teachers and administrators were still paid more than African American teachers and administrators in the same positions in many public school systems throughout the South.

As expected, the 1954 Supreme Court ruling banning racial segregation in public schools was not well-received by White professing Christians throughout the Bible Belt. In response to this ruling, Whites throughout the South abandoned public schools en masse. With White church support, Whites established private all-white academies to maintain racial segregation. As earlier noted, many White churches opened their facilities as temporary segregated school facilities until the academies could be built. In many school systems throughout the South, controversial state-approved public funding to support private White school academies was provided. An example of state-approved public funding for White academy tuition grants was the private academy scholarship fund approved by the all-white Mississippi State Legislature in 1964. Thankfully, the Federal government intervened and stopped this unjust act.

The church-supported Cruger-Tchula Academy was the first to be established in Mississippi and was soon followed by many others throughout the state and Bible Belt.

Though professing to be Christian, the rebellion by Whites in Holmes County and throughout the Bible Belt against God's "Great Commandment" reflected Satan's desire to create a more acceptable pseudo-Christianity, void of unconditional sacrificial love for all humanity and disguising the absence of eternal salvation.

As a reminder, God's "Great Commandment" stated, *"You shall love the LORD your God with all your heart, with all your soul, with all your mind, and with all your strength. This is the first commandment. And the second, like it, is this:* **You shall love your neighbor as yourself.***"*

This commandment is foundational for all professing believers of Christ. Any professing believer modeling racial relations contrary to God's clearly understood love requirement for all humanity must not be considered legitimate. Obviously, this pseudo-Christianity blatantly opposed God's established love parameter for His creation.

[As a **side note**, Jesus changed this requirement of love in John 13:34-35 for Christian discipleship and Christianity. (Ref. *"The Fanaticism of Christian Discipleship"* for more detail and differences between believers and Christians)]

***************************

**Many of the segregated academies throughout the South falsely advertised themselves as "Christian," primarily because of White institutional church support and involvement. The purpose of doing so was to influence public opinion and convince White families who professed Christianity to believe that this evilness was acceptable to God.**

**Indeed, since the Garden of Eden, Satan has been the great deceiver at the expense of eternal salvation for many unsuspecting souls.**

***************************

**(There is an important statistic to consider as we review this appendix summary. As noted earlier, unlike today, a startling 95% of adults in America professed Christianity in 1955, according to a Barna survey.**

**It is also important to note that the Christianity professed by most Whites throughout the Bible Belt did not just oppose God's requirement for love, justice, and righteousness but was also a strategically designed**

deceptive smokescreen disguising eternal damnation for far too many deceived and unsuspecting souls.

**This rebellion against God was attested by the many segregated White-church supported school academies and all other attempts to maintain racial segregation.)**

\*\*\*\*\*\*\*\*\*\*\*\*\*\*\*\*\*\*\*\*\*\*\*\*\*\*

God's foundation for humanity was grounded on sacrificial, unconditional agape love for all others, regardless of race or any other differences. This foundation was under the eternal umbrella and Biblical understanding that we were all created by God in His image (Genesis 1:27). We were to live in union as sisters and brothers in oneness under the sacrificial cross of Christ (John 17:20-21), considering and responding to the needs of all others before our own (John 13:34). This was and still is, the defining characteristic of authentic Biblical Christianity as modeled by Jesus.

Though professing Christianity, by and large, Whites throughout America could never bring themselves to the compassionate position of loving other races as they loved themselves, especially when considering African Americans. **In spiritual reality, they were not just rejecting African Americans but rejecting God.** To reinforce this rejection, the ungodly spirit operating through them would never allow sacrificial love for minority races to become a reality through various deception schemes focused on their manufactured fears and hunger for self-focused advantages.

By and large, conservative, White, professing Christians in America have traditionally supported ungodly policies reflecting racial injustice, division, and White supremacy, but unbelievably, they still desired and expected God's approval.

Contrary to the word of God, in most settings, Whites would separate themselves from minority races throughout history whenever threatened with oneness, except when the god of monetary gains was involved.

As a case in point, White-owned plantations were prevalent throughout Holmes County, Mississippi. African Americans were allowed to live with the White owners and their families because African American labor was required for the plantation's workforce. The White plantation owners would even provide their housing, though most of the accommodations were substandard. However, African Americans were prohibited from living in their communities outside the plantations.

White plantation owners in Holmes County were very influential in the White community and the local White churches. Though the White owners of the plantations would often allow their children to play with the African American children on the plantation, those same African American children were not allowed in public playgrounds or to live in their residential communities outside of the plantations.

Perhaps harder to believe, Whites in Holmes County (including the plantation owners), as throughout the Southern Bible Belt, would not allow African Americans to attend their segregated churches (Matt. 25:45). Whites throughout the South faithfully but falsely worshipped (John 4:24) the all-loving God Who they could never accept and persistently disobeyed. Though many were students of God's word, like the Pharisees of the gospels, most never understood justice or God's love or developed a personal relationship with Him.

As noted, this hypocrisy and historical confusion regarding justice and righteousness reflected in blindness to God's will could only have been orchestrated and successfully instituted by Satan throughout the history of America. Though difficult to accept by many modern-day theologians, this is the only explanation that survives Biblical scrutiny. Injustice in America has historically been perpetrated by far too many professing Christians who could make a huge difference in the lives of hurting humanity.

Though the reality of professing White Christian rebellion against God was prevalent throughout America's history, to varying extents, their unwillingness to stand and voice unyielding support for justice and righteousness exists today to address the many needs of injustice in America.

At the time of this writing, 32 Mississippi school districts are still under federal desegregation orders. Many school districts in Mississippi and throughout the Bible Belt are still denying African American and other minority students equal access to educational programs and opportunities. Across the

United States, schools with at least 90% nonwhite students spend $733 less per student than schools that are 90% White. These and many other injustices continue to exist without meaningful opposition from conservative White professing Christians or conservative lawmakers who profess Christianity. In obedience to God's will, they could effect the necessary changes for justice and righteousness to prevail.

Segregation is still prevalent throughout the Bible Belt, as reflected in the fact that many all-white private academies formed in the 1960s are still in existence and are primarily White today. Though many now have an African American presence, the spirits of division, self-considered superiority, and Divine entitlement reflecting Satan's evil influence and design are still present in many hearts. The African American enrollment is usually at an acceptable level under 2% to give the appearance of inclusiveness for a financial benefit and positive public perception.

As stated, many of these private academies erroneously identify themselves as being "Christian." This deception is another strategy of Satan to undermine God's foundation for His kingdom on earth. This strategy gives the many willing participants, including innocent and deceived students, a false understanding of God, Biblical love, interracial oneness, and salvation. The unrepentant perpetrators, masterminds, and religious leaders who condone this deception will indeed be held accountable by God.

Most of the Whites under Satan's deceptive influence, perhaps due to generational ties, are unwilling and unable to break free from his inspired evilness of condoning racial injustice and are still unable to discern his deceptions. There are still many residential and business communities throughout the United States where minorities are not welcomed by professing White Christians. White churches across America are now opening their doors to minority races, but many hearts remain closed. May God help us all.

Father God, may *"Thy kingdom come, and Thy will be done, on earth as it is in Heaven."* Amen.

# **Personal Reflections and Final Plea**

Since retiring from active pastoral ministry in 2006, God has afforded me many opportunities to visit many primarily White churches throughout south Louisiana, Mississippi, and Texas. On many occasions, I was the only African American in attendance. The receptions ranged from welcoming to actually being turned away at a rural church in south Louisiana. However, during that God-appointed visitation season, I did not hear a sermon acknowledging and revealing the seriousness of White church-supported racial injustice in America or even one that closely touched upon the subject. In far too many of those ministries, the sin of racial injustice was seemingly ignored altogether. From my many conversations with White spiritual leaders, it is apparent that many consider racial injustice to be a manufactured false narrative by minority races to gain sympathy and unmerited advantages. Many have voiced their displeasure that minorities continue to bring up the past injustices of the White race, and they feel it is time to forgive and move on.

Race relations have historically been a dividing issue in religion throughout the Southern Bible Belt, attested by the overwhelming majority of racially segregated White churches throughout America's history before the 1970s. Though most churches throughout the Bible Belt have opened their doors to minority races, it is frustrating to see that race relations are still a spiritual-hindering issue in religion today.

The institutional White church in America has traditionally not provided for the spiritual needs of the remnant of true White believers by catering to the manufactured fears and self-focused hopes of the majority. Many irrelevant and worldly topics are elevated as more important issues to be addressed. The effects of racial injustice and sin, in general, are rarely discussed. This omission is purposed to avoid conflict and maintain the unity of each church congregation. Regretfully, as viewed by many pastors, addressing these topics may jeopardize their pastoral careers (2$^{nd}$ Tim. 4:2-5).

This writing gives the Bible's response to the age-old question, "What is wrong with Christianity in America?" Perhaps shocking to most professing Christians, true Biblical Christianity has never existed in America broadly, but primarily a convincing satanic-induced deception that, perhaps unrealized by most professing Christians, is void of eternal salvation. Hopefully, this writing will generate much-needed interracial dialogue.

While writing this book, I experienced a wide range of emotions ranging from sadness to bewilderment and, yes, anger. As a clarification, my anger was not directed at the White race in America but at the evil spirit that is confusing the majority of White professing Christians spiritually and successfully using them, as throughout America's history, to disrupt God's kingdom order for human relations. As noted earlier, God's word clearly reminds us, *"For we do not wrestle against flesh and blood, but against principalities, against powers, against the rulers of the darkness of this age, against spiritual hosts of wickedness in the heavenly places"* (Eph. 6:12). Spiritual warfare is a reality within the body of the professing church of God in Christ. Regretfully, the focus of the leadership of the institutional White church in America is strategically directed away from the spiritual battlefield of racial injustice. Far too often, the focus is misdirected from the total inclusiveness of the sacrificial cross of Christ and the "Great Commandment" of God to the more desirable topics of self-focused empowerment, worldly prosperity, and family concerns, generally, living a better life. The historical racial injustices of America's White forefathers and the ongoing divisive racial injustices of today's society are not generally seen as major spiritual concerns to be addressed by America's White pulpits.

While experiencing various emotions during the writing of this book, there were times that I had to step away from this task to maintain my spiritual equilibrium.

Portions of this book present undesirable and somewhat gruesome details of America's history of satanic-induced racial injustice perpetrated through America's White society and historical racially segregated White church. However, there were other details and examples that I chose not to include so as not to give a feeling of "overkill" to White readers. However, some of them were just as revealing, just as damning, and just as distressing.

I soon realized that racial injustice is the elephant that has historically been sitting on the front row of America's institutional White church that everyone is seated behind and trying to look over or around to see the cross of Jesus on the altar. Because he obstructs their spiritual view, they have a distorted image and understanding of Jesus' sacrificial cross and are unaware of its salvation requirement for sacrificial love, justice, and righteousness.

**Many White professing believers in Christ throughout the history of America have not been informed by their spiritual leaders of a critical Biblical truth. Without a life-focus of**

sacrificial love for all humanity, justice, and righteousness, there is no salvation, regardless of all other spiritual focuses.

As large and spiritually blinding as the elephant is, it is difficult to understand why his presence is insanely allowed and, even worse, joyfully celebrated since the European occupation of America. Institutional religion in America remains frustrated in its attempts to manufacture God's presence on its distorted and rebellious terms, which exclude God's kingdom's requirements for sacrificial love for all humanity, justice, and righteousness. Understandably, this effort has only resulted in more frustration, unnecessary suffering, national chaos, and the loss of eternal salvation for far too many unsuspecting souls.

**Indeed, Satan has mastered the art of religious deception through misinformation and spiritual blindness.**

After realizing the magnitude of this problem and understanding the dire consequences in the lives of far too many professing Christians, more than ever before and with the empowerment of the Holy Spirit, I am determined to be an active agent of God for the spiritual deliverance of as many as possible. **The spiritual deliverance of the religious captives is a primary goal of this writing.** I am committed to ending this historical and ongoing spiritual madness orchestrated by the kingdom of darkness and evilness against God's kingdom.

The awesome power of God is without measure. Yet, very few have the freedom to experience it because of spiritual bondage resulting from demonic-influenced religious confusion. As Satan realizes and has feared since his first deceptive encounter with Adam and Eve, a united and empowered people of God could become a tremendous, overpowering, and victorious force against the principalities, powers, rulers of darkness, and spiritual hosts of wickedness.

As a concern of many White Americans today, the racial minority population of America is projected to become the majority by the middle of the $21^{st}$ century if the current trends of growth continue. Many assess the current religious, political, and civil rebellion and unrest in the U.S. by White Americans as an effort to replace America's democracy with an authoritarian form of government. The understood intent is to reinforce the diminishing White control of America's society and economy and firmly secure the historical benefits of White supremacy. This assessment, though controversial, has historical support from the many injustices of America's past, as documented in this writing.

As earlier noted, there is a consistent pattern of evil-induced history repeating itself as Satan consistently repeats his successful schemes. As a warning of wisdom, *if you ever want to know what he may be planning to do, look at what he has already done.*

In 1948, the occupying minority European population of South Africa established an apartheid system that led to an authoritarian type of government. This was done to secure and maintain political, social, and economic control of the indigenous people. Apartheid was characterized by an authoritarian political culture that ensured that South Africa was dominated politically, socially, and economically by the nation's minority White population (Also, a careful review of the initial European occupation of Australia in the 1700s and many other countries reveals a similar pattern of seizing complete control from the indigenous people and securing it through the political process. The political process was consistently reinforced by religious dogma as seen throughout the history of America).

"Apartheid was a system of institutionalized racial segregation and discrimination that was enforced through legislation by the National Party government.

Under apartheid, the government implemented strict laws that segregated and marginalized the non-white population, particularly black South Africans, in various aspects of life including where they could live, work, go to school, and even whom they could marry. The regime used a combination of laws, police brutality, censorship, and other means to maintain control and suppress opposition *(This same system was instituted by America's White society and professing Church of God under the Jim Crow Laws in America's past and is methodically being revised today through the political process supported by conservative White professing Christians).*

The apartheid regime restricted political freedoms, limited the rights of non-white citizens, and used violence and repression to maintain its power. Opposition to the regime was met with harsh measures, including arrests, torture, and even killings. The government also controlled the media and limited freedom of speech, further consolidating its power.

Overall, the apartheid regime in South Africa exhibited characteristics of authoritarianism through its control over political and social institutional suppression of dissent, and restriction of civil liberties."[1]

Such a foolish endeavor in America, if successful, would lead to a level of racial anarchy that America has never experienced and from which it would never recover. This would lead to the destruction of America's spiritually fragile society and provide the ultimate victory that Satan's schemes throughout the history of the United States of America were designed to accomplish.

**In spiritual reality, the rebellion and unrest of America's White society are a continuation of the ongoing evilness orchestrated by Satan against Almighty God, which commenced after the creation of this world in the Garden of Eden. And, since the resurrection of Christ, they are a continuation of the satanic-orchestrated spiritual war against Biblical Christianity.**

## Wake up, people of God!
How long will you remain in this demonic-induced spiritual stupor? America, this world, and God's professing people are perishing while our spiritual leadership remains asleep at the steering wheel of control God affords His faithful and united warriors.

The sins of America's fathers and the sins of the professing church of God have reinforced the spiritual divide between God and His rebellious church, and America and the world are paying the price. The bulk of Satan's relentless attacks are focused on our children and youth, the most vulnerable ones in our society, God's unprepared future army. God's spiritually floundering and divided church in America is unable to mount a counter-offense to save them and develop them into the image of Christ. Satan is destroying a young generation across this nation, across all race groups, through various means of spiritual deception and confusion (ref. the book *"Just Like Jesus"* by this same writer). Let us now come together with all urgency to repair the breach and save the United States of America from demonic-initiated self-destruction.

After sitting before God during this writing, I now sense the importance of this precious time that God is allowing for repentance and correction. I plead with you and for you in my prayers from the bottom of my heart. Our remaining time is short. Thanks to the mercy of God, there is still time. We must acknowledge and repent of our current and past ungodliness and come together as one united body in Christ, reflecting His sacrificial love for all humanity. Contrary to the historical focus of religion in America, **<u>sacrificial love for all humanity, justice, and righteousness must be prioritized by all professing believers of Christ.</u>**

During the time frame of this writing, political and divisive rhetoric is already in 'full swing' to influence the outcome of the 2024 presidential election in America. This election is considered by many to be the most important presidential election in America's history for sustaining its fragile democracy and truly developing God's Kingdom's design of interracial oneness in America. Again, conservative White professing Christians as well as the entirety of White America will have the opportunity to demonstrate their willingness to turn from the divisive and self-focused evilness of the injustices of America's past and present. They can boldly renounce and turn from their longstanding desire to maintain the unjust, evil-gotten advantages of White supremacy as reflected throughout America's history and truly display the interracial sacrificial love of Christ and the cross-centered sacrificial tenets of Biblical Christianity. They will have perhaps their final opportunity to reveal to the world, but more importantly, to Almighty God, their commitment to His kingdom's order of justice and righteousness and Christ's unconditional, sacrificial love for all humanity as required in God's "Great Commandment."

The faithful united interracial remnant of Christ in America must "lead the charge" while reflecting the image of Christ. They must model the sacrificial love of Christ before America's faltering society, the spiritually challenged professing church of God in Christ, and the world. This demonstrated commitment to God must become America's professing Church of God in Christ's new foundation to develop the required interracial oneness and sacrificial love that has never existed throughout America's history. Indeed, a new day is dawning, not just for America but for God's entire creation.

I remain prayerful for a mighty move of God to truly open blinded spiritual eyes and change cold, resisting hearts, not just throughout the Southern Bible Belt, but throughout America and the entirety of God's creation before the long-awaited return of Jesus. We must act now with all urgency. At His return, the opportunity for spiritual correction will no longer be available.

Please join me in prayer and dedicated action for this vision to become a reality. Everyone has a God-appointed role. Pray for clarity regarding yours.

## *God will be glorified in the "United States" of America.*

# Postscript

Many have attempted to provide a spiritual analysis of the historical resistance by conservative White professing Christians in America to interracial equality, justice for the racially oppressed (Isa. 56:1, Mic. 6:8), interracial sacrificial love (Mk. 12:31), and as documented throughout this writing, their historical ungodly hunger for racial supremacy and societal control at the expense of the "least of these," the most vulnerable, in God's creation (Matt. 25:45). Since these are foundational components of Biblical Christianity and indicators of one's unbelief in Jesus through their rejection of God's commandments for human relations, an unbiased spiritual analysis is critically important. It is needed not to just gain understanding, but to secure permanent deliverance for the many rebellious captives to be set free and truly honor Jesus as Lord. In spiritual reality, their resistance is a continuation of the longstanding evil-orchestrated spiritual warfare against the holy, just, and righteous throne of Almighty God and the sacrificial cross of Christ that commenced in the Garden of Eden.

This segment of spiritual warfare commenced in Europe in the $4^{th}$ century AD through warfare strategies of appeasement against the undiscerning, self-focused, and power-focused Roman Catholic Church's leadership. It was reinforced by the unbiblical oversight and political and financial influence of the pagan inspired Roman Emperor Constantine. He was the first Roman emperor to convert to Christianity. The generational seeds of spiritual rebellion and self-focused religious confusion were sown within the Roman Catholic Church and European society through the spiritual channels of access provided by the sins of their misguided Roman Catholic spiritual leaders. This successful strategy enabled Satan to secure a stronghold over the Roman Catholic Church and the continent of Europe. This spiritual access was not recognized as an issue of concern during the Protestant Reformation in the 1500s, therefore the sprouting seeds remained and were not included for disposal by the fledgling Protestant church leadership. This evil strategy launched against the holy throne of Almighty God has been successful throughout the world for over 2,000 years. It was enhanced by many evil-orchestrated and violent European invasions of countries throughout the world (as listed in Ch. 5) by undiscerning generations of European professing believers in Christ, both Catholic and Protestant. They primarily remained unaware of Satan's evil stronghold over their lives and actions.

The U.S. is experiencing the results of Satan's deceptive strategy for America and what the early European leaders who wrote the U.S. Constitution did not realize; **the experiment of democracy will not work without interracial sacrificial love, justice, and righteousness. In other words, America's fragile democracy will fail without God!**

---

After reviewing the mostly suppressed history of the racially segregated White (European) professing Christian churches in America, perhaps the most anticipated question is, "How could such an enormous level of spiritual blindness and confusion exist within the White professing body of Christ throughout America's history which successfully influenced their participation in racial segregation, White supremacy, and the unjust lynchings of innocent African Americans?"

The racially segregated White churches in America's history and the spiritual confusion that exists today among many White professing Christians throughout the Southern Bible Belt reveal the unimaginable extent of the blinding persuasion and confusion of Satan's stronghold power and control. This is the short explanation.

For more detail and better clarity, when allowed by God, Satan's legal access into the lives of humanity often results from rebellion against God as was revealed through the fourth-century hierarchy of the Roman Catholic Church. Their sins of self-focused advancement at a sacrificial cost to their undiscerning parishioners and their ungodly hunger for spiritual control of humanity and God's creation provided the avenues of legal access for Satan's evilness to take root as a spiritual stronghold. Through this spiritual access, Satan initiated his evil course of action through their ungodly future which the Roman Catholic Church and world are still influenced by today. Satan's stronghold over Europe created the longstanding European desire for worldwide supremacy, spiritual dominance over humanity, and worldwide control of the earth's natural resources to supply European economies. This evil-induced strategy was "played out" over the course of American and world history to the detriment of the indigenous populations of the lands of their forced occupations. In many of their invasions, the indigenous people were utilized as forced labor as a means to accomplish their goals of self-focused fulfillment and permanently securing complete control. As earlier noted, in the lands of their invasions their complete control was secured through the political process which was intentionally designed for that purpose and was consistently reinforced by religious dogma as seen throughout America's history. Biblical Christianity was demonically redesigned as an instrument of deception to maintain racial supremacy and secure control over God's earthly kingdom. However, the body of Christ has entered into the end-time period of correction and restoration as we prepare for the long-awaited return of Jesus. God has begun to effect the painful but necessary changes of correction as many areas with unaddressed historical injustices are beginning to experience.

Satan's evilness is not always easy to detect, however, it is commonly revealed in the eyes of the expressions of anger, confusion, and dominance (Those who are anointed in deliverance ministry will understand that statement). Many under his influence or control are helplessly bound and perhaps destined for damnation without the intervention of God-anointed deliverance, as is revealed and modeled throughout the four Gospels. To serve the Lord unhindered, and to live according to His will, the spiritual captives must be set free from spiritual bondage. The ungodly phenomenon of perpetrated evilness as witnessed in religion throughout America's history highlights the importance of the required threefold ministry of Christianity, **preaching, healing, and deliverance** (Luke 4:18). This threefold requirement was revealed and modeled by Jesus, the first-century apostles, and the first-century church.

As orchestrated by Satan, most twenty-first-century ministries in the United States of America only focus on the ministry of preaching with little to no focus on the required ministries of healing and deliverance. Therefore, the required guardrails are not in place to prevent his intrusion, which always results in spiritual confusion, spiritual bondage, and many unnecessary sicknesses and premature deaths. Satan has effectively prevented the development of the ministries of healing and deliverance from every religious institution in America in which he has influence and/or control. However, these requirements of Christ are mandatory for spiritual viability and wholeness, and are especially required for effective preaching. They can only be developed through the indwelling presence, power, and oversight of the Holy Spirit. The lack of His power reflects His absence and Satan's deceptive influence.

Perhaps the follow-up question is, "Could this historical level of spiritual blindness and spiritual confusion among the professing body of Christ exist today?" The regretful answer is "Yes," it does. The separation from Christ and the influence of Satan is revealed time and again throughout the twenty-first-century professing body of Christ. It is witnessed in race relations, in resistance to providing for the needs of the oppressed, the high rate of marital divorce and sexual immorality among professing Christians, the ungodly high rate of mental and physical sickness, the acceptance of the sins of worldliness, abortion, and homosexuality by professing Christians, etc. The spiritual ineptness of the twenty-first-century church reflects the absence of the required power and guidance of the Holy Spirit.

In reviewing church history through the lens of our twenty-first-century spiritual awareness, it is easy to recognize the spiritual confusion of the past and gasp with amazement at the documented events of church-condoned evilness. Our current awareness resulted from God-ordained forced racial integration and more interracial inclusivity that commenced with the Brown vs. Board of Education Supreme Court ruling in 1954. This God-inspired ruling was followed by other legal rulings that mandated interracial inclusivity that was enforced by God-fearing governing authorities. Associating with others will always lead to a better understanding of each other. The lack of interracial understanding proved to be an ungodly hindrance to racial integration in America, even among the professing body of Christ. When viewing America's history, we can clearly see the spiritual blindness that easily results from racial segregation, especially when undergirded with evil mesmerizing, and confusing influences from Satan. However, before we make the assumption that things are now better within Christ's professing body and America's society, we must have a correct Biblical context to apply this assumption.

Scripture informs us that God does not change (Heb. 13:8). Professing Christians must be mindful that Satan, and not humanity, is our true enemy (Eph. 6:12) and he does not change either. He is the same yesterday, today, and forever. He only comes to steal, kill, and destroy (Jn. 10:10) and is willing to utilize every evil weapon in his limited arsenal. He must be renounced at every encounter. He is restless and realizes that his time on earth is soon ending. He realizes that many of his evil strategies of the past are no longer providing his desired results. In response to the growing awareness of the professing body of Christ, he has changed his long-standing primary deceptive evil strategy for religious confusion. Satan has changed his evil strategy for professing White Christians in America from unprovoked violent confrontation and genocide against minority races which resulted in mob violence and murderous lynchings as documented in this writing. His new strategy is spiritual apathy, which is just as deceptive and eternally damning.

This lack of concern and indifference strikes at the heart of the sacrificial cross of Christ which is action-focused sacrificial love (James 2:14-25) for the entirety of humanity and God's creation.

As earlier noted, Jesus clarified Christian discipleship and Christianity in His new commandment to His disciples. In John 13:34 and 35 Jesus stated to His disciples, *"A new commandment I give to you, that you love one another;* **<u>as I have loved you, that you also love one another.</u>** *By this all will know that you are My disciples, if you have love for one another."* To love all others as Jesus loves us is Jesus' validating requirement for true Christian discipleship and Christianity. This foundational truth has been disregarded among Christ's professing body throughout America's ungodly history. Jesus loves us so much that He obediently honored the will of the Father and sacrificially gave His life for us when He died on the cross for our sins. As Christians, we are required by Jesus to likewise love all others for the advancement of God's true kingdom on earth and the benefit of all humanity. This new commandment indicates that Jesus loves us more than He loves Himself, as professing Christians are also to love all humanity and reflect that love in all of life's concerns. This is a required validation for our profession of faith and a sign to all humanity that Jesus is truly our Lord and has captivated our hearts and allegiance.

With this Biblical understanding as our foundation, we can clearly see that spiritual apathy is in opposition to the heart and will of Christ and the eternal message of love from His sacrificial cross. Spiritual apathy towards the needs of all others is Satan's new strategy for the deception of Christianity in America. Apathy can be subtle and difficult to pinpoint as it has been normalized in today's compromising religious environment. It can steal our ability to feel compassion and empathy for the oppressed. People who are different from us can eventually be seen, not as brothers and sisters in Christ, but as our competitors who are less deserving of God's entrusted resources, as witnessed in religion in America today. If we don't see our resources as entrustments from God to be used for His glory, and we don't see ourselves as entrusted stewards of His resources who one day will give an accounting for our stewardship, then we can easily be led astray by Satan through unbiblical, self-focused, false teachings on Christian financial stewardship. We can wastefully use God's resources on excesses and unneeded personal desires to the detriment of those who are in need (ref. Matt. 25:14-30, Lk. 19:11-27, Jn. 21:15-17). This worldly-focused misunderstanding by professing Christians in America disregards the true message of the sacrificial cross of Christ. It remains a fallacy of today's self-focused prosperity gospel (ref. *"The Fanaticism of Christian Discipleship"* by this same writer for clarity and additional information). The Bible teaches that apathy is a sin.

James 4:17 states, *"So whoever knows that right thing to do and fails to do it, for him it is sin."*

Ephesians 4:19 states, *"In their spiritual apathy they have become callous and past feeling and reckless and have abandoned themselves to unbridled sensuality."*\

Revelation 3:16 states, *"Because you are lukewarm, and neither hot nor cold, I will spit you out of my mouth."*

Proverbs 18:1 states, *"Whoever closes his ear to the cry of the poor will himself call out and not be answered."*

Indeed, spiritual apathy is in opposition to the will of God and is a clear example of Satan's deceptive influence. Spiritual apathy must be understood as an attribute of unrighteousness. Our legitimacy as Christians is determined by our response to Jesus' commandment of self-sacrificing love for humanity, loving all others more than we love ourselves, regardless of our differences. In this place of oneness with Christ, we begin to recognize the needs of all others before our own, which is contradictory to most religious teachings today and generally is rejected by today's self-focused professing Christian body.

As a professing Christian, if we are struggling with spiritual apathy towards the needs of all others, this may indicate that we need to seek God on a higher and more personal level. This may necessitate a break from our current spiritual environment and influences and prayerfully seek the guidance and empowerment of the Holy Spirit in our new walk with God, as He molds us into the image of Christ. This walk will begin when we renounce the ways of this evil world and surrender our "all" to God and trust Him in all matters of life. God is faithful.

I apologize for the length of this postscript. Traditionally, they are short statements. However, these are desperate times that require a setting aside of traditions. Professing Christians throughout the history of America have been led astray and many are perishing today because of satanic-induced traditions. This postscript of spiritual insight regarding the current spiritual state of Christianity in America was too important to omit (Ezek. 3:18-19). Hopefully, it will be beneficial to each reader by providing the required focus for a personal spiritual evaluation to lay the foundation for oneness with Christ. May God be glorified in your new life in Christ.

# **Bibliography**

## **Chapter 1**

1. "NKJV Study Bible." Second Edition; 2007; page 450
2. "On Views of Race and Inequality, Blacks and Whites Are Worlds Apart," by the Pew Research Center; June 27, 2016
3. "Racial Segregation in the Church," eji.org; January 1, 2016

## **Chapter 2**

1. "The Beacon," dated April 16, 1998; pages 1&8, The Macon Mississippi newspaper
2. "In Southern Towns, 'Segregation Academies' Are Still Going Strong," by Sarah Carr; December 13, 2012
3. "White Churches Involved at Every Step," by Ellen Ann Fentress, The Academy Stories Editor

## **Chapter 3**

1. "Smith Wigglesworth Devotional," Whitaker House; pg. 449
2. From *The NKJV Study Bible,* copyright 1997, 2007 by Thomas Nelson, Inc. Used by permission; pg. 1,942

## **Chapter 4**

1. "Zondervan NIV Exhaustive Concordance," by E. Goodrick & J. Kohlenberger, 1999, page 1576
2. "Clarke's Commentary," by Adam Clarke, Volume 3, pages 215 & 216
3. "Matthew Henry's Commentary on the Whole Bible," 1998; page 1731
4. "Clarke's Commentary," by Adam Clarke, Volume 3, page 620

## **Chapter 5**

1. "https//ar.usembassy.gov
2. "Colonial enslavement of Native Americans included those who surrendered, too," by Linford D. Fisher, Brown University; February 15, 2017
3. "All my Slaves, whether Negroes, Indians, Mustees, or Molattoes. Towards a Thich Description of Slave Religion," by Patrick Neal Minges; 1999
4. www.history.com/topics/native-american-history/Indian-reservations, Authors, History.com editors. October 11, 2022, Publisher, A&E Television Networks

## Chapter 6

1. "The Major Role The Catholic Church Played in Slavery," by Stacy M. Brown, September 18, 2018
2. "Church involvement in the trans-Atlantic slave trade: its biblical antecedent vis-à-vis the society's attitude to wealth," by Emmanuel Kojo Ennin Antwi; www.scielo.org.za
3. "The Bible was used to justify slavery. Then Africans made it their path to freedom," by Julie Zauzmer Weil; April 30, 2019
4. "The Major Role The Catholic Church Played in Slavery.," by Stacy M. Brown; September 18, 2018; The New York Amsterdam News
5. "Southern Baptist Seminary Documents History of Racial Injustice," December 12, 2018; eji.org
6. "Mormonism and Slavery," https://en.m.wikipedia.org
7. "Book of Mormon," Chapter 19: Repentance, churchofjesuschrist
8. "Churches played an active role in slavery and segregation. Some want to make amends," by Michela Moscufo; April 3, 2022; NBC News.

## Chapter 7

1. The Suppressed Truth About The Assassination of Abraham Lincoln," by Burke McCarty,1922; pages 82, 83
2. "The Suppressed Truth About The Assassination of Abraham Lincoln," by Burke McCarty,1922; pages 49, 50
3. "The Suppressed Truth About The Assassination of Abraham Lincoln," by Burke McCarty, 1922; pages 36, 37

## Chapter 8

1. "Ku Klux Klan," splcenter.org
2. "History of the KKK," oldgloryknights311.simdif.com
3. "KKK Constitution Bylaws," digitalgallery. bgsu.edu
4. "KKK application form, 1924 – Credo," credo.library.umass.edu
5. "100 Years of Lynchings," by Ralph Ginzburg, 1988; pages 53, 55
   "A History of Racial Injustice," calendar.eji.org+
6. "Jim Crow South's Lynchings of Blacks and Christianity," slate.com
7. "100 Years of Lynchings," by Ralph Ginzburg, 1988, pages 65

## Chapter 9

1. "Amaso Leland Stanford," thelatinlibrary.com
   "Leland Stanford," encyclopedia.com
2. "The First Asian Americans," Asian-nation.org
3. "Covid 'hate crimes' against Asian Americas on the rise," BBC News; February 26, 2021

4. *"Japanese Imprisonment at Amache,"* www.historycolorado.org
   *"Japanese Internment War Hits California Farm Lands – 1942,"* www.sfmuseum.org
5. *"White Christian Privilege: The Illusion of Religious Equality in America,"* by Khyati Joshi; 2020

## Chapter 10

1. *"The Week Magazine,"* "It Does Happen Here," by Susan Caskie; August, 2024
2. "The Long History of Anti-Latino Discrimination in America," by Erin Blakemore; August 29, 2018
3. "Racism and Latinos: The Wall of Separation and Fear," by the Rev. David Maldonado; September 16, 2020

## Chapter 11

1. "Faith on the Hill," Pew Research Center; Jan. 4, 2021
2. "Presidents Who Owned Slaves," dhmi.org
3. "Best states 2024 ranking;" U.S. News and World Report
4. "Study finds Mississippi is nation's worst state in which to live, again." www.gulflive.com >2022/08

## Chapter 13

1. "Social Justice and Biblical Justice Are Actually One and the Same," by Rebekah Thompson; Oct. 6, 2021

## Chapter 14

1. "Freedom Riders," by history.com editors; updated, January 20, 2022 / original: February 2, 2010
2. "Americans of all colors contributed to civil rights movement," by Lloyd Bradley; February 5, 2015
3. "White Antiracist Activists," Compiled by Elizabeth Denevi and Lori Cohen, Eastern Educational Resource Collaborative
4. "Jessie Daniel Ames": www.britannica.com
5. "Anne McCarty Braden," womenwork.library.louisville.edu
6. "Biography of Jonathan Daniels / City of Keene," keenenh.gov.
7. "bendingthearctojustice.com"
8. Wikipedia, "Murders of Chaney, Goodman, and Schwerner"
9. "How Dick Gregory Forced the FBI to Find The Bodies of Three Civil Rights Workers Slain in Mississippi," by David Dennis, Jr.; August 30, 2017
10. "The Voting Rights Martyr Who Divided America," cnn.com
11. "James Zwerg," Spartacus Educational; spartacus-educational.com
12. "White Pastor Who Supported the Montgomery Bus Boycott," npr.org

## Chapter 16

1. "White American Christianity Needs to Be Honest About Its History of White Supremacy," Jan. 13, 2021, Time Magazine
2. "Priests, Pastors & Preachers Who Prey on Their Parishioners," clorelaw.com; February 24, 2019
3. From *The NKJV Study Bible,* copyright 1997, 2007 by Thomas Nelson, Inc. Used by permission; pg.1235

## Chapter 17

1. "Georgia's U.S. Senate Race Should Have Never Been This Close," by Kali Holloway, "November 9, 2022
2. "Matthew Henry's Commentary on the Whole Bible," 1998; pg. 1645
3. "Smith Wigglesworth Devotional,"1999; pages 166, 167

## Personal Reflections and Final Plea

1. "Quora.com/Was-Apartheid-South-Africa-an- authoritarian-regime?"

This book serves as a companion resource for *"The Fanaticism of Christian Discipleship"* by this same writer, which clarifies true Biblical Christianity. The *"Fanaticism of Christian Discipleship"* also reveals and analyzes many of the erroneous teachings of twenty-first-century Christianity that have enhanced and disguised the deception of Christianity in America and worldwide.

---

All profits from book sales are used to support the ministries of the Louisiana Prayer Institute in Covington, Louisiana. All of our services are for the glory of God and the advancement of His kingdom on earth and are free to the general public.

---

*"Finally, brothers, good-by. Aim for perfection, listen to my appeal, be of one mind, live in peace. And the God of love and peace will be with you."*
2nd Corinthians 13:11

May God remain your guide through the spiritual turbulence of this journey.

# Shalom

# Notes

Made in the USA
Columbia, SC
14 November 2024

164f3576-3f04-458e-b386-4e411a02e292R02